# Kierkegaard and Modern Continental Philosophy

'This bold attempt to secure for Kierkegaard the same kind of role in contemporary continental philosophy already enjoyed by Nietzsche is a challenge both to those who leave him out of current conversations altogether and to those who treat him as if he were just another French poststructuralist.

It is lucidly written and remarkably free of jargon. Weston's expositions of the major figures he discusses will be accessible to undergraduates, while his argument will require specialist scholars to take note. Both as a teacher and as a scholar I want to keep this book ready-to-hand.'

Merold Westphal, *Fordham University*

In *Kierkegaard and Modern Continental Philosophy: An Introduction* Michael Weston argues that, despite being acknowledged as a precursor to Nietzsche and post-Nietzschean thinkers such as Heidegger and Derrida, the radical nature of Kierkegaard's critique of philosophy has been missed.

Michael Weston examines and explains the metaphysical tradition, as exemplified by Plato and Hegel, and the post-metaphysical critiques of Nietzsche, Heidegger and Derrida. He shows how Kierkegaard's ethical critique of philosophy undermines the former and escapes the latter. He considers another ethical critique of philosophy, that of Levinas, before identifying ethics as the non-philosophical site from which philosophy can be criticized. *Kierkegaard and Modern Continental Philosophy: An Introduction* argues that by refusing to allow philosophy jurisdiction over ethics and religion, Kierkegaard's critique applies as much to modern continental thought as to the metaphysical thought it seeks to undermine.

**Michael Weston** lectures in philosophy at the University of Essex. His previous book was *Morality and the Self* (1975).

# Kierkegaard and Modern Continental Philosophy

## An Introduction

Michael Weston

London and New York

First published 1994
by Routledge
11 New Fetter Lane, London EC4P 4EE

Simultaneously published in the USA and Canada
by Routledge
29 West 35th Street, New York, NY 10001

© 1994 Michael Weston

Typeset in Baskerville by
Ponting–Green Publishing Services, Chesham, Bucks
Printed and bound in Great Britain by
T.J. Press (Padstow) Ltd, Padstow, Cornwall

Printed on acid-free paper

*British Library Cataloguing in Publication Data*
A catalogue record for this book is available from the
British Library.

*Library of Congress Cataloging-in-Publication Data*
Weston, Michael, 1946–
    Kierkegaard and modern continental philosophy: an
introduction / Michael Weston.
        p.    cm.
    Includes bibliographical references and index.
    ISBN 0–415–10119–0. – ISBN 0–415–10120–4 (pbk.)
    1. Kierkegaard, Søren, 1813–1855–Influence.
    2. Philosophers, Modern–Europe.    3. Philosophy,
    European–History.    I. Title.
B4377.W46      1993
198'.9–dc20                                93–21649
                                                CIP

ISBN 0–415–10119–0 (hbk)    ISBN 0–415–10120–4 (pbk)

For Margaret, William and James.
For my Mother and to the memory
of my late Father.

And they said, Go to, let us build a city and a tower, whose top may reach unto heaven; and let us make us a name . . . And the Lord came down to see the city and the tower, which the children of men builded. And the Lord said, Behold, the people is one, and they have all one language; and this they begin to do: and now nothing will be restrained from them, which they have imagined to do. Go to, let us go down, and there confound their language, that they may not understand one another's speech.

Genesis 11: 4–8

The fact of the matter is that we must acknowledge that in the last resort there is no theory.

S. Kierkegaard, *Journals and Papers*, entry 2509

# Contents

# Preface

Kierkegaard had a premonition of the fate of his writings:

> Alas, but I know who is going to inherit from me, that character I find so repulsive, he who will keep on inheriting all that is best just as he has done in the past – namely, the assistant professor, the professor.
>
> (*Journals* 6818)

He was right about this. After it became available in major European languages at the beginning of this century, his work helped to form and was absorbed into some of the new tendencies in philosophy then developing, existential phenomenology and existentialism. (I look at some of the structural parallels with Heidegger's earlier work in Chapter 2.) But this appropriation by philosophy meant either ignoring Kierkegaard's repeated attacks on philosophy, or claiming that they were directed against Hegel and the metaphysical tradition and no longer applied to a philosophy which was post-metaphysical in intention. These attacks in the published writings are, however, carried out by pseudonyms exploiting Kierkegaard's prodigious talent for ironic characterization and downright comedy, and need, therefore, for their assessment a consideration of why Kierkegaard expressed himself in this, for philosophy, rather bizarre way. When we attend to this, we come to see, I think, that Kierkegaard's objections are directed at aspects of the philosophical enterprise which post-metaphysical thought shares with its predecessors, and yet do not, precisely because of their mode of development in a pseudonymous literature characterized by comedy, open themselves to the claim that any purported attack on philosophy must itself be, implicitly, philosophical. This latter claim has been characteristic of post-metaphysical thought from Nietzsche on, which has seen the possibility of a critique of metaphysics as requiring a strategic thinking which undermines the fundamental categories of metaphysical thought from an impetus received, paradoxically, from the metaphysical enterprise itself. Perhaps Kierkegaard shows us the 'other' of philosophy in such a way that it does not depend on philosophy for its determination, but rather reminds us that philosophy, whether metaphysical or post-metaphysical, always comes too late. I hope what follows may introduce Kierkegaard's thought in its radicality, whilst aware that I too have succumbed to what he would have seen as a 'speculative' mode of expression which is 'a temptation, the most dubious of all' (*Concluding Unscientific Postscript*, p. 192). For, as he remarked, 'Existence . . . is a difficult category to deal with; for if I think it, I abrogate it, and then I do not think it' (Ibid., p. 274). I hope too that the accounts given of the philosophical thinkers I deal with may prove useful in themselves, for Kierkegaard would have stressed that liberation from the temptations of philosophy requires experiencing its power of seduction and so a treating of it with seriousness.

Where the person is understood within metaphysical conceptuality which emphasizes autonomy, or post-metaphysical thought which involves an historical self-situating determining the present task of an intervention into metaphysically formed structures of thought and life, I have used the third person masculine form. Where the person is understood religiously, or positioned within Kierkegaard's existential dialectic, and so in terms of the notions of giving and 'grace', and thus of the primacy of 'love', I have used the feminine.

I am indebted to discussions with Michael McGhee of the University of Liverpool over the years since we were students together, to Professor Peter Winch who first encouraged my reading of Kierkegaard and Simone Weil, to Professors Robert Bernasconi and David Krell who incited an interest in Heidegger and Derrida, and to Simon Critchley of the University of Essex for his expertise in modern French thought. The Department at Essex has provided a varied and stimulating working environment, whilst the University's provision of sabbatical leave enables its teachers to develop their research interests. I am grateful too to all my students over the years who have helped, in their interest and opposition, the formation of my understanding of Kierkegaard. Linda Day typed the manuscript and good-humouredly put up with my constant alterations and revisions. Adrian Driscoll of Routledge has been a supportive and encouraging editor. My thanks finally to the most important, if indirect, contributors to this book, Margaret and our children William and James.

# Introduction

Consider the following estimations by philosophers of the significance of their work:

> Unless . . . either philosophers become kings in our states or those whom we now call our kings and rulers take to the pursuit of philosophy seriously and adequately . . . there can be no cessation of troubles, dear Glaucon, for our states, nor, I fancy, for the human race either.[1]

> All that proceeds from thought – all the distinctions of the arts and sciences and of the endless interweavings of human relationships, habits and customs, activities, skills and enjoyments – find their ultimate center in the *one* thought of *God* . . . philosophy *is* theology, and [one's] occupation with philosophy – or rather *in* philosophy – is of itself the service of God . . . we should *know* God cognitively . . . and should esteem this cognition above all else . . . these lectures have . . . the purpose of knowing God.[2]

> no one before me has known the right path, the *ascending* path: only after me are there again hopes, tasks, prescribable paths of culture . . . Precisely therewith am I a destiny.[3]

> man essentially occurs only in his essence where he is claimed by Being . . . Thinking lets itself be claimed by Being so that it can say the truth of Being.[4]

> the essence of man consists in thinking the truth of Being.[5]

> the treatment of the concept of writing . . . [gives] us the

assured means of broaching the de-construction of the *greatest totality* – the concept of the episteme and logocentric metaphysics – within which are produced, without ever posing the radical question of writing, all the Western methods of analysis, explication, reading or interpretation . . . It is therefore the *game of the world* that must first be thought, before attempting to understand all the forms of play in the world.[6]

'everyday language' is not innocent or neutral. It is the language of Western metaphysics.[7]

Deconstruction is, in itself, a positive response to an alterity which necessarily calls . . . Deconstruction is therefore vocation – a response to a call.[8]

These quotations express their authors' conviction of the supreme importance of philosophy for human life. At the beginning of Western philosophy, Plato created a famous image of philosophy's relation to the rest of human life which may help to show the plausibility of this at first sight perhaps rather surprising claim.[9] We are to picture, Plato tells us, prisoners fettered at the neck and ankle facing the end wall of a cave upon which are reflected, by the light of a fire behind them, shadows of images held aloft by other human beings. The cave, however, has an opening out into the clear light of day, towards which a prisoner, if released, may, with considerable difficulty, progress, eventually to emerge from darkness into light. There, initially blinded by the sunlight, she will first become aware of shadows, and then, as her eyes become accustomed to the light, of the objects which cast them, and so to look then towards the heavens, finding this easier at first at night beholding the moon and stars, until at last she is able to see the sun itself. This image, Plato tells us, is of our condition in relation to education and its lack. By the prisoners, then, who take the shadows on the wall to be what is real, Plato presumably intends to picture a state of unreflective life enchained to opinions it has received and whose source lies elsewhere. Such opinions are reflections, distorted as are shadows cast by firelight, of beliefs which have been consciously formed by other human beings, 'made images', as Plato puts it. Here we may suppose are, on the one hand, the beliefs of the practically knowledgeable, those who have an ability, acquired by experience and training, to bring about changes in the world, the craftsmen of all kinds, the farmers, generals, captains and navigators of ships, and so forth, all those to whose expertise we defer when we want to get something done in the world. And on the other hand, here we should find the opinions of the morally and politically knowledgeable, those who have been well brought up in the customs and laws, the *nomoi*, of the city and who have developed the capacity to perceive what is needed in ever-changing circumstances to maintain social life and promote the city's interests, those to whose views we may defer in the Assembly when matters of policy are discussed or in the law courts where questions of justice are to be decided. The particular judgements both kinds of individual make are justified either by their experience of what has worked in the past or of their inherited tradition, or by appeal to their trained perception, acquired through past experience, of what will work in new circumstances or of how their tradition is now to be applied. They know, we might say, *about* the natural and social worlds, a knowledge of how to bring about certain kinds of results, and, in the light of this, they can make particular judgements about what to do on specific occasions.

The fire of the cave represents, we may suppose, the sun, by reference to which we form the divisions of time. The reason-giving of the unreflective and of the practically knowledgeable, Plato seems to be suggesting, both take place by reference to what is temporally situated, on the one hand, to the current state of popular opinion, on the other, to past experience of their crafts or the city's traditions. The former are thus subject to the vagaries of popular opinion as it changes in time, the latter to tradition, whether that of their particular craft or of the custom and law of the city. Both are thus in thrall to time experienced as a fate to which they are subject.

Yet our capacity for reflection can provide a liberation, a rising above this senseless governance by time. The unreflective, in appealing to general opinion, nevertheless claim that what they say is *true*, and in this tacitly accept the authority of those who claim to know, the practically and morally knowledgeable. But the knowledge possessed by the latter, acquired by training and experience, as one *about* the natural and social worlds, nevertheless invokes a kind of question it is unprepared to answer. Such a knowledgeable individual may know how to grow a certain kind of plant, rear sheep, or how to apply the nomoi of the city in order to produce judgements that are just. But such knowledge, being about plants or sheep, or the law, seems to presuppose a prior kind, that of what a plant, sheep or justice is. These latter questions are not about the plants, sheep or laws of which we have had experience, but, we might say, about their ideas: that which we must understand in order to encounter anything *as* a plant, sheep or case of justice. Our present knowledge has been gained from past experience, from initiation and practice in the traditions of crafts and of social living, and will be justified by appeal to that experience. But *these* questions cannot be answered by such an appeal, since that experience itself presupposed the application of such ideas, in identifying what one encountered as plants, sheep, or as laws which embodied justice. Such questions therefore seem to require us to appeal to what can measure, judge, experience in time itself.

But in order to set about answering such questions, we must know how to do so. Plato envisages an arithmetical training to prepare us for raising and responding to these questions since arithmetical truths appear divorced from the constraints of time and yet we use numbers, and so implicitly refer to such truths, in making judgements about things, actions and events in time in a quite unrestricted way. Numbers perhaps correspond to the 'shadows' we first encounter outside the cave, for here we find a realm of timeless truth concerning units which are, as Plato says, 'always the same' and which thus prefigure the forms as timeless unities for our intellectual apprehension. To raise our capacity for thought from the level of judging about what is in time to asking 'What is justice?' is to direct it towards the task of formulating timeless truths, as definitions of these purely intellectual objects. Such attempts themselves must furthermore take place in terms of the ideas concerned with such ideas themselves, those of sameness, difference and unity, which cannot be defined since all definition presupposes them. But at the summit of such reflection lies what makes this process more than just an intellectual game, a playing with equivalences of marks which we arbitrarily determine, but rather a reflection about the nature of the reality with which we began and through a concern for which we embarked on our intellectual journey. For we began with our everyday judgements through which we ordinarily live our lives, and proceeded through realizing that these judgements presupposed we knew what justice and the rest were 'in themselves'. In order to judge that this or that act, institution or person is or is not just we must know what justice is. Our reflection is thus directed towards apprehending the intellectual structure of the reality we un-reflectively inhabit and so ultimately towards the relation be-tween what is in time and the purely intelligible, the ultimate principle of all that is, that can in any way be as an object of perception or thought.

We return from such heights to the cave therefore apprehend-ing the *true* standards in terms of which judgement about things in time can be made. Plato says that philosophers:

> have a pattern in their souls and so can, as painters do, look to their models, fix their eyes on the absolute truth and with reference to that establish in this world also the laws of the beautiful, the just and the good, when that is needful and preserve those that are established.

> (*R* 484d)

If the judgements we ordinarily make presuppose that we know the forms of the things about which we speak, then clearly we must be able to *justify* such a claim, by being able to formulate them (or explain why they cannot be formulated) and to justify these formulations as the *right* ones, as *the* truth. Only so can we judge about things in the world, including, of course, ourselves, in the best way possible. Philosophy is thus the development of a capacity without which we could not live our ordinary lives, that of giving reasons for our beliefs and actions. Indeed, it responds to a necessity involved in such reason-giving, since the everyday reason-giving as exemplified in the cave cannot *ulti-mately* justify its judgements and so can support only an illusory sense of certainty.

We can note four general features of this project. First, it aims at finality, at the apprehension of the *totality* within which we can trace out the necessary lines of justification for any par-ticular judgement we might make. We may begin with judge-ments about external objects or cases of justice, but we cannot put a stop to our questioning at a terminus peculiar to that class of cases, for the question will arise as to why that should constitute the ground of reasoning there. We are driven to show that this terminus is required here in terms of something more fundamental, and unless there is some ultimate point we can reach which brings reflective questioning *as such* to an end, then the questioning will recur leaving all justification insecure. Second, in so far as all other activities stand in need of philosophy, as the quest for this totality, in order to determine whether or not what passes for reason-giving there truly is, or with what degree of approximation, philosophy itself needs no such certification. It rightly stands in judgement upon all other human projects. Third, since the totality is to claim jurisdiction over all our non-philosophical activities and modes of thought we must arrive at it through a process of *reflecting*, bringing out what is in some way implicit or hidden in those activities and thought themselves. Philosophy can appeal to nothing beyond this process of self-reflection itself, and thus has the character of 'recollection'. And this leads to the fourth feature we can remark. If human beings need to justify their beliefs and actions, then the form of human life which could *truly* do this would *govern* itself, rather than being in thrall to something beyond its own understanding. It would apprehend of its own power the true standards for its everyday judgements through which it could govern its life, and so would become autonomous. But such a form of life can only be practised as philosophy, for only philosophy aspires to this ultimate justification. In philosophy, human existence aspires to its ultimate goal, self-determination in terms of a measure it finds within itself, as the end of its capacity for reflective thought. Philosophy fulfils the human ambition for autonomy.

Of course, post-metaphysical thought regards this conception of the totality and its attendant interpretation of life in terms of autonomy as, in a certain sense, naive. For Heidegger, for example, it does not recognize its *own* historicality, that it is merely the way in which Western man has understood himself and his world from later antiquity until the recent past. But the revelation now of its historicality opens up a new possibility for man, that of living in terms of this historicality itself. Rather than occupying the position of an autonomous humanity with its possibility of apprehending the unity of reality, man is to live as historical, facing a future which is essentially open on the basis of a past understood as a source of possibility for the emergence of the new within the present. Truth is no longer timeless, but the unconcealing of possibilities held by the past which allow the new to come forth. This view in its turn is questioned by Derrida who tries to reveal it as the culmination of attempts to determine *the* meaning of man and his world, a project which nevertheless depends on the *production* of meaning, a differential process which renders the idea of a determinate meaning at once necessary and impossible. We will look at these positions in greater detail later. But we can immediately note that they emerge through a further, intensified reflection, directed now at the fundamental concepts of metaphysics themselves, those of totality, truth and the autonomous individual.

Although going beyond what it understands as metaphysics, post-metaphysical thought nevertheless responds to the same kind of question; it is part of what Derrida calls the 'universal problematic'.[10] For metaphysics, man's capacity to live in terms of reasons opens him to the necessity for attaining the concept of the totality which would bring such reason-giving to an end and render man autonomous. If Heidegger and Derrida go beyond this, it is because they see a possibility of questioning this idea of the totality and its corresponding notion of the nature of man and so of replacing them with something adequate to the nature of that question. These replacements, the notion of an historical humanity and its attendant conception of truth as unconcealment, or of a humanity for whom meaning involves the 'non-concept' of differance, play a parallel role to those they displace. They give us, that is, the way in which we can relate to ourselves and our world truly, or where this notion itself is rendered questionable, appropriately, in accordance with our historical situation or with the differential 'nature' of meaning itself: the way which terminates the possibility of reason-giving. There is in both metaphysical and post-metaphysical thought a single underlying conception which determines the way in which we can rightly or adequately relate to anything whatever: the totality, historicality, differance. And when we do relate to things in that way, we use properly our capacity as humans, for whom the question of coming into such a true or adequate relation necessarily arises. Since it is in the articulation of these fundamental conceptions that we express what ultimately determines the adequacy of any such actual relation, man's 'nature' finds its most complete manifestation there. Hence the primacy of philosophy, of Thinking, or decon-struction, for man, even if this is, as in the latter two cases, an historical primacy determined by our historical situation. These provide the measure for the adequacy of his other activities since they issue in the resolution to the problem which is human existence, the problem of living in a way which is justified before itself.

In what follows, I shall consider two responses to this 'universal problematic'. Wittgenstein tries to show that there is no *philosophical* need for it. Reason-giving takes place in terms of what *counts as* a reason, as a move, within particular language-games. There is thus no totality: what counts as such a move is irreducibly diverse. The language-games within which the variety of reason-giving and appeal to the real is played out have themselves, therefore, no reason: they are there 'like our life'. And since the totality is an illusion, the reflective move of post-metaphysical thought to a yet more encompassing position must be equally so. This critique is well enough documented, and I shall be concerned with it only relatively briefly. But the Wittgensteinian response may be felt not to address the basic attraction of these forms of thought. They respond, surely, to a need we indeed have, of situating ourselves in relation to ourselves and to the world. We have lives to lead which require that we have an understanding of the *meaning* of that life, and one through which we *must* relate to all else so that such relations can be justified in the appropriate way. The 'universal problematic' seems to emerge from the very nature of human life, from the problem which human existence is for itself. It is in relation to this that the second response, with which I shall be primarily concerned, is directed. For Kierkegaard there is indeed such a need, but it is wrongly understood as philosophical: it is existential, and finds its ultimate resolution, or more properly, dissolution, not in an intellectual apprehension of man's nature (or non-nature) and its correlative fundamental notion of reality or its post-metaphysical heirs, but in religion. A Wittgensteinian treatment of this is perfectly appropriate, for it would lie in returning the notion of a 'universal problematic' from its metaphysical use to the contexts within which it has its *living* home, in the various ways in which human beings come to understand the meaning of their lives and the kind of dispute that can take place there. Such disputes are not intellectual, at least in the philosophical sense: they are not resolved by philosophical argumentation. Rather, they are conflicts occasioned by the degree to which individuals are willing to *commit* their lives to *a* meaning, and their resolution lies, in so far as there can be such, in a transformed relation of the individual to his or her life. A relation to God for Kierkegaard is that relation within which the *whole* of the individual's life can be given meaning: its difference from other existential resolutions lies, therefore, in the degree of commitment which they manifest, and in terms of which we can understand the nature of their opposition to religion. Metaphysical and post-metaphysical thought are the result of a misconstruction of the nature of the need which they attempt to address.[11] That need manifests itself not in intellectual doubt, but in the problem the individual has with the meaning of her or his life. And in relation to that philosophy simply bypasses the issue. A youth, wrote Kierkegaard, who is 'an existing doubter' hovering 'in doubt and without a foothold for his life . . . reaches out for the truth – in order to exist in it . . . a philosophy of pure thought is for an existing individual a chimera, if the truth that is sought is something to exist in'.[12]

In what follows I shall try to show why Kierkegaard thought this to be so, and thereby clarify the nature of the chimera and of the problem to which it is an illusory response. The book, that is, tries to show the nature of Kierkegaard's *ethical* critique of philosophy, and thus the actuality of a non-philosophical site from which philosophy can be criticized. The plan of the book is as follows. Chapter 1 tries to show the character of the metaphysical project, according to Kierkegaard's description of it, through a discussion of its start in Plato and culmination in Hegel: I then develop a certain interpretation of Kierkegaard's critique of this project which seems to open the possibility of a post-metaphysical philosophy. This interpretation formed, I think, a major inspiration for Heidegger's early work, and Chapter 2 tries to illustrate his development of it and the nature of his own critique of Kierkegaard. However, I then suggest that this interpretation fails to read Kierkegaard in terms of the strange form his writings on philosophy take, being pseudonymous works characterized by irony and comedy. The rationale for this form is shown to lie in the primacy of the first-person in terms of which even a philosopher must speak and which resists philosophical conceptuality. Chapter 3 takes up the apparent similarities between Kierkegaard's and Nietzsche's critiques of philosophy, but tries to show that Nietzsche too fails to remain faithful to the primacy of the I. Chapter 4 develops an interpretation of Heidegger's later thought, indebted as it is to Nietzsche rather than to Kierkegaard, and shows it to be subject to a Kierkegaardian criticism of a philosophy articulating 'what the age demands'. Chapter 5 discusses Derrida's relation to Heidegger and, whilst claiming that Derrida too would fall within Kierkegaard's critique, tries to develop a contrast between his thought and that of the later Wittgenstein in order to clarify the fundamental existential motivation of post-metaphysical philosophy. This motivation is interpreted in Chapter 6 as hubris, and the apparent similarities between Kierkegaard and post-metaphysical thought are shown to mask a fundamental difference: Kierkegaard's emphasis on the first-person position from which any individual must speak. Chapter 7 compares Kierkegaard with Levinas who too stresses the primacy of the I and develops like Kierkegaard, an ethical critique of philosophy. The issue of the appropriate form of language in which such an ethical critique can be carried out is raised, and in the concluding brief chapter this question is shown to rebound on *myself*.

# Chapter 1

# Kierkegaard and the metaphysical project

In *Concluding Unscientific Postscript*, Kierkegaard remarks that in his earlier *Philosophical Fragments* he had ignored the difference between Socrates and Plato:

> By holding Socrates down to the proposition that all knowledge is recollection, he becomes a speculative philosopher instead of an existential thinker, for whom existence is the essential thing. The recollection principle belongs to speculative philosophy, and recollection is immanence, and speculatively and eternally there is no paradox.[1]

Plato and Hegel mark the beginning and culmination of a particular project of human thought, metaphysics, which, for Kierkegaard, in its claim to reveal the truth of human existence represents a misunderstanding, and in its character as a human enterprise, expresses a deficient mode of human life. In erecting that mode, 'relative' or 'conditioned' willing, to a position of pre-eminence, it constitutes a confusing of human existence whose proper criticism is ethical or religious. We can begin to see why he thought this to be so by examining the character of this project in Plato and Hegel.

## I

Philosophy, Plato said, begins in wonder, for, as Aristotle later put it, 'wondering involves a desire to understand, so that a thing that rouses wonder is a thing in connection with which we feel desire'.[2] What it is which prompts the philosophical wonder and desire to understand is shown in Socrates' account of his development in the *Phaedo*. Initially his interest had been aroused by the investigation of nature (*peri phuseus*) directed towards understanding the causal conditions for the coming to be, maintenance and perishing of the things he found around him.[3] But the possible results of such an investigation do not seem able to satisfy the desire to understand which underlies his inquiry. He first gains an insight into the nature of this desire upon hearing someone reading from a book by Anaxagoras in which it was said that it is the mind (*nous*) that arranges and causes all things.[4] This seemed to Socrates 'somehow right', but upon investigating Anaxagoras, he is disappointed, for 'the man made no use of intelligence, and did not assign any real causes for the ordering of things, but mentioned as causes air and ether, and water and many other absurdities'.[5] According to Socrates' account, Anaxagoras appears to have been engaged on a more general version of his own initial inquiry, attempting to explain natural phenomena in terms of very general causal principles. What such inquiries neglect, and what Socrates comes to realize is the object of his own desire to understand, is 'the good, which must embrace and hold together all things'[6] and it is in relation to this that he leaves the investigating of beings (*ta onta*) and turns to that of conceptions (*tous logous*) in order to understand the truth of beings.[7] Socrates' interest lay not in the causal conditions for the existence of things, which could be formulated in general empirical principles, but in what it is that makes these things the things they *are*: something is 'beautiful for no other reason than because it partakes of absolute beauty; and this applies to everything'.[8] It is this sense of cause or reason (*aitia*) which provokes his desire to understand, and which is more fundamental than that of the causal conditions which the investigations of beings concerns itself with.

Why this should be, Socrates indicates when he says 'not only the abstract idea itself has a right to the same name through all time, but also something else, which is not the idea, but which always, whenever it exists, has the form [*morphe*] of the idea'.[9] When we say 'Simmias is greater than Socrates' this is true by reason of the greatness he happens to have.[10] But not only can the idea of greatness not admit of its contrary and so also be small, but 'the greatness in us will never admit the small'.[11] If 'Simmias is greater than Socrates' is true, then this truth has the character of *changelessness*, even if at one time Simmias is greater and at another smaller than Socrates. If a proposition is true, then it cannot become false, and the appearance to the contrary is the result of forgetting that statements about things in the world are always claims as to what is true of them at a particular time and place, and clearly what is true of them at one time and place may be different from what is true at another. The question which prompts Socrates' wonder and so his desire to understand is *how it is possible for there to be truth about beings*, a possibility which is presupposed by the empirical inquiries into the causes of things which attempt to tell us particular truths.

The issue which concerns Socrates Wittgenstein called 'The agreement, the harmony, of thought and reality.'[12] 'A wish seems already to know what will or would satisfy it, a proposition, a thought, what makes it true – even when that thing is not there at all! Whence the *determining* of what is not yet there?'[13] This question lay at the foundation of Wittgenstein's early work, and in the preparatory studies for the *Tractatus* he had written: 'My whole task consists in explaining the nature of the proposition. That is to say, in giving the nature of all facts, whose picture the proposition is. In giving the nature of all being.'[14] How is it possible for a proposition, a thought, to be true, to be satisfied by what is? As the reference to the proposition as a 'picture' suggests, Wittgenstein thought at this time that it must be because reality and thought share a common form. Propositions could only be true or false, correspond or fail to correspond with what is, if reality had *intelligible* form. A proposition, a thought, represents a situation, and is true if the situation exists. It can only agree or disagree with reality if this representing is possible, and that requires that there be an isomorphism of thought and reality: reality must essentially have the character of thought. The wonder that provokes Socrates' desire to understand is that what is, 'all being', is thinkable, that truth is possible. What must the nature of all being be that this should be so?

When Socrates is explaining this in the *Republic* he begins by saying:

> We predicate 'to be' of many beautiful things and many good things saying of them severally that they *are*, and so define them in our speech . . . And again, we speak of a self-beautiful and of a good that is only and merely good, and so, in the case

of all the things that we then posited as many, we turn about and posit each as a single idea, assuming it to be a unity and call it that which really is.[15]

Man is the being possessing *logos*, a word which means word, account, reason amongst others. He speaks and because he speaks he can be asked for and give reason, justification, for what he says. The most fundamental form of saying, for it appears any other kind must be built upon it, is identification, saying 'This is that':[16] this is a cow, this colour is red, and so on. Even an utterance like 'This is sweet' is not merely a squeal of delight or disgust. It appears to involve a *claim*: that this taste satisfies what is meant by 'sweet'. And that meaning appears to be something quite different from the taste itself. The taste comes to be and passes away, it is mine and not yours, it occurs here and at this time. But the meaning is not somewhere or at some time, is not mine or yours. It 'is' in a different way. Whereas the 'is' of the taste or of this table, this room, means 'is here and now, at such and such a place and time', the 'is' of the meaning does not. It is apparently a timeless 'is'. And whereas the taste is tasted, the table seen and felt, the sound heard, the meaning can neither be tasted, seen, felt nor heard: 'And the one class of things, we say can be seen but not thought, while the ideas can be thought but not seen.'[17] The ideas are objects of the intellect, *nous*, the taste, the table, the colour are objects of sense, *aisthesis*.

And yet this is not a matter of different capacities being directed at quite unconnected objects. For we *say* the objects of sense *are*: the table, the colour, the taste. But that object is a table only in so far as it satisfies the idea of the table: its very being *as a table* depends on the idea. But should we say: very well, we experience by sense not the table but a brown physical object, then the same can be said. It is only a brown physical object in virtue of the ideas of brownness and of physical object. And if it is said, nevertheless we at least experience 'this', then that too, as something said, standing as it does for an object, is only possible in so far as there is a congruence with the idea of an object. Without the ideas we could not even say 'This'. To say, or think, there *is* something is already to use language, and so presuppose meaning. Without meaning, without the ideas, there is ____ not even nothing, since for there to be 'nothing' there must be meaning. Nevertheless, we are forced at the limit to recognize what cannot be conceptualized. In order for there to be temporal beings through their relation to the ideas, there must be presupposed that which is first formed in accordance with ideas, 'the Mother and Receptacle of this generated world',[18] which as it 'is to receive all kinds' is 'devoid of all forms'[19] and so only 'in some most perplexing and most baffling way partaking of the intelligible'.[20]

When we speak of 'the class of things that can be seen' we are already in the realm which presupposes the objects that can only be thought. Those objects are the meanings which, as timeless, cannot be subject to change, which can only occur in time. Hence, Plato says, they are 'always the same'. But their sameness is, at the same time, *difference* from other ideas, so that if we can state a meaning we do so by a definition, a distinguishing, and if we cannot state it, but merely intellectually apprehend it in its indefinability, we nevertheless do so in its distinction from all else. A definition, say 'A triangle is a three-sided plane figure', is a truth which is neither spatially nor temporally delimited, as are all truths about objects 'that can be seen' which are in the realm of 'becoming'. And we can see that the definition is a distinguishing of the triangle within a more general idea, that of plane figure, which also encompasses squares, rectangles, and so on. The idea of the plane figure is itself distinguished within a more general idea, that of figure, within which we have both two-dimensional plane and three-dimensional figures. A definition, or the apprehension of an indefinable distinction, is always a distinguishing within the context of a more general idea, of a part from the other parts of this whole. This more general idea itself, that of figure, can only be distinguished as part within the realm of a yet more general idea. We rise from the idea of a triangle to plane figure to that of figure itself, the idea of geometrical ideas. But the idea of figure is itself a part of the more general category, the ideas which make possible things within time, within which it may be distinguished. That more general category is itself a part of the general category of idea itself, the other part being composed of those ideas which relate both to ideas themselves and to the application of such ideas to the realm of the temporal: sameness, difference, unity.

But ideas, temporal beings, and that which must be presupposed for the application of ideas within the temporal at all, are all themselves parts of being: they can all be said to 'be'. But we cannot say what 'being' means by distinguishing it as part within a larger whole, for there can be no such whole. Rather, to say what being is, is to give its own parts, the temporal 'is' and the timeless 'is', in their *relation*. Thus Plato tells us that 'becoming' is for the sake of 'being' in the timeless sense, and 'that for the sake of which anything comes to be is in the class of the good'.[21] *The* Good is not an idea but the relation between temporal beings and the ideas which makes the latter the condition of possibility of the former. Hence 'the good itself is not essence but still transcends essence in dignity and surpassing power',[22] granting existence and essence, their role *as* essence, to ideas, and so making possible our knowledge of them as essences, as what makes possible the objects we unreflectively take as real.[23] Of course, Plato speaks of the *Idea* of the Good. But this is not something which can be apprehended by thought, since it is presupposed in the possibility of thought itself. If we do speak of the idea of the Good, it is in the sense of the Idea of idea itself, that which makes ideas essences either of what is not an idea or of subordinate ideas themselves, and that is the relation between the temporal and the timeless 'is'. The realm of Being is not simply divided into two unconnected realms, of Becoming and timeless Being. They are a *whole* which we understand when we see that the latter makes the former possible. And when we recognize the idea of the Good, of this very dependency of the world we take unphilosophically to be the real one upon the realm of what is only available to the intellect, then we 'arrive at the limit of the intelligible'.[24]

Here we see the Platonic resolution of our question: how is truth possible? Plato's answer is that what we speak of non-philosophically and so produce 'truths', the realm of becoming, is 'for the sake of timeless being': that what is in time is made possible by the timeless being of the ideas, the proper objects of thought, and so 'participates' in the intelligible. 'The table is brown' can be true only because there are tables and brownness in the world as temporal and spatial instantiations of the ideas of table and brownness, because the realm of becoming is a 'copy' or image of that which is available to thought alone. This 'harmony between thought and reality' we address in directing ourselves towards the idea of the Good:

'Wise men tell us that heaven and earth and gods and men are held together by communion and friendship, by orderliness, temperance and justice, and that is the reason why they call the whole the Kosmos [order].'[25] Philosophy as love of wisdom thinks 'the whole' (*to holon*) and it does so in terms of order, without which the wholeness of the whole cannot be thought. This thinking takes place as 'dialectics': 'For he who can view things in their connection is a dialectician, he who cannot, is not.'[26] The dialectician is one who systematically determines what each thing really is,[27] the great difficulty lying in doing this correctly. The key to this is not 'to separate everything from everything else' which is 'the mark of a man who has no link whatever with the Muse of Philosophy'[28] but to be governed by the aim of truth, the unity of the whole: 'Whom do you mean, then, by the true philosophers? Those for whom the truth is the spectacle of which they are enamoured.'[29]

The philosopher is enamoured of the spectacle of truth for he is directed not towards the production of truths but towards resolving the question of the possibility of truth, towards the truth of truth. Our everyday truths are possible because the reality we there address is intelligible, formed in accordance with what is truly intelligible, the ideas.

But what, then, of ourselves? We speak not only of other things around us but of ourselves, and we can do so only if there is, timelessly, the idea of the human, of what in relation to the whole distinguishes man from other beings. Man is within the 'visible and tangible' and so has a body.[30] Beings within space and time are either inanimate or living, the latter having the power of self-directed change, *psuche*, through which they approximate their ideas. If the Good is the relation of purposiveness which relates the temporal realm to the unchanging, then this process of imitation is the way in which temporal living beings reveal it. Their 'good' is their satisfaction, to the extent this is possible within the changeable, of the requirements of their idea. *Psuche* as the power of self-direction towards their good may be present unconsciously, as in plants,[31] or with a degree of awareness of their end, as with animals which seek what is beneficial and flee from what is harmful. The animal has both sensation, which plants have too, and an unreflective consciousness of their good. But man, whilst sharing these forms of *psuche*, has too *nous*, intelligence, and *logismos*: that is, the ability to *know* ends by intelligence and to calculate means towards them. This gives him both the power of knowledge of other beings and of self-mastery of himself. Intelligence distinguishes man amongst living beings, and manifests itself in the very capacity for speech which requires some form of apprehension of meanings, ideas,[32] but takes its proper form in knowing these intelligible objects explicitly and in knowing their relation to temporal beings. At its highest development, this is the capacity for philosophy, knowing the nature of the All:

> We should rectify the revolutions in our head by learning the harmonies and revolutions of the All, and thereby making the part that thinks like unto the object of its thought, in accordance with its original nature, and having achieved this likeness attain finally to that goal of life which is set before men by the gods as the best life both for the present and the time to come.[33]

Man's end, through which he best participates in his idea, that of an intelligent living being, lies in philosophical knowing within which all other beings, both temporal and unchanging, appear as they *are*. In this way, he reveals in its appropriate form the relation of purposiveness, the Good, which holds beings together in harmony. Hence 'the greatest study' is 'to learn the idea of the Good',[34] through which it is possible for the good of man, apprehension of the truth of the whole, to be achieved. Those 'who are uneducated and inexperienced in truth have no single aim and purpose in life to which all their actions, public and private, must be directed'.[35] Human life finds its end in philosophical knowing of the truth of the All, and this is wisdom:

> The soul alone by itself departs to what is pure and always existent and immortal and unvarying, and in virtue of its kinship with it enters always into its company. Then it has ceased from its wandering and when it is about these objects it is always constant and unvarying because of its contact with things of a similar kind: and this is called wisdom.[36]

Truth is possible about the world since it is formed as an image of the purely intelligible, the ideas. But it is available to *us* because we have a 'divine element', intelligence, which enables us to apprehend what is changeless and so inhabit a world of becoming at all, for that depends for its being on changeless being. Unless there were this harmony between ourselves and the ideas, thought would be impossible for us. The soul must, therefore, be 'unchangeable or something close to it',[37] for its judgements, and those upon it, if true, are changelessly so. Our possession of *nous* makes possible not only our capacity for the apprehension of what is true about the world surrounding us, but also about ourselves, whose being is itself made possible by the idea of the human. Taking this as our pattern, we can attain 'self-mastery and beautiful order' making of ourselves 'a unity, one man instead of many'.[38] The idea of the human, that which distinguishes man from all else within the whole, is that of an intelligent embodied being, for whom, therefore, 'it belongs to the rational part to rule, being wise and exercising forethought on behalf of the entire soul'.[39] But that rational part engages in its own proper activity in understanding: so the capacity for ruling is identical with that of learning and knowledge.[40] But understanding, as the progress of Socrates towards self-knowledge in the *Phaedo* shows, culminates in philosophy, which aims at comprehending the principle which holds together all being, man himself included. Philosophical contemplation, *theoria*, the fulfilment of this inquiry, thus constitutes the highest activity for humanity, the end of human life: it lies in making the cause of the harmony between thought and reality, the Good, manifest.

Yet man can only play this role in the scheme of things, revealing the intellectual order of the whole, the truth, if there *is* such truth. The idea of the Good is the central principle of this order, that Becoming is for the sake of Being, that what is in time depends for its being upon non-temporal forms. That this is so is recollected through reflection upon the realm of becoming: we already say temporal beings are, and this is only possible in so far as forms *are* non-temporally. Without the forms we could not say anything, and so there would be no realm of Becoming. Nevertheless, this appears to rest on an assumption which it must, at the same time, be beyond intelligence to justify, since intelligence can at the most apprehend the forms and their relation to temporal being. Thus, Socrates, being asked to speak about the Good, asks: 'do you think it right to speak as having knowledge about things one does not know?'[41] Given that we do say temporal beings are, then perhaps we must assume the existence of the forms and of their relation to such beings. But mightn't it be that such initial saying were *itself* illusory, so that reflection upon it merely compounded the illusion? Of course, we could never know whether this is so or not. But if our reflection is to reveal the truth of the whole, we must begin with something which is itself, albeit imperfectly, true. Given that our aim is truth, how can we justify this initial starting place? Doesn't the pursuit of truth involve us in an assumption which that very pursuit requires us to justify whilst at the same time prevents us from doing just that? How can we know we have any contact with truth at all? Only if the pursuit of truth could reveal itself as presuppositionless could its instability be rectified, and that, of course, is Hegel's aim.

## II

This sceptical question can only occur from within the pursuit of truth itself: even if it appears as necessarily unanswerable, it must first be formulated, and so brought within what is sayable. If it is to raise the possibility that all our saying of beings may be illusory, it not only presupposes that at least something can be said, but that that something has a particular form, namely, that it is a possibility that we have no contact with truth at all. The very formulation of this possibility involves our understanding a notion of truth in terms of which we can see that, in relation to it, the proposal is indeed a possibility. For Plato, the truth of the whole is understood as already and always existing to which our intellect may, if it comes to understand the truth, correspond. Understood in this abstract way, it appears possible to raise the question whether we could know there was such truth at all, and if there were whether we could come adequately into relation to it. There always remain the possibilities that there isn't or that we couldn't. But since the formulation of such sceptical questions must use the notion of truth, they can be defused if we can show that that notion precludes these possibilities. The abstract notion of truth precisely abstracts it from our saying and thinking, whilst it is only there that it has any sense: it is what we say and think that is true or not. Truth has to be understood in terms of our thought: what it means, we might say, has to be determined by its role there. The sceptic depends on that meaning in formulating his question, whilst attempting at the same time to question the viability of thinking in its entirety.

Replaced within the context which gives it its sense, 'truth', Hegel says, is seen as the end of thought. It is revealed where thought attains its *telos*, which is something to be determined by *thinking itself*. The truth is not something external to thought to which it may correspond and which would allow the possibility of the sceptical question, but is rather the immanent goal thought is itself directed towards and in terms of which it overcomes inadequate formulations in a progressive realization of what that goal is. Thought here really does recollect the truth, since it is its own, whilst Platonic recollection presupposes an adequacy of the intellect to the truth which must simply be accepted.

For Plato, the possibility of the truth we non-philosophically assume lies in the intelligibility of the world, in its being 'thought-like', which is constituted by its 'participation' in the ideas, so that things *are* within the world only as instantiations of ideas. Truth concerning the ideas lies in an adequation between our thinking and these fully knowable objects, just as truth about the world lies in the correspondence between our thought and the things in the world which the ideas make possible. But as recollection, the apprehension of the former assumes that the truth we non-philosophically suppose is actual, something we cannot assume if our inquiry is into the possibility of truth itself. For what could show that our philosophical thought is true, rather than merely drawing out the presuppositions of a thinking about the world we non-philosophically take to be so? We need to demonstrate the impossibility of such a doubt, which we can only do if the notion of truth itself precludes it. And that is possible only if the question of the possibility of the truth we assume non-philosophically is at the same time that of *the notion of truth itself*. The truth we assume must, that is, be shown to be inadequate in its own terms, so that reflection compels us towards the revelation of the notion of truth itself. The intelligibility of reality as we non-philosophically take it to be is not a matter of the harmony between thought and reality for Hegel but a moment in a unitary dynamic which reveals what is 'true' only in the progressive emergence of the notion of truth itself.

In its immediate form, thought is consciousness, within which truth is understood as a correspondence between itself and an independent and indifferent reality. But truth is what is known, and in attempting to articulate what it is that it knows, consciousness in the successive forms of sense-certainty, perception of stable things, and the understanding of forces and laws, comes to understand that its object is not an 'in itself' but a 'for us'. It comes to the realization that in order to relate to the given as given, it must use itself, its own forms of objectivity. Were reality absolutely indifferent, consciousness could have no contact with it. Nature is the Concept externalized, that is, it is *for* thought, it is 'something posited'. Thus, sense-certainty claims to know the tree immediately. But what it claims to know, the tree here, *is* only *qua* tree, and so in its difference from other things, and only here as opposed to there, and now as opposed to other times. And what it claims to know only is such for a perceiving subject, which is itself a universal. Comparison of sense-certainty's own criterion of knowledge, immediacy, with what it claims to know results in a new understanding both of the object known and of what 'knowledge' and so 'truth' is. What is known is thus revealed as an object for a perceiving subject. But, again, what the perceiving subject claims to know is, *qua* object, unavailable to perception, since this can only know properties and not the object of which they are properties. What is known thus appears now as the object of understanding, an inner reality which underlies the appearances sense-perception can apprehend. Initially this is understood as force which produces the appearances, but this fails to explain the effects, being simply whatever accounts for them. The object of knowledge appears, therefore, as law, a necessary relation between appearances which constitutes them as the appearances of an object, and which as the organizing principle of appearances requires a consonant conception of subjectivity as transcendental. Thus in pursuing the truth, consciousness becomes self-consciousness, coming to have itself as its object.

Self-consciousness initially emerges in the *momentary* mutual realization of freedom from finitude, the given, in the risking of life in the struggle to the death of the heroes of Greek epic. Such freedom, in its essential opposition to the given, obtains a universality in the form of life of the master and slave, within which the slave, in constant fear of death, encounters the limit of human finitude, and, in knowing it, goes beyond: 'Man as spirit *knows* its limit, and in this passes beyond the limit.'[42] And in moulding materials to his master's demands, he comes to know himself as essentially other than external nature. This individual knowing of one's freedom over against nature, both external and human, becomes concrete in the Stoic way of life, and expresses its essential negativity in being actualized merely in freeing oneself from care about worldly things, in a conquest of one's own nature. But self-consciousness as thought is directed towards truth, and truth is of a unity. The desire for truth aspires to a unity transcending the division of Stoic consciousness. This desire for a state in which we should be both free and whole emerges in the unhappy consciousness of the post-Roman world. Since freedom is still freedom from nature, such a unity is not to be attained in our natural existence, but only in a state beyond this life, in relation to which our earthly existence is as nothing.

The desire for truth now takes the form of Reason, in which the individual selfhood defines itself, not in opposition to a given human nature, but as its positive appropriation. As theoretical reason, it expresses itself in natural science, 'observing' a given world, but overcoming its givenness with the ambition to conquer it completely in a total knowledge, an ideal frustrated by the irreducible irrationality of contingency. As practical reason, it attempts, not to master in thought a given world, but to transform the given human world in its own image. That image, in so far as it is an ideal, something to be held before thought in its transforming activity, is of a universal individuality. But such universality, in the light of the particularity of the given individual's desires, remains abstract, leading to no concrete and binding laws on all.

The self must understand itself, not in terms of individual selfhood, but rather in terms of a concrete unity of individuals, a concrete self-conscious universality. Man's desire for truth initially reveals himself to himself as Spirit in the unreflective unity of a people, defining itself over against others. But as an *explicit* unity of all, it is manifested in its abstract form in the legal community of the Roman Empire. As no content derives from such an abstract unity, the emperor has total power to determine the rights of individuals. The content of the unity is arbitrary, deriving from the given particularity of the emperor. The ethical unity of the constituent peoples is destroyed, but this reveals, in the Stoic consciousness, the freedom of individuals from any given social form. Such free individuals must now create a community in their own image, the Christian community which despises the world and looks towards fulfilment of its true nature in the Kingdom of God beyond this life, whilst the actual community of this world is created by individuals in the image of their given individual desires for power and wealth. Such determination by one's given nature is overcome in the negative freedom of the early Enlightenment, in which the self understands itself as free of any given social form and, in its aspiration for unity, conceives of everything given as material, to do with as it will. The French Revolution shows that this absolute freedom, which as a form of Spirit, is universal and must express itself in collective activity, can, being divorced from any concrete content, only manifest itself in the community of destruction, of the past order and then of itself.

Man as Spirit must develop a social order which unites its freedom from the given with the given: to produce a community of free individuals. In Kant's philosophy, the self understands its unity with humanity as a whole through the conception of duty, the submission of a given human nature to the demands of universality. Yet here the universal of humanity is opposed to the particularity of the individual: being defined in opposition to nature, man is divided from himself, and the ultimate goal of an ethical commonwealth in which nature and duty would be one remains always and only as an ideal. The conflict between ideality and reality is overcome in the unity of the post-Kantian conscience, in which the abstract Kantian unity of mankind becomes a concrete community of individuals, acting in particular circumstances in the light of their consciences. Yet such a community is inevitably characterized by conflict, the consciences of different individuals determining different courses of action. And since anything can be considered good, there can be no certainty, either for others or for the individual himself, that he follows the dictates of conscience rather than his individual desires. The 'we' of humanity can only obtain a concrete form which satisfies the desire for truth, and so unity, in a *community* of free individuals. The apprehension of this Hegel finds manifest in the rationality of the bureaucratic state.

But although this apprehension is present, it is so as moral certainty, a certainty of contemporary action. It does not understand its own necessity: that it is the truth. It could do so only by rising above the given, present as the material for universalizing action, to see the essential unity of the given and humanity's nature as universalizing reason, in an *absolutely* free activity of self-knowing. Such an activity knows nature as *for* humanity's self-knowing, and knows the various forms of human life as stages in man's coming to know himself: it sees the unity of the finite natural and human world as constituted in the universalizing activity of humanity which attains *its* own appropriate form, as thought, in knowing itself. This absolute knowing is God: 'God is spirit, the activity of pure knowing.'[43] The individual, in raising himself to knowing the essential unity of what is, can become, although only in such knowing, divine: 'humanity is immortal only through cognitive knowledge'.[44]

Yet what God is is known only in the absolute knowing which is philosophy. Religion and philosophy both have the same object,[45] 'reason in principle',[46] but it is known as what it is only by the highest form of cognitive activity, where the rationality of the world finds its appropriate form of articulation, in rational thought. Religion apprehends the unity of the world, but it does so only in an incompletely rational form of thinking, representation,[47] in which it is conceived as something external: 'faith expresses the absolute objectivity that the content has for me';[48] 'The content . . . has and retains the form of an externality over against me. I make it *mine*, [but] I am not [contained] in it, nor identical with it.'[49] Christianity is the 'absolute religion' for there 'God has made known what he is; there he is manifest':[50] God reveals himself in a man. The 'unity of divine and human nature comes to consciousness for humanity in such a way that a human being appears to consciousness as God, and God appears to it as a human being.'[51] Since religion is the manifesting of God, it finds its fulfilment, its truth, in the rational articulation of that manifestation, in knowing what God is. Christianity itself reveals this as its end, for its doctrines proclaim that 'we should *know* God cognitively, God's nature and essence and should esteem his cognition above all else'.[52] But that rational knowledge can only take place in philosophy: 'philosophy is theology, and [one's] occupation . . . *in* philosophy . . . is of itself the service of God'.[53]

The Platonic idea of the Good, the relation of purposiveness which binds the temporal and the intelligible into a whole, is identified by Hegel with the activity of human thought itself. The timelessly true is the principle of rationality of the world which comes to its own self-consciousness in human philosophical knowing. It is, therefore, both *ousia* in the Platonic sense, existing 'solely through itself and for its own sake. It is something absolutely self-sufficient, unconditioned, independent, free as well as being the supreme end unto itself',[54] and, at the same time, Spirit.

> Spirit *is* in the most complete sense. The absolute or highest being belongs to it. But Spirit is . . . only in so far as it is *for* itself, that is, in so far as it posits itself or brings itself forth; for it is only as activity . . . in this activity it is knowing.[55]

The rationality of the world is both substance, an intellectually apprehensible order which 'is' in a more than merely temporal sense, and subject, for it is essentially a thinking which must come to know itself. Reality becomes self-transparent in man's absolute knowing. And there man attains true self-consciousness, finding *within himself* the ground which can justify his cognitive, practical and political activities, for these represent the concrete manifestations of Spirit's universalizing activity which are for its own self-knowledge. And man can, in absolute knowing, become self-conscious Spirit.

For Plato and Hegel, man, characterized by thought, must act and think in accordance with truth. Truths about what is in the world depend on the latter's intelligibility, and the truth of this intelligibility is first to be formulated either in terms of the ideas of what is in the world, or in the characterization of the nature of the objects of sense experience and understanding. But the truth about the intelligibility of the world requires further that of the harmony between the things of the world and the ideas, or of the principle of reality which makes the objects of sense experience and understanding aspects of reality. The truth is ultimately of the whole, and the truth of any part lies in its place there. Man, however, is not merely a being apprehended by thought because its nature is intelligible, but rather the thinking being through whom all other beings become known in their intelligibility, and this is possible only through knowing the whole. Man's truth, his determination in terms of the whole, is, thus, to apprehend the truth of reality, or to be its principle through which reality knows itself. Hence, the activity of philosophy constitutes the fulfilment of human life.

For both Plato and Hegel, man's highest form of activity is philosophical knowing in which the ground, in terms of which all other forms of knowledge and truth can be understood, is discovered as at one with man himself. For Plato, this ground is the idea of the Good, of the purposiveness which binds together all that can be said to be and which provides us with the notions of a final truth and unchanging being. The philosophical life appears as the highest because it fulfils man's nature, his distinction from all else in the whole of being. The divinity within man lies in his intelligence, his capacity to participate in the timeless in its *appropriate* form, *as* intelligible, and so reveal the purposiveness which binds the temporal and timeless together. For Hegel, this purposiveness becomes the activity of unifying thought itself, which reveals external nature as *for* the universalizing activity of man's scientific knowing, and man's own as to be imprinted with the image of man *as* such a universalizing being, and so as self-determining. Man, as the being who is capable of knowing his end and acting accordingly, knows his nature as such only in the activity which brings this capacity to fulfilment. And that can take place only in absolute knowing, when external and human nature have been revealed as they *are* through the coming to self-consciousness of the organizing activity of reason. Man does not just possess a divine element, but can in such knowing become God as the ultimate ground of all being, self-conscious Spirit.

## III

Referring to Hegel, Kierkegaard remarks in his *Journals* that 'Philosophy is the purely human view of the world, the human standpoint'[56] which tends 'toward a recognition of Christianity's harmony with the universally human consciousness'.[57] It leads, that is, towards an identification of the human with the divine, a process which has its roots in the Platonic conception of a divine element in man's nature. Hegel's thought, for Kierkegaard, is the culmination of this tradition of philosophy, within which the nature of that human project becomes transparent, for there the human being thinking 'the system of the universe'[58] becomes divine. In such thinking he becomes one with self-conscious Spirit. And that is God.[59]

Kierkegaard, notoriously, found Hegel *comic*: 'someone who is really tested in life, who in his need resorts to thought, will find Hegel comical despite all his greatness'.[60] This comedy results from the incompatibility between the sort of question which our existence is for us and how that question is conceived by metaphysics. Metaphysics seeks to *answer* the question, by providing a ground, a determination of the nature of man, as embodied intelligence, or as Spirit, universalizing unifying activity, through which a concrete form of human life can be justified as life's end, its meaning and purpose. The argument to this ground takes the form of locating the human in relation to the whole, the truth of truth. Thought of the whole, as Hegel emphasizes, precludes appeal to presuppositions, and so must have the form of recollection of what is implicit in thought. The problem of existence as part of this general project appears as an intellectual one, to be resolved by thought revealing what is implicit in existence. This is why metaphysics assumes 'that if only the truth is brought to light, its appropriation is a relatively unimportant matter, something which follows as a matter of course'.[61]

I shall be concerned throughout this work with the rami- fications of Kierkegaard's critique of this understanding of the problem of human existence. However, that critique begins with his insistence that it is just this matter of appropriation which poses for us the question of the truth of existence: 'The inquiring, speculating and knowing subject . . . raises a question of truth, but he does not raise the question of a subjective truth, the truth of appropriation and assimilation.'[62]

The truth which metaphysics seeks is to be revealed through reflection, and having been apprehended is then to be *lived*. But to say this is immediately to mark a difference between the categories appropriate *within* reflective thought and those con- cerning our *relation* to it through which it becomes part of our life. Whereas the metaphysical project attempts to determine life's measure through situating the human in relation to the whole of being, Kierkegaard emphasizes that such thought as a human activity itself is part of life. Life's measure would be what can give meaning to life as a whole. The question then arises as to whether what must for its *own* significance be situated by the individual in relation to this whole can itself reveal the truth of life. 'If a man occupies himself all his life through with logic, he would nevertheless not become logic: he must therefore himself exist in different categories.'[63] These categories are those of 'subjectivity', the relation of the individual to her *own* activities and relationships and so forth which issues from the relation she has to her life as a whole. If an individual occupies herself with logic, we may ask not merely what results ensue but *how* she involves *herself* with it. This question initially prompts an account of the sort of commitment she has to the activity. But this in turn raises a question about that relation itself: is it of the *right* kind? The individual must relate *herself* to this activity as she must to *any* activity or relationship or to anything which occurs to her. Is her form of relationship, then, appropriate for a being subject to such a necessity *throughout her life?* The individual has a conception of her life as a whole, that she has a life to lead, and the question as to the truth of existence relates to this, through which an appropriate relation to activities and relationships *within* life can be determined. But for the individual, her life as a whole cannot be present: 'life constitutes the task. To be finished with life before life has finished with one, is precisely not to have finished the task.'[64] One cannot, therefore, relate to one's life as a whole in terms of a *result* or *fulfilment*, for this is to treat life as a task which can be *completed*, even if this is conceived as an ideal. But this is precisely what metaphysics does, understanding life's task as the achievement of knowledge of the whole or as the end of the process whereby the whole achieves explicit rationality: 'objective thought translates everything into results, subjective thought puts everything into process and omits results – for as an existing individual he is constantly in process of coming to be'.[65]

Metaphysics in construing life as having an immanent goal fails to recognize that the wholeness of life from the point of view of the *living*, the *existing* individual cannot be so conceived. Its view is a result of seeing the question of human life 'objectively', a relation which we as living beings may take up in relation to past human existence, as when we concern ourselves with the objective truth about historical events, but which we cannot take up in relation to our *own*. 'Hegel . . . does not understand history from the point of view of becoming, but with the illusion attached to pastness understands it from the point of view of a finality that excludes all becoming.'[66] The metaphysical project treats human life in the mode of pastness and only so can it think of it in terms of a final result. But whereas it makes sense to relate to the past in terms of disinterested inquiry and so in terms of the objective truth, such a relation is only possible for a being who has a quite different relation to her or his own life.

> Whenever a particular existence has been relegated to the past, it is complete, has acquired finality, and is in so far subject to a systematic apprehension . . . but for whom is it so subject? Anyone who is himself an existing individual cannot gain this finality outside existence which corresponds to the eternity into which the past has entered.[67]

His historical inquiry is an activity he engages with and to which he relates: but this latter relation cannot be one of the 'disinterested' inquiry through which he addresses the objects of his research, but one we can only understand in 'subjective' categories. That is, we must understand such a relation in terms of life as it is related to by the one who is *living* it and not in terms of the relation of a living being to a life which is not her or his own. The comedy of the System, Kierkegaard says, is that it forgets that philosophy has to be written by human beings[68] who have necessarily a different *kind* of relation to their own lives than they can have to anything else: 'The only reality to which an existing individual may have a relation that is more than cognitive is his own reality.'[69]

How, then, are we to understand existence when it is seen 'subjectively', that is, when it is a matter of an individual regarding her or his own life? Kierkegaard's answer to this is: as 'becoming'. Whereas objectively life is regarded as if it were in the past, completed and so surveyable by the contemplative gaze of the philosopher, subjectively life is not completable, since one is not done with it until it is done with one. From the existing individual's viewpoint, her own life appears as 'constantly in process of becoming',[70] without an achievable or ideal end. To live, therefore, consistently in terms of this subjective view, 'it is essential that every trace of an objective issue should be eliminated'[71] and so all trace of living as if such goals could give significance to one's existence as a whole. To do otherwise is not simply an error of the metaphysical interpretation of life, but characterizes human beings' relations to their lives generally, in ways I shall note in the next chapter: 'It is enough to bring a sensuous man to despair, for one always feels a need to have something finished and complete.'[72] But to live clear-sightedly in terms of the subjective view, to live as an *existing* individual, is to live one's life *as* constantly in process of becoming, and so not towards a goal.[73] Whereas objectively, one's future is seen in the 'illusion attached to pastness' as if it were directed towards an end surveyable from the present and so *closed*, subjectively the future is open. For the living individual, her future is not already mapped out, tending towards an end: 'The incessant becoming generates the uncertainty of earthly life, where everything is uncertain.'[74] To live related to the essential openness of the future alters too the character of the past. To be so related is to 'strive infinitely'[75] so that one's concrete activities are not dependent upon the realization of some finite goal for their significance. As no finite goal can have such ultimate significance, the past, whether of achievement or its lack, can have no such significance either, but is merely the base from which one's present striving into the openness of the future takes place. The present, then, is where the past is taken over as one's *own* and so in relation to the absolute openness of one's future. We shall see what this means more concretely for Kierkegaard later.

His critique of metaphysics rests, then, on the contrast between the objective conception of life, where it is seen as if it were already in the past and so complete and surveyable at least in principle, and the subjective, that way one's life is seen from *within* it, from the point of view of the one who has to live it. And it might appear that Kierkegaard analyses the difference in purely temporal terms. Life as 'becoming' involves, as 'constant striving', the non-ending taking over of one's past into an open future, whereas life objectively conceived is at best progress towards a predetermined future. But it has to be emphasized that Kierkegaard's understanding of these temporal notions is *religious* or ethico-religious: 'all essential knowledge is essentially related to existence. Only ethical and ethico-religious knowledge has an essential relationship to the existence of the knower.'[76] That is, for Kierkegaard, the individual who truly lives as 'becoming' relates to the future as open only in so far as this relation is one to the Infinite or God, and his 'constant striving' constitutes therefore a relation to God, an offering up of his life to the Deity. So that he remarks in the *Journals*: 'To be contemporary with oneself (therefore neither in the future of fear, or of expectation nor in the past) . . . is . . . the God-relationship.'[77] A present within which one takes over one's past in relation to the open future is only possible as such a God-relation since 'the Deity . . . is present as soon as the uncertainty of all things is thought infinitely':[78] that is, the future is only truly open through one's relation to God. And Kierkegaard is far from believing, therefore, that life does not have a *telos*. One who lives his life as always becoming is, because this requires a relation to God, directed towards the end bestowed by God, an 'eternal happiness', although this is, unlike the end understood by the objective views of life, unattainable through our own efforts and so does not close off the horizon of the future.

I shall discuss these notions in greater detail later. But mustn't the suspicion immediately arise here that Kierkegaard is involved in reinstating precisely those 'objective' concepts he has shown to be incompatible with the subjective standpoint? Life does not have an end within it, but is now said to have one beyond it. And in that case, life is surely part of an order which is determinate and fixed, even if, unlike the order of metaphysics, it is one we cannot apprehend: 'Reality itself is a system-for God; but it cannot be a system for an existing spirit. System and finality correspond to one another, but existence is precisely the opposite of finality.'[79] But given Kierkegaard's critique of the objectivity of metaphysical conceptions, why should the existing individual who understands his existence as constant becoming without a finite end believe in an infinite one, guaranteed by the author of an order beyond our comprehension? Isn't this religious construction a last vestige of the hold of objective thinking? Mightn't we hope to move to a properly existential understanding of existence freed of the metaphysical notions of a determined end within a given order? Certainly Heidegger did.

# Chapter 2

# Kierkegaard, Heidegger and the problem of existence

Despite the paucity of references to Kierkegaard in *Being and Time* and Heidegger's earlier works, it is nevertheless clear that he played a major role in the formation of Heidegger's thought. Indeed, it is possible to extract from Kierkegaard's writings statements which at least appear to articulate the central structural features of Heidegger's earlier thought. Consider the following:

(i) 'These entities (i.e. ourselves) in their Being, comport themselves towards their Being.'[1]

   The self is a relationship which relates itself to itself.[2]

(ii) its [our being's] essence lies . . . in the fact that it has always to be its Being as its own.[3]

   An existing individual is constantly in process of becoming.[4]

(iii) Everyday concern understands itself in terms of that potentiality-for-Being which confronts it as coming from its possible success or failure with regard to whatever its object of concern may be . . . Dasein has forgotten itself in its own most *thrown* potentiality for Being.'[5]

   The immediate man (in so far as immediacy is to be found without any reflection) is merely soulishly determined, his self or he himself is a something included along with 'the other' in the compass of the temporal and the worldly . . . its concepts are: good fortune, misfortune, fate.[6]

   Properly speaking, immediacy has no self, it does not recognize itself.[7]

(iv)  anxiety discloses Dasein as Being-possible.[8]

Freedom's possibility announces itself in anxiety.[9]

Freedom means to be capable.[10]

(v)   [The appeal of conscience] calls Dasein forth to the possibility of taking over in existing even that thrown entity which it is.[11]

authentic disclosedness, which is attested in Dasein by its conscience . . . we call 'resoluteness' . . . In resoluteness we have now arrived at that truth of Dasein which is most primordial because it is authentic.[12]

everyman is a spiritual being, for whom the truth consists in nothing else than the self activity of personal appropriation.'[13]

The second quotation of each pair comes, of course, from Kierkegaard. But however suggestive these may be, they obviously differ in a fundamental way from Heidegger's own words. Kierkegaard appears to restrict his attention to the individual self engaged in the task of 'personal appropriation', whereas, Heidegger, however, is concerned with the Being of human being, so as to reveal the manner in which that being can be most primordially its Being. But what, then, is the relation between these two projects?

The 'official' explanation is given in one of the few references to Kierkegaard in *Being and Time*, where Heidegger remarks that whereas Kierkegaard 'explicitly seized upon the problem of existence as an existentiell problem, and thought it through in penetrating fashion', he was prevented from an adequate philosophical interpretation of that problem through his adherence to traditional metaphysical conceptions, 'the existentiell problematic' being 'so alien to him'.[14] That is, Kierkegaard thought about the problem of existence as the problem the individual faces in relation to his own existence, and sees certain possible ways in which this may be conceived and resolved by the individual: aesthetically, ethically or religiously. But he is prevented from seeing how the ontic possibilities he discusses are grounded in the Being of human being, and hence from apprehending a more radical interpretation of what those possibilities are and their relation to that Being, through his use of ontological notions which are drawn from intra-worldly beings and are quite inappropriate for the discussion of that being which is in its 'essence', Being-in-the-World. (I shall explain these terms shortly.) Nevertheless, I think such an account of the relationship between Kierkegaard and Heidegger will hardly do. If it is the case that Kierkegaard thought through 'in penetrating fashion' 'the problem of existence' as an individual problem, it is also true that he thought this led to a recognition of religion, and ultimately, Christianity, as constituting its resolution. The reason for this lay, according to Kierkegaard, in the peculiar nature of the problem of existence faced by the individual which precluded a resolution in terms of what human beings, of themselves, could do. And it therefore precluded the familiar philosophical resolution: that is, of determining the essence of human being and claiming the problem of existence at the individual level to find its solution in living, to whatever degree possible, in accordance with that essence. Heidegger himself, in a lecture given in 1927 and 1928, recognized the disparity between the philosophical and religious conceptions of human existence in contrasting the religious believer who 'can only "believe" his existentiell possibility as one which human existence is not master over'[15] with that pre-scientific mode of human existence which gives rise to philosophy, 'a human's free appropriation of his whole existence'.[16] Philosophy, 'as the free questioning of purely self-reliant human existence'[17] can hardly *itself* recognize faith as a genuine existentiell possibility, at least in the terms with which it describes itself. Faith, Heidegger says, is a mode of human existence 'which, according to its own testimony – itself belonging to this mode of existence – arises not from Dasein or spontaneously through Dasein, but rather . . . from what is believed'.[18] Philosophy, however, according to *its* testimony cannot share such a self-description in terms which cannot be grounded in man's own Being. There is, then, a fundamental lack of communication between philosophy and faith: 'Faith is so absolutely the mortal enemy that philosophy does not even begin to want in anyway to do battle with it'.[19] But if this is the case, how could it be that Kierkegaard had described the existentiell problem so penetratingly when his account is directed towards showing faith as its resolution? Could it be that Heidegger's pursuit of the 'existentiell problematic' is in fact in contradiction with Kierkegaard's description of the problem of existence?

# I

The problem of existence Kierkegaard deals with is one faced by the individual in relation to his own existence. Heidegger's problem of existentiality, however, concerns the Being of human being, that which makes possible the concrete problem or problems we can identify at the individual level, and it is addressed within the context of an attempt to reactivate the question of Being.[20] But that question involves the problem of existentiality only because it is a 'radicalization' of an essential tendency that belongs to man's Being itself.[21] In order for us to relate in any way, theoretically or practically, to 'nature, history, God, space, number', in fact to anything whatever, we must already have an understanding in some way of the Being of these beings.[22] 'Something like Being reveals itself to us in the understanding of Being, an understanding that lies at the root of all of our comportment toward beings.'[23] Such comportment towards beings of whatever kind is a mode of Being of a particular being, ourselves. But whereas other beings have the understanding of their Being in another being, the human, we do not. Rather, we must understand ourselves in our Being: we have an essential relation to our own Being.[24] And as all our comporting towards other beings is something *we* do, it involves at the same time such a relation of ourselves to our own Being. Now, the problem of existence raised at the existentiell level is the question about the meaning of my individual existence, directed towards guiding the conduct of my life. As a relation towards my existence, the question will already involve some understanding of my Being, the Being of human being. The possibility of my conceiving and responding adequately to the existentiell question will depend on the adequacy of my pre-understanding of the Being of the human. And that means, in turn, on the adequacy of my understanding of Being: 'the question of Being, the striving for an understanding of Being, is the basic determinant of existence . . . the question of Being is in itself . . . the question of man'.[25] Of course, it is not necessary for me to be able to *interpret* this understanding of Being: that task is one for philosophy, for the existential interpretation of the Being of man in the service of recalling us to the question of Being. Nevertheless, it remains the case that the existentiell 'problem of existence' depends for its adequate understanding on an adequate pre-ontological understanding of Being. In this way, however radical a departure from traditional philosophical conceptions Heidegger's thought represents, it remains within the context of that 'human's free appropriation of his whole existence' which Kierkegaard himself identified as the peculiarly philosophical project: 'the ignorant person merely needs to be reminded in order, by himself, to call to mind what he knows. The truth is not introduced into him but was in him.'[26] The problem of existence raised at the existentiell level involves an understanding, although not necessarily conceptually articulated, of existentiality, the Being of the human, and that, in turn, of an understanding of Being. I shall briefly sketch Heidegger's treatment of these latter issues in order to bring out how it develops a particular conception of 'a human's free appropriation of his whole existence' which identifies a general mode of human existence within which man is in accord with his Being. Such an understanding would provide the necessary guidelines for the resolving of an existentiell problem of existence, even if the individual concerned were himself incapable of engaging in that mode.

An understanding of our Being is involved in any relating of ourselves to other beings, and so in whatever we do: we always live under the auspices of some understanding of our Being, of the possibilities of human being. Such a Being is not something we are related to as something to be apprehended, but as something to *be*. We are the sort of being which has its Being to be: we have to live our understanding of our Being. Since it is through man that the Being of other beings is disclosed, whilst his Being is disclosed through himself in having to be that Being, Heidegger calls human being Da-sein, *to be* there. (The significance of the 'Da' will appear shortly.) As its Being is always to be for Dasein, that Being cannot lie in some determinate state or condition which could be actualized in some particular Dasein: Dasein has always to be its Being and is never finished until it ceases to exist. And as it always has its Being to *be*, Dasein is essentially *concerned* about its own Being, which means too that its Being is in each case *mine*: that each Dasein must live itself its own understanding of its Being.

Nevertheless, although we must always live our understanding of Being, we do not in the first place and generally do so through an explicit attention to that Being. Rather our initial understanding lies implicit in the way we exist prior to any reflective appropriation of ourselves or of the things we encounter, that way in which we first and for the most part give ourselves immediately and passionately to the world. Dasein is Being-in-the-World. The world is that wherein we dwell, the familiar environment made up not of things but of relations of purposiveness. Only in so far as we exist within these relations do we encounter things at all. In so far as we are in these relations in the appropriate way, living purposively, the things we encounter, and the relations themselves, are there in an unobtrusive and unthought manner. Through living these relations we encounter not merely things having the character of equipment for carrying out our purposes, but materials we use which refer ultimately to what is simply found and not made, to Nature, but a Nature having the character of usefulness, detrimentality and indifference. The particular environment which is our own world refers beyond itself, to other humans for whom our work is intended, and so to the public world of 'wearers and users', a world which is also ours. With the public world we encounter too environing Nature, the Nature in terms of which we construct shelters, set up lighting, and so on.

Since Dasein has its Being to be, and so such a Being is always 'mine' rather than a 'what' which I might merely apprehend, the question arises as to 'who' this Being is which I make mine. Within the form of existence which we most immediately are, I take over my Being as a Being which *anyone* could take over. I am what I do, so that I am my world, the particular context of purposive relations which is familiar and mine: I am a shoemaker, teacher, banker, and that others can be and are. In a similar way I enjoy myself, make judgements, and so on, as 'one' does, in a way available for anyone. I am my Being as something already given and familiar which can be taken over by me as by anyone: an already existing environment of modes of work, customs, opinions into which I fit myself. Such a manner of existing, the way we immediately are, involves a general understanding which encompasses all beings: my own and that of other Dasein, and that of intra-worldly beings, whether equipment, materials or environing Nature. It is only on the basis of such a mode of existing, immediately absorbed in the world of purposive relations, that any more reflective appropriation of my own Being and that of things revealed in the world can take place.

Dasein has its Being to be, and so in its way of Being, in its concrete forms of acting in and relating to its world, it has some understanding of its Being. Such understanding of its potentiality to *be*, of the potentialities of its general form of existing, is the primary sense of understanding since it is involved in anything Dasein may do or be. Having such an understanding, it 'knows' what it is capable of, what its potentiality for Being is. Within our immediate absorption in the world, in everydayness, this understanding of one's potentiality for Being does not derive from Dasein itself, from the Being of a being which exists as having a relation to its Being. In its immediate form of existing, Dasein is simply absorbed in its world, understanding its Being unreflectively in terms of what it can do there. It understands itself, that is, in terms of its success and failure in living within the purposive relations of its world. This in-authentic self-understanding, not drawn from the Being of Dasein itself, has an essential temporal structure: Dasein awaits the revelation of itself in what the future may bring in terms of success or failure, lives a present absorbed in its world, and has behind it a past which, however much it may be a matter of satisfaction, regret or indifference, is something finished and determinate.

Within everydayness, Dasein's self is reflected back to it from what happens or has happened in its world. But this is only possible in so far as Dasein is Being-in-the-World, is as absorbed in the purposive relations of world. And it can be so absorbed in these relations, in the in-order-to which reveals equipment and materials, the for-which of the work, and the for-the-sake-of which refers to Dasein's potentialities themselves, in so far as Dasein itself has an essentially temporal structure, which in the world takes on the particular mode of expecting itself from within its world. But Dasein has to *be* its Being, and it has to so long as it is. Hence, its Being cannot achieve concretion in any state or condition which could be granted to it by what occurs in the world. Understanding one's Being in this way removes the possibility of understanding it in terms of something to be manifested, in the way of other beings, from within the world.

Dasein realizes it is not to be identified with any concrete possibility its world offers, but that it is the simple possibility of having to *be* its world. Within the world, and understanding itself not from itself, inauthentically, Dasein is at home, in the familiar. Understanding itself from itself, it recognizes itself, however, as *unheimlich*, not at home and essentially so: as having, not to be *in* its world, absorbed in its familiar relations, but to *be* its world. Such a realization takes place only out of its inauthentic absorption in the world, so that Dasein must take over authentically, in terms of its own Being, that Being which it already inauthentically has been.

Such authentic existing, resoluteness, is the pre-eminent form of human temporality. Dasein does not await itself in what the future may bring in the world, but always comes towards itself: that is, it takes over what it has been as what must always be taken over, so that the future is open, the past a source of possibility and the present that within which a new revelation of a possibility of its past can occur. Dasein takes over what it has been, its world, so that it exists in relation to the world in a new way, in terms of its *own* potentiality. It takes over the concrete possibilities provided by its world but *as* possibilities and not as finished modes of being into which Dasein must fit. It appropriates its past not as something finished, but as possibility: and this it can only do by relating to the past as open, by maintaining it as possibility. Since its world is a common one, such engagement with the world constitutes the renewal of a common heritage, a tradition.

Human being is a kind of being which, unlike other beings has a relation to its own Being: it can only relate *itself* to other beings in whatever way it does through having some understanding of itself. Since it must always comport itself in this self-referential way, its Being can be nothing which Dasein could be as complete. We can only conceive such a self-referential notion of Being, which the being concerned always has to *be*, as temporality: as a *way* in which what one has been is to be taken over. Inauthentic temporality takes over what one has been as the simply past and completed, which shows itself in what one has accomplished or failed to do, whilst looking towards one's future as something determinate which will be settled *in* time, by what happens. But to understand oneself in this way is not to understand oneself *as* temporality, but as a being within the world like any other. It is the incompatibility between such an understanding of one's Being and the *way* that Being must always be projected in one's dealings with beings in the world which compels a recognition of one's Being as temporality. To understand one's Being as temporality is radically to distinguish it from the being of intra-worldly beings. It is to realize that one can only *be* that Being as one's Being in the appropriation of the past without issue. And that can only take place if the past is regarded as itself without issue: not as finished and determinate, but as constant possibility of being taken over. To understand oneself in this way is to engage in one's past as an ever renewable source of possibility, to engage in the constant renewal of one's heritage. It is in this that genuinely new creation lies and which enables man to have a history.[27] Man has a history because he is historical: that is, exists as a being which must constantly take over its past as possibility. Of course, for the most part a human being must exist inauthentically, simply living at home in the familiar world. But he lives in accordance with his Being, lives it *as* his Being, in creation, in the bringing forth of what is new out of the possibilities made available by his past. In this way he lives his Being as *unheimlich*, as essentially not at home in the world. Man is not a being among other beings: rather he is as the appropriation of what has been, as *existing* world, within which any other being can have its Being, its own temporal mode.

We can see in this way the sense underlying Heidegger's claim that the question of Being has been forgotten. What has been forgotten in philosophy is that Being *is* a question. Human being only has access to beings through his nature as Being-in-the-World; it is only in so far as he is at first and for the most part absorbed in relations of purposiveness that beings are revealed at all to him. In this manner, they are revealed in the mode of unobtrusiveness and familiarity, as ready-to-hand, and only through modifications of this can they reveal themselves in other ways: as objects of theoretical contemplation, for ex-ample. But he can be as Being-in-the-World only in so far as his Being is temporality itself. Explicitly existing as such, he takes over his past as possibility to allow the new to come forth. In this way, the past always exists as a question, as what poses a question to Dasein, an open possibility. If Being is what we must under-stand in order to have access to anything that is, including ourselves, then that is the essential question which our past is for us.

## II

This may indeed appear as a thinking into the Being of human being which underlies Kierkegaard's criticisms of Hegel in terms of the 'existing individual', a thinking Kierkegaard himself was unable to carry out being still in the grip of certain metaphysical conceptions. In defence of this one may point to a central part of Kierkegaard's attack on Hegel: that Hegel's speculative activity aims at the formation of the System, the articulation of the Truth, the principle of reality making itself manifest in thinking that Truth, thought thinking itself. But 'system and finality correspond to one another, but existence is precisely the opposite of finality'.[28] And this surely is because the existing individual is 'constantly in process of becoming'[29] and this should receive 'an essential expression in all his knowledge. Particularly, it must be expressed through the prevention of an illusory finality, whether in perceptual certainty, historical knowledge or illusory speculative results.'[30]

Surely, then, Kierkegaard is in the process of developing a conception of the nature of human being which would undermine those notions of truth and being contained in Hegel and the metaphysical tradition which, according to Heidegger, underlie our concrete ways of relating to ourselves and other beings. Those notions are inappropriate for a being which must exist as constant self-appropriation':[31] 'the knower is an existing individual for whom the truth cannot be [an identity of thought and being] as long as he lives in time'.[32] Rather, that truth must lie in man's nature as becoming, which requires, therefore, an understanding in temporal terms rather than the traditional categories associated with substance. Kierkegaard's reflections upon this, couched as they are in terms of 'the real subject' directed towards an 'eternal happiness' granted through a relation to God as absolute Goodness and so to an apparent fulfilment beyond time, betray the radicality of his beginning.

However tempting such an interpretation may be for philosophy, it is not, I think, compatible with Kierkegaard's own thought. The first thing that strikes the reader of those works in which Kierkegaard discusses the nature of philosophy is their peculiarity of *form*. They are written pseudonymously, and their predominant tone, where philosophy is at issue, is one of humour. The pseudonym of the *Concluding Unscientific Postscript* speaks of the 'incessant activity of the irony' in the *Philosophical Fragments*, referring to the plan of that work as a 'parody on speculative philosophy', and remarks of such philosophy

> not that it has a mistaken presupposition, but that it has a comical presupposition occasioned by its having forgotten, in a sort of world-historical absent-mindedness, what it means to be a human being. Not indeed, what it means to be a human-being in general; for this is the sort of thing that one might even induce a speculative philosopher to agree to; but what it means that you and I and he are human beings, each one for himself.[33]

The pseudonymity and the comedy have their grounds, Kierkegaard says, in the nature of his critique of philosophy, that it is *ethical*.[34]

To engage in such a critique is in itself to deny the claim of philosophy to have jurisdiction over the ethical. Philosophy has traditionally claimed such jurisdiction over the question of the meaning of life, as it has, by its nature, over all forms of thought. Plato's contention at the beginning of the *Republic*, that his topic is the nature of the good and the bad life and that it is philosophy's job to answer it, is not at issue in Hegel's thought. This claim, seen from within philosophy, seems reasonable enough. The good life, presumably, is that which fulfils or is appropriate to our nature as human beings, and it is surely philosophy's task to determine what that nature is. But this very project, Kierkegaard claims, involves the 'confusion' of 'over leaping the ethical',[35] which in Hegel's case is then compounded by 'proposing a world-historical something as the ethical task for individuals'.[36] This confusion is revealed, not when we engage with speculative philosophy in an investigation of the truth of its thought, but when we ask about the *relation* of the individual thinker to speculative thought itself and so 'ask ethically, and assert the claim which the ethical has upon the existing individual'.[37] When we raise this question, we see that philosophy requires the adoption of the same relation of the inquirer to their project as do other cognitive inquiries: 'Abstract thought requires him to become disinterested in order to acquire knowledge.'[38] An essential requirement of such disinterest, and so subordination to the subject matter in pursuit of knowledge, lies in the way the inquirer must treat the results of their inquiries:

> Although the historical material belongs to the past, it is as subject for cognition not complete; it is constantly coming into being through new observations and inquiries, new discoveries are constantly brought to light, compelling not only additions but also revisions.[39]

But the philosopher attempts to treat the issue of *life* itself as the object of such a project of thought within which 'knowledge of the world-historical is, as a cognitive act, an approximation'.[40] Thus the philosopher's results can only have the same status as that of other forms of intellectual project: they are essentially hypothetical and to be treated as such, as always capable, by further inquiry, of being overthrown. But philosophy claims, by its nature, the priority of the general over the individual: only if one knows the nature of the human being in general can the individual have the essential guidelines for working out what life is good in his own case. To be consistent, then, the philosopher's attitude *to his own life* would have to be *uncommitted*, since any result may prove unfounded. But such a relation to his own life is impossible,[41] since the philosopher as an existing individual lives and so manifests in every action a conviction of the value of his existence which, in terms of his ostensible project, should be suspended: 'existence has the remarkable trait of compelling an existing individual to exist whether he wills it or not'.[42] In particular, of course, the philosopher has to commit himself to speculation, a commitment which cannot ensue on the basis of its results. Such a confusion is the expression of an essential lack of seriousness about the very problem the philosopher claims to be addressing. For if he believes, as the nature of the philosophical project requires, that without an intellectual result the individual's problem about the meaning of his own life cannot be resolved then he must *himself* have such a problem and so be *genuinely* at a loss as to the significance of his life in its *totality*, which would thus *include* his intellectual pursuits. Such a state, far from being 'disinterested', would be one of total despair, which indeed Kierkegaard thinks is the genuine appearance of the problem.

The philosopher does not have a genuine problem about 'what it means to be a human being in general' for his embarking on his intellectual project shows he does not have a problem about his own life, yet the one presupposes, on his own terms, the other. And indeed the very nature of such a problem completely escapes him. The philosopher thus becomes either what Kierkegaard calls a 'fanatic', who treats the results of his thought not in the appropriate disinterested way and so always liable to be overthrown, or lives himself in quite different terms, erecting his palace in thought and living in a hut outside. Either way, such a *relation* of the individual to his project involves categories that lie outside it, the categories of 'subjectivity', for 'if a man occupied himself, all his life through, solely with logic, he would nevertheless not become logic; he must in himself exist in different categories'.[43]

The 'categories' of subjectivity relate to the relation of an I to her *own* life and are ones Kierkegaard says concerned with 'passion': 'It is impossible to exist without passion',[44] even the confused passion of the philosopher. And the issue of the 'meaning' of life, to which the search for life's measure in philosophy is directed, has to be understood in this context. That is, 'meaning' here is not a matter of something to be known or understood, but rather refers to what we speak of when we ask what a relationship, activity and so forth *means* to someone, where we are asking how committed they are to it, a matter of the passion of their involvement. Such passion may be partial, in the sense that one's involvement may depend on the prospect of certain results expected for oneself, which themselves matter in terms of a desire for them. Such a desire, however, as part of one's life, raises again the question of one's relation to it: since such a desire may come and go, one can only have a temporary and conditional involvement with it. Thus, where we speak of the meaning of *life*, we raise the issue of the sort of passion which could be appropriate to encompass one's life in its totality, to the content of one's life, its 'what', whatever it may be, and so is consonant with the individual's recognition that they have *a* life to lead: 'life constitutes the task. To be finished with life before life has finished with one is precisely not to have finished the task.'[45] The 'spheres of existence' Kierkegaard identifies, the aesthetic, ethical and religious, represent different degrees of passion with which the individual may live their life, and which determine the forms of passion with which they relate to the various contents their life may have. The 'dialectic' of these stages is due to the inadequacy of certain 'stages on life's way' to confront the 'subjective' problem, of having one's whole life to lead, whilst the revelation of inadequacy and the move to another sphere remain matters of passion and not ultimately of thought. The revelation of inadequacy, that is, has the character of despair, which can be overcome only through passion, commitment of a more encompassing nature.

Kierkegaard says 'while aesthetic existence is essentially enjoyment, ethical existence essentially struggle and victory, religious existence is essentially suffering'.[46] Aesthetic existence identifies its meaning with what happens to it, its categories being he says 'Fortune, misfortune, fate, immediate enthusiasm, despair',[47] without reflecting on what gives these events their significance. This lies in the desires of the individual for them, which however can project significance themselves only in so far as there is the implicit *consent* of the individual concerned, something which may become apparent if one's desires are not merely unsatisfied but appear unsatisfiable and one's allegiance to them suddenly appears transferable. Instead of such transference, it may be possible for a subjective reflection as to the source of the value of the things one longed for, one which recognizes that it lay in the *temporary identification of oneself* with the longing. Aesthetic existence thus constitutes a particular degree of the passion with which the individual may live their life, involving the unreflective, unconscious attachment to externalities through the temporary identification of oneself with the desire for them. Such reflection out of despair makes possible the raising of the subjective problem, since abstracted from one's present desires, the issue of what can give significance to *any* content of one's life as a whole can now appear. This is the moment of the ethical either/or, within which the self itself may be chosen, through which choice I impose the very form of the I, which I am throughout my life, on the facticities of my life. This is done by choosing oneself, and thus rendering oneself independent of external or internal conditions which may or may not come about. The ethical individual 'can impart to [his history] continuity, for this it acquires only when it is not the sum of all that has happened to me but is my own work'.[48] Such choice, appropriate to the source of value lying in the imposition of the individual self, is thus not dependent on conditions and so takes the form of unconditional resolutions, of commitments of *myself*. Such passion thus has the form of the conscious commitment of myself, the imposition of the unity of the I upon the content of my life, which Kierkegaard calls 'self-assertion'. Yet such passion cannot be adequate to the totality of one's life since it involves a split between myself as imposer of commitments and myself as the subject of such imposition: hence its categories are 'struggle and victory' of myself over myself. 'The ethical finds the contradiction', the source of despair, 'within self-assertion',[49] which can again only be overcome through a more encompassing passion. But the individual brought to ethical despair must now recognize that the passion which would be adequate to one's life in its totality can have *no object*, since the presence of an object marks a split in subjectivity, whether between the subject and an external object as in the aesthetic, or within the subject as in the ethical. Thus Kierkegaard says 'it is essential that every trace of an objective issue should be eliminated'.[50] Such a passion would be total and so *for* nothing. But this very form shows that it *cannot* be something *taken on* by the individual, for what can be taken on has the form of a project and so of objectivity. This is the recognition that the 'truth' for the meaning of the individual's life, that is, the most extreme form such passion can have, is something the individual cannot undertake and so involves a total self-transformation which, if it can take place, has the character of a gift. Kierkegaard thus says the existential dialectic culminates in 'the subject's transformation in himself', and 'Subjectivity is truth' as such total transformation from orientation to objectivities to nothing. This is the point of Kierkegaard's repeated emphasis that 'the subjective problem is not something about an objective issue, but is the subjectivity itself'.[51]

To recognize this is thus to recognize that in relation to such 'truth' the individual can do nothing of themselves, so that one's only possible mode of relation to it is non-instrumental: that is, to 'imitate' it in the form of what Kierkegaard calls 'infinite resignation', to live fully whilst attempting to resign one's concern with objectivities. Such a relationship to life's meaning, in which one recognizes that one is absolutely not the source of such meaning, is what Kierkegaard calls the 'God-relationship', as opposed to all other views of life which in one way or another locate the human and its capacities as the source of significance. The 'meaning' of life is thus for the individual a paradox: 'inwardness in an existing subject culminates in passion; corresponding to passion in the subject the truth becomes a paradox'.[52] The 'first paradox' is 'the absolute difference' between God and man,[53] whilst the absolute paradox is the absolute transformation, which as it cannot be taken as an objective, is beyond human capacities, and so beyond under-standing. 'God' is thus not a name,[54] but a term which has its significance in the context of expressions like 'the God-relationship', that is, in characterizing a form of human existing which recognizes its inadequacy in relation to the question of the meaning of life and expresses this is the form of infinite resignation. 'Christianity' he says in the *Journals* 'is not a doctrine but an existence',[55] and:

> God himself is this: *how* one involves himself with Him. As far as physical and external objects are concerned, the object is something else than the mode: there are many modes. In respect to *God*, the *how* is the what. He who does not involve himself with God in the mode of absolute devotion does not become involved with God.[56]

This absolute devotion recognizes the inadequacy of the indi-vidual to bring about the total transformation of themselves, by living life as sacrifice or worship, the essential religious categories – the sacrifice of objectivity, of the assumption that human projects constitute or are the means towards the meaningful life. 'The subjective existing thinker ... is always negative – his positiveness consists in the continuous realization of the inward-ness through which he becomes conscious of the negative.'[57]

Perhaps some remarks of Simone Weil's may be of use here. The human being, she says, 'doesn't regard his existence as a good, he always wants something else than simply to exist'.[58] This is why it is that the issue of 'meaning' in life arises. Thus she says, 'Man always devotes himself to an order', and outside the religious, this order has at its centre something, a person, party, people, an abstraction, a theory, whatever, with which the individual identifies him- or herself. The 'meaning' which these impart is thus a matter of the way, the 'how', with which the individual gives him/herself. But none of these constitute what I could totally give myself to, and indeed such *total* giving is beyond my powers, which is why the issue is a paradox: 'It is a question of being delivered from self, and this I cannot do by means of my own energy.'[59] Such 'deliverance' would be living for nothing: 'Obedience to God [and] since God is beyond all that we can imagine or conceive, to nothing.'[60] If we recognize our inability, our relation to such deliverance, the passion we can take on, is 'To detach our desires from all good things and wait . . . to will the void. For the good which we can neither picture nor define is a void for us.'[61] Such an activity, she says, 'has nothing to do with an intellectual process . . . The intelligence has nothing to discover, it has only to clear the ground. It is only good for servile tasks.'[62] By 'clearing the ground' she means recognizing that no conceivable end or project, such as, say, one suggested by philosophical reflection, can constitute that to which I can give myself totally, since they are all the objects of some particular desire or capacity I possess.

The question which human life faces us with is, as far as life itself is concerned, paradoxical: life cannot determine its own significance in terms of itself. This realization compels the recognition that meaning can only be given to one's life as a whole by relating it *as* a whole to an *absolute* good. An absolute good is one to which I can relate my *whole* existence, in terms of which I recognize that nothing I can do, and so no capacity I may or could possess, and nothing that happens to me can give meaning to my life as a whole. One can know nothing concrete about such an absolute Good[63] since it does not lie in the exercise, fulfilment or result of any human capacity, except that to relate to it requires that one unconditionally gives up the presumption of the human to be the source of its own significance and so ceases to look for any result, and hence for anything, including one's victory over oneself, which one would deem good. And this means that one's activity in relation to this good *cannot* be regarded as means towards its achievement. Rather, recognition of this absolute good can, in so far as it results in one's activity, only take the form of the *negative* movement of removing within one's life the illusion of a humanly projected goodness, and so ultimately of total self-renunciation: 'in self-renunciation one understands one is capable of nothing'.[64]

This 'absolute Good' for the individual is what Kierkegaard means by an 'eternal happiness'. But this notion cannot play a similar role to that of 'happiness' within the aesthetic and ethical forms of existence. There it would make sense to ask in what happiness consists, for it would be used to refer to some state attainable *within* life or conceivable as an ideal which one must conceive in order to pursue. But the notion of an 'eternal happiness' merely identifies 'the good which is attainable by venturing everything'[65] in relation to which our activity cannot be the utilization of means towards the achievement of an end. Hence, Kierkegaard says 'therefore the resolved individual does not even will to know anything more about this telos than that it exists, for as soon as he acquires some knowledge about it, he already begins to be retarded in his striving'.[66] To will to 'know' something about it is to construe the 'absolute Good' as if it were something we could achieve or approach of our own powers and so would need a prior conception in order to direct our activity. But the absolute Good is that which requires us to venture everything and only so can it give significance to one's *whole* life. It cannot therefore be construed as within the reach of our powers, whatever they may be, which are necessarily a *part* of the life which is to be given up in its *entirety* to this good. What could give such significance must, therefore, have for us an essentially *negative* form: all we can know about it is that it cannot be known and all we can say about it is that it requires us to venture everything. I shall return to this issue of the 'negatively determined concepts' in the next chapter.

An 'eternal happiness' marks this absolute *telos* for the individual, his absolute good. The goodness of this good is that to which the individual must relate in order to have his own absolute end, and this is the notion of absolute goodness itself, God. 'God is a highest conception, not to be explained in terms of other things, but explicable by exploring more and more profoundly the conception itself.'[67] That absolute goodness, the measure for my life *as a whole*, can, that is, be related to only in 'the mode of absolute devotion', and that to which we can be so related is 'God'. 'Self-annihilation is the essential form for the God-relationship.'[68] I cannot, therefore, relate to God through my understanding, as if I could *grasp* the measure for my life as a whole and its reason and so set about making my life in accordance with it, since then my activity would be a means towards the achievement of the individual good determined by that measure. God is, seen from the point of view of reason, the 'limit to which Reason repeatedly comes', the 'unknown with which Reason collides'[69] since, as the measure for life in its entirety, all reason can know is that God requires, *as* God, the *whole* of life, and therefore the recognition by the individual 'that he is nothing before God, or to be wholly nothing and to exist thus before God'.[70] The relation to God requires the sacrifice of our reason and understanding in the sense of a giving up of their claim to be able to establish and reveal a measure for life as a whole which human powers may achieve or advance towards: 'The contradiction which arrests [the understanding] is that a man is required to make the greatest possible sacrifice, to dedicate his whole life as a sacrifice – and wherefore? There is indeed no wherefore.'[71] The limit of our reason is to reveal this contradiction, the impossibility of a human resolution to the problem of the meaning of existence, and that the relation to the absolute measure requires the active giving up of such presumption. Such an understanding of existence, which really does encompass life as whole, is, therefore, according to Kierkegaard, essentially religious.

Since the issue of answering the problem of the significance of one's life requires venturing everything, no *reason* can be given for undertaking the absolute commitment to an end for life as a whole. 'At first glance the understanding ascertains that this is madness. The understanding asks: what's in it for me? The answer is: Nothing.'[72] Whether we recognize this description as placing a requirement on us depends not on argument, but on our own relation to our lives: that is, whether we *will* have an end for our lives as such or not. No reasons can be given someone why they should, since the transformation in existence involved requires one in what the individual *counts as a reason*, and any reason which could now be given could only appeal to what is seen as such in their present condition. Seen from the point of relative willing, that of all determination of the end of life in the fulfilment of human capacities, it is 'madness'. If it does not seem mad, it is because one wills to have a meaning for one's life as a whole. This is, however, something we *can* do, although it can only result in the exercise of our powers directed towards self-annihilation, the dying away from the significance of finite results. Our activity in relation to the absolute measure, God, and the good it determines for the individual, becomes not the employment of means towards the achievement of an end but rather *worship*: 'the only appropriate expression for God's majesty is worshipping him . . . worshipfully to give up everything . . . is what it means to worship'.[73]

The apprehension of the relation to God as constituting *the* meaning for human life is the religious understanding. It has two forms for Kierkegaard. The universally religious, or 'Religion A', understands what this requires in human terms, a turning away from all humanly determined goods as constituting *the* good. It thus conceives of the demand as one of 'infinite resignation', an active offering up of human life as it is lived to God. This involves seeing the task of life as one of the constant exercise of the renunciation of absolute concern with finite results, and so of dying away from the world: 'the individual who sustains an absolute relationship to the absolute telos may very well exist in relative ends, precisely in order to exercise the absolute relationship in renunciation'.[74] Christianity, or 'religion B', goes beyond this, by involving Faith, the belief that, having offered one's self to God in the striving of infinite resignation, it will be given back, so that one's life is no longer characterized by striving against one's tendencies to will relatively, but by an absolute purity within the world. 'Faith, after having made the movements of infinity . . . makes those of finiteness.'[75] Christianity is the 'absolute religion' for Kierkegaard because it recognizes in its most radical form the difference between man and God,[76] the nothingness of man before God: that nothing that man does, not even 'infinite resignation', can have any value unless it is given by God to man. And the transformation of the individual to absolute purity is not something which the individual can accomplish of himself, since it involves a *total* transformation of the self away from relative to absolute willing. I shall return to these notions in the next chapter.

Let me return to the issue of the form of Kierkegaard's writings about philosophy, that they are pseudonymous and their characteristic tone humorous. As to the latter, the pseudonym of the *Concluding Unscientific Postscript* says 'wherever there is contradiction, the comical is present',[77] and the ethical critique of philosophy is partly a matter of bringing out the comedy involved in the contradiction between the philosopher as an existing human being and the character of his discourse. The latter purports to deal in a disinterested way with the intellectual problem of the nature of the human being and its appropriate form of life. But the very form of this inquiry is at odds with the question which it itself claims must face the philosopher as an individual, the significance of his own life. Kierkegaard may be regarded as claiming that philosophy in its concern for the 'problem of life' is involved in what Wittgenstein would call a 'grammatical confusion'. It tacitly assumes the problem is intellectual, and hence involves a privileging of the intellectual human being. What Kierkegaard tries to get us to remember is that the 'problem' in this context is one an individual *has with her or his own life*, and is thus manifest as despair rather than intellectual puzzlement, whose resolution lies, not in an 'answer', but in a redirection or intensification of passion. Such despair admits of degrees. One can despair of getting what one wants, and simply direct one's desire elsewhere; or, one may despair of *any* internal or external condition as providing one's life with meaning, and see then the necessity, for emerging out of such despair, of committing *oneself*. And such ethical life has its own form of despair, where the problem becomes that of one's life in its totality, an absolute despair. The sense of 'reflection' in relation to such 'existential' problems, ones an individual has with her/his own life, is that of reflecting on the nature of the despair, how it arises through one's attachment or involvement with people, things, activities and so on, and what has left this disrupted. Such reflection opens up the space for the removal of despair through a realignment of one's involvement, and so passionately, where the degree of passion required depends on the extent of the despair. The nature of the total despair which emerges out of ethical existence is over *any* object as adequate for the total commitment of life, which thus reveals that the despair emerges out of the desire for such an object and the recognition of its impossibility. Such despair thus makes possible a new kind of passion, directed towards resigning this desire, such a passion being the only one possible for the individual to undertake in relation to her/his life as a whole. This passion is the first form of the 'God-relationship', passion without an object, or the negative form of love, infinite resignation. But again I will return to these issues later.

The pseudonymity of the works too has its ground, Kierkegaard says, in the 'character of the production'.[78] What is at issue here is bringing out the nature of the problem of life in its totality, but in such a way that it is recognized that this is not a general intellectual problem, but one that can only be faced by an individual in relation to her own life. This, Kierkegaard says:

> must not be done in a dogmatizing manner, for then the misunderstanding would instantly take the explanatory effort to itself – in a new misunderstanding, as if existing consisted in getting to know something about this or that. If communicated in the form of knowledge, the recipient is led to adopt the misunderstanding that it is knowledge he is to receive, and then we are again in the sphere of knowledge.[79]

The pseudonymity is part of a 'polemic against the truth as knowledge'[80] which requires 'an indirect form' of communication.[81] 'The very maximum of what one human being can do for another in relation to that wherein each man has to do solely with himself, is to inspire him with concern and unrest',[82] to create a situation which faces the individual with the question of the significance of her own life, whilst recognizing that the writer is himself merely one human being addressing another. Such a communication endeavours

> to say something to a passer-by in passing, without standing still and without delaying the other, without attempting to persuade himself to go the same way, but giving him an impulse to go precisely his own way. Such is the relation between one existing individual and another, when the communication concerns the truth as existential inwardness.[83]

The pseudonyms are 'a means of keeping the reader at a distance',[84] so that the responsibility for their relation to their own lives, on the part of *both* reader and author, is recognized in the very form of the communication. Perhaps this requires a fictional form within which the author asserts nothing in his own voice and which *involves* the reader in the expression of the possible views of life[85] from the aesthetic to the religious and thus leaves her or him with the subjective reflection about their own life. I shall return to this issue of the form of Kierkegaard's writings in Chapter 6.

Kierkegaard would surely have regarded Heidegger's appropriation of his thought as a continuation of the philosophical project in relation to the problem of existence. The philosophical conception of the problem the individual faces in relation to their own life places the conception of the essence of the human being at its centre: only if we have an adequate, even if unarticulated, understanding of this can we resolve the problem in the required way. This problem of existence is first and foremost that of 'what it means to be a human being in general' and only through that, what it means for you or me to be a human being. This structure is not altered where the human being is understood as Dasein and so as essentially temporality, even if this does undermine metaphysical conceptions of the human. But what that structure fails to capture, Kierkegaard would claim, is precisely the relation of the individual to their own life within which there can be a 'problem' of existence at all. Within that context, that of the 'existential', the notion of 'problem' is essentially characterized as 'despair', 'reflection' as directed towards its causes in one's situation and one's 'life view', and 'solution' as the realignment or intensification of passion which could remove that despair. Such 'problems' thus emerge only through the necessity of the individual giving themselves so that their life acquires 'meaning' in the sense of a certain quality or degree of commitment. Seen 'existentially', in terms of the relation the individual has to her own life, 'the problem of existence' is thus that of the passion through which one could commit one's life in its totality. The impossibility of this on the part of the individual is what identifies the resolution as lying in 'being delivered from self', a recognition which can only be expressed through 'infinite resignation'. The philosopher, in raising the question of the Being of the human in general, bypasses the nature of the 'problem of existence' which only has sense in terms of the passion with which the individual lives their own life. He is thus involved in 'a confusion of the categories'[86] transforming 'the communication of capability and oughtness capability', which requires indirect communication 'by an *I* to an *I*',[87] 'into the communication of knowledge. The existential has disappeared.'[88] What has disappeared is the individual's relation to her or his own life, the primacy of giving oneself which is prior to any project, relationship or activity for the individual human being, including, of course, philosophy. There is thus a prior question which escapes philosophy, namely whether engaging with it is compatible with the question which their existence poses for the individual: 'Abstract thought requires him to become disinterested in order to acquire knowledge; the ethical demand is that he becomes infinitely interested in existing',[89] and thus engage in 'the enthusiastic resolve for the whole of life'.[90] But 'The existing individual can never wholly attain this state [of disinterestedness] qua individual; and ethically he is not justified in trying to attain it existing approximando, since the ethical seeks contrariwise to make the existential interest infinite.'[91]

Underlying this confusion of categories, however, is, Kierkegaard believes, a very human desire, for pursuing the essence of the human is motivated by a desire that the problem of existence at the individual level can be resolved by referring to some particular mode of existence as an exercise of human powers which would constitute the highest life for humanity. For to speak of the being of the human is precisely to speak of what could justify appeal to such a mode in solving that problem. For this reason, Kierkegaard speaks of metaphysical inquiry as a form of aesthetic existence, albeit one which lacks the self-understanding of more straightforward pursuits of worldly ends. The problem of human life is of how the individual can commit his life in its entirety, and the resolution of this precludes the very *form* of the philosophical response which attempts, in terms of a determination of man's Being, to give a privilege to certain of man's own powers. Kierkegaard does not give an account of a problem at the existentiell level which can only properly be addressed through an adequate understanding of the existentiality, the Being of human being, since no such understanding could allow a resolution of the problem that account is directed towards. What that problem requires is giving up the *presumption* of such an understanding to resolve it, since it requires, quite simply, the giving up of *all* human presumption to be able to give meaning to human life. It is not merely that religious existence is the 'mortal enemy' of 'a human's free appropriation of his whole existence'[92] but rather that the problem which human existence is shows that no such 'free appropriation' is possible.

If the earlier Heidegger's thought is indebted to Kierkegaard, that of the later Heidegger is a response to Nietzsche. Before considering whether that later thought, which involves an emphasis on the divine absent from the earlier writings, provides an adequate response to Kierkegaard, I should, therefore, like to identify the structure of Nietzsche's thought. I shall do this with respect to a Nietzschean rejoinder to much contemporary analytical moral philosophy. This is often held to be free of metaphysical and post-metaphysical concerns, a view which may appear by such a confrontation to be overly optimistic. However, although Nietzsche's argument can indeed be seen to undermine the plausibility of such an immanent interpretation of value, the question remains whether Kierkegaard too is equally vulnerable. I hope to show he is not.

# Chapter 3

# Happiness, self-affirmation and God
## Nietzsche and Kierkegaard

## I

'Put as briefly as possible, to think morally is, at least, to subject one's own interests, where they conflict with those of other people, to a principle which one can accept as governing anyone's conduct in like circumstances.'[1] Hare here identifies what is, I think a pervasive understanding of the nature of morality within the analytic tradition. There morality is conceived as a constraint upon the individual's pursuit of his own interests, one which nevertheless, in terms of those interests themselves, he can see as binding on himself. Such a binding constraint is only intelligible in so far as I recognize a certain measure for the pursuit of my own interests and one which is equally binding on anyone's pursuit of theirs. To think morally is to subject the pursuit of my interests to a measure which derives from the idea of pursuing interests as such, and so involves seeing my pursuit from a universally applicable point of view. There are, of course, disagreements as to the form and justification of this measure with whose details I shall not be concerned here, although I will later try to sketch the general approach within which these various solutions are formulated. However, it is clear that on this view I can only think morally if I *have* interests, and what these are is to be determined independently of what is required by morality, and so of a conception of moral goodness. The notion of moral goodness must, in some way, be derived from that of a non-moral goodness, and the latter from that of the interests of the agent.

From the agent's point of view, it may be suggested, what is good is what is required for the pursuit of his activities, some of which are good as required for the pursuit of others which are regarded as good in themselves. The satisfactory engagement with the latter is what constitutes for the agent his *own* satisfaction, his happiness. What pursuits are deemed 'good' in this sense is for the agent himself to determine. Where his interests lie is a matter of the choice of the individual, of his determination of which activities, of those made possible by his capacities, he will go in for, and with what scale of priorities. Non-moral good is a matter of satisfying *me*. From my own determination of what activities I deem most important stems their goodness, and in the light of this I will see the goodness of what is required for their pursuit. 'Good' invites the question: 'For what?' It is a term which identifies a relation between certain conditions and an interest. My overriding interest lies in *my own* satisfaction, in identifying, amongst activities available to me, those which I shall take as fulfilling *myself*. My happiness lies in pursuing these activities, not necessarily successfully in terms of some standard lying outside of me, but to my *own* satisfaction, to limits which I myself determine. Not only which pursuits are ultimately good is determined by my choice, but also the degree to which they are to be pursued, and the way in which their success or lack of it is to be regarded. What is ultimately good for me is, in this way, something which I determine, for what is at issue is what is required to satisfy *me*, which may well be quite different and quite deficient when looked at from someone else's point of view. What will satisfy me is something on which I am ultimately the authority. Of course, it is true that I may think I shall be satisfied by the pursuit of certain activities, to a certain degree and with a certain amount of success, and yet find I am not. But whether I am or not is something only I can say, and in the light of my own determination of this, I shall either continue the course I have set or change tack. Such activities, again, need not be egotistic in the narrow sense of pursuing goals to be possessed solely by me, but may involve the pursuit of the satisfaction of others. What satisfies me may well, in part, consist in enabling others to be satisfied. But whether that is so or not is, again, up to me: as regards my own happiness, I am my own measure. If there are to be any requirements which may constrain what I deem to constitute my happiness or restrict its pursuit, they must issue from what is already involved in my self-determination of what counts as good for me.

The general idea underlying the various accounts of these constraints is this. I give value to, deem good, certain activities and relationshps as required for my happiness, and so also to the conditions which enable me to pursue this. The moral question now is: do I accept that, and so am willing to act as if, that which gives me reason to act has the same value, and so is to be deemed good, in the case of any other person? Man's overriding desire is for happiness, understood as the satisfaction of the agent with his pursuit of his various activities. But this end, and the activities he thereby engages in, are not pursued instinctively. Rather, man takes happiness *as* his end and pursues his activities for the *reasons* which it provides. But I can only act for reasons if I recognize that what I count as a reason in my own case is so for anyone in the same circumstances. If, in the light of the pursuit of my happiness, I see I have reason to choose those activities which seem to offer the prospect of self-satisfaction, and to desire that I can pursue them to my self-satisfaction, so I must recognize that the same goes for anyone who takes happiness as their end. Similarly, in so far as I take that as my end, I see I have reason to preserve my life and to satisfy the basic requirements without which I cannot pursue my chosen activities: health, clothing, housing, security, and so on. But if I have reason for desiring these things, and so attempting to secure them, I must recognize that the same goes for anyone else. However, I can only recognize that these *are reasons* in the case of other people if I am willing to *act* on them, just as I take them as reasons for action in my own case. So in terms of my pursuit of self-satisfaction, I have reasons to act to secure the possibility of choice of activities for others and to aid their pursuit: this will give me reason, for example, to act to maintain or institute social arrangements for the arbitration of conflicting claims and for the protection of individual choice. In the same way, I have reasons to act so that the lives of others are preserved, that they are fed, housed, clothed, and so on. I recogize these requirements in saying I 'ought' to act in this way in relation to others. But this 'ought' simply marks the presence of reasons provided by the overall end I pursue, and is basically the same 'ought' as marks the reasons which that end provides for actions in relation to my own self-satisfaction. If I pursue this end, then I ought to act in ways which are required by it. In my own case, this means I ought to choose activities I think are likely to produce my self-satisfaction. But in taking self-satisfaction as my end, I recognize its capacity for giving reasons as such, and so that I ought to further it generally and act accordingly in the case of others. We see in this way why it is that we take ourselves to be under obligations to help those in need, to preserve freedom of choice, and so on. The constraining nature of the 'ought' is a result of our incompletely rational nature, that we must set our ends but often fail to act in ways for which they give reason. I may act in ways for which the overall end of my self-satisfaction offers reasons against, as when some projected activity puts in jeopardy an essential condition, like health, for its pursuit. But, and more commonly, I am apt to pursue my self-satisfaction as though that of others had no claim on me. The moral 'ought' simply articulates these wider requirements in relation to others which my taking self-satisfaction *as* my end, and so capable of giving me *reasons*, involves.

Allowing the cogency of this, what are we to say about the overall end of happiness? Since all reason-giving flows from it, it would appear that we cannot have reason for its pursuit. Nevertheless, if it is taken as our overall end, the end for our lives as such, then we can at least ask what it is about human life that means it finds its appropriate end here. In describing this end, Mackie tells us:

> We can . . . say firmly that for any individual a good life will be made up largely of the effective pursuit of activities that *he finds* worthwhile, either intrinsically, or because they are directly beneficial to others about whom he cares, or because he knows them to be instrumental in providing the means of well-being for himself and those closely connected with him.[2]

The good life, as I remarked above, is one to be determined by the individual in terms of his own satisfaction. The meaning of human life is given by the individual *setting his own limits*: selecting certain activities of the ones which his capacities make available to him, determining the degree to which they are to be pursued and what is to count as their satisfactory performance. Happiness is the unhindered pursuit of such activities and relations within these self-set limits. But how are we to understand the setting of these limits? They mark what contents *me*, and not momentarily, but, in so far as happiness is the end for my life as such, in a stable and abiding way. What is at issue is a satisfaction of *myself*, one which, therefore, is adequate to cope with my life as a whole. I can achieve some stable plan of this kind only if I exercise my capacities with an eye to settling on limits, and on ones which I can be reasonably confident that I shall find lastingly satisfying. Having determined these, my future is to be a continuation of my past, since it is to be organized in the light of what that has led me to believe will prove satisfying for my life. Of course, I may change my mind about this, but I shall do so, in so far as I look to happiness as the end, in terms of arriving at some overall conception of what satisfies me through which I can then live my life. Happiness as the end for my life as such involves a certain conception of the problem of my existence: it is one of discovering through my experience a general conception of what will prove of lasting satisfaction which I can then use in order to plan and relate to my future. But does this represent an adequate understanding of the problem? Nietzsche would not have thought so.

## II

Nietzsche's thought presents a radical critique of previous philosophy, the terms of which may well seem close to that of Kierkegaard. The metaphysical notion of truth, Nietzsche claims, presupposes a transcendent position, 'One would have to be situated outside of life',[3] unavailable to a living human being, yet metaphysics is itself a human activity. It is thus a particular human perspective on life, and one formed in terms of an illusion. To see life clear-sightedly requires seeing it in contrast not to a timeless notion of being, but as constant becoming; and not to a timeless notion of truth and its attendant notion of a general humanity, but in terms of individual life. But, of course, in contrast to Kierkegaard, Nietzsche tried to reveal religion too as implicated in the same perspective as previous philosophy. In doing this, he does not reject the project of philosophical reflection, but claims rather that, at its extreme development, such reflection undermines itself, opening up the possibility of a form of life beyond reason and truth. The *claim* on us of such a life can, however, only be felt from *within* the claim of reason, of reflection, itself, so that the thinker must be situated at once both within and without the discourse of reason. Such a position precludes access to life beyond reason, placing us rather under the necessity of an interventionary thinking, the active undermining within our received forms of thought of the hold of reason and truth. In this general structure, as we shall see, Nietzsche's thought becomes determinative for the later work of Heidegger and Derrida.

Nietzsche *situates* his thinking in relation to a nihilism which he diagnoses as implicit in contemporary European culture: 'Everything lacks meaning . . . The *aim* is lacking: why? finds no answer.'[4]

The immediate cause of this lack of meaning is that 'God is dead', by which Nietzsche means 'that the belief in the Christian God has become unbelievable'.[5] This is not merely the claim that science has been divorced from religion so leaving nature merely a field of 'causalism, mechanism'[6] and not of purpose, and that ethics and politics have become secular. Rather, Nietzsche's claim is that this very development in our relation to the human and the non-human is *itself* part of the progress towards the loss of meaning. This could only be so if these secular relations themselves involve an essential reference to God where belief in God has become untenable. Since these secular relations may well be thought of as themselves proceeding from the perception of such untenability, this may seem paradoxical. But Nietzsche claims that the unbelievability of God has left morality with no sanction[7] so that it 'no longer knows how to maintain itself'.[8] The reason why this leads to nihilism is that 'it was upon moral judgements that *value* was based so far'.[9] By 'so far' Nietzsche means 'the history of Europe since Socrates': 'the common factor' in this thinking 'is the attempt to make moral values dominate over all other values: so that they should be the guide and judge not only of life but also of 1) knowledge, 2) the arts, 3) political and social endeavours'.[10] Under some understanding of 'moral values', then, these are held to underpin our current relation to the human and the non-human, whilst 'God' in turn is held to be necessary to provide their sanction. Nihilism is, however, *implicit* in this whole structure, which is why the secularization of these relations finds its *telos* there: 'Nihilism as the necessary consequence of our valuations so far.'[11] The secularization evident in our science, ethics and politics is part of the manifestation of this implicit nihilism, and is thus part of the process whereby moral values *undermine themselves.* The significance of nihilism, Nietzsche says, lies in the fact that here 'The highest values devaluate themselves.'[12]

This process of devaluation indicates what is meant pre-eminently by 'moral values' here, for it proceeds through *truthfulness* 'turned against morality' thus discovering 'its teleology, its partial perspective'.[13] The history of Europe since Socrates has been the attempt to make the value of *truth* determinative for knowledge, human relations and the arts. But this project now turns against itself by questioning the pursuit of truth itself. How, then, could the pursuit of truth undermine itself?

Where truth becomes the supreme value, it implies finality: knowledge is directed towards a final state of perfect knowledge, and life is directed towards some final perfect state, the 'fulfilment of some highest ethical canon in all events', itself underwritten by a claim to knowledge.[14] This is the 'teleology' of moral values which is revealed when 'truth' is turned towards the whole structure of our relations to ourselves and the non-human. But that this reflective glance should undermine that structure requires further that it reveals the 'unbelievability' of such final states. The belief in finality requires a justification, that there are such states and in what they consist. This justificatory role has been played in Western culture by the appeal to God or Reason, and yet the progress of the pursuit of truth has rendered these 'unbelievable', thus undermining the whole structure. The process by which this came about is given in brief in *Twilight of the Idols*[15] in a 'history of the ideal world'. The ideal of the final state of knowledge is, in ancient philosophy, assumed to be available to the human intellect; but this assumption could only be *justified* if we and the world had indeed been formed in accordance with this ideal: hence the perceived necessity later to assume a belief in God as creator whose plan is apprehended by our thought. But this is merely to try to support one hypothesis which we can have no reason to believe by another, a subterfuge which modern thought has uncovered in its demonstration that there are no reasons for believing in the existence of God. In this juncture, nihilism manifests itself for 'then the categories of aim, unity, being, which we used to project some value into the world, we pull out again, so the world looks valueless'.[16]

Such nihilism Nietzsche calls 'passive', a bringing out of what was already implicit in the original project to make 'truth' the supreme value. It is only a consequence of a paradox at the heart of this project itself which makes questioning and ultimate justification a necessity and so must constantly seek to provide an ultimate foundation for its ideals. But this very questioning must discover the illusory nature of these very ideals: they cannot be believed by a human being. The 'value of life cannot be estimated. Not by a living man, because he is party to the dispute, indeed its object, and not the judge of it.'[17] Truth as supreme value must postulate its final states, but human beings are not in a position to believe in them:

> One would have to be situated *outside* life, and on the other hand to know it as thoroughly as any . . . to be permitted to touch on the problem of the *value* of life at all – sufficient reason for understanding that this problem is for us an inaccessible problem.[18]

The supreme value of truth involves claiming access to a position beyond life in terms of which it may be judged – hence the necessity of the appeal to 'God'. But the pursuit of truth itself will discover that for human beings no such access is possible so that the claim to apprehend that there are final states and the justification for this belief are illusions. It is this process, of a coming to such a self-understanding of the project of truth as a *human* project and so an illusion, which is underway in the secularization of our forms of knowledge, ethics and politics. Where this realization becomes inescapable, the notion of such final states becomes unbelievable, and then, because our whole way of life is founded on them, life and the world appear devoid of meaning. It is in this context that Nietzsche intends to transmute 'passive' nihilism into an 'active nihilism'[19] which itself is a preparation for something further.

The pursuit of truth directed towards itself, a movement made possible by its own undermining of a belief in God, reveals the ideal of truth, of finality, as the object of the 'will to truth', rather than, as that will understands itself, the supra-human standard for human life itself. That pursuit reveals the 'history of Europe', the history of the primacy of the value of truth, as a human project. The valuing of life in terms of the ideal of truth is thus 'only a value judgement on the part of life', and so the question now arises, itself motivated by 'truthfulness', 'Of *what* life?' And the answer Nietzsche gives to this is 'of declining, debilitated, weary, condemned life. [Morality] is the *instinct* of *decadence* itself.'[20] The life which needs to give a supreme value to truth and so be directed towards an ultimate goal is one which experiences its existence as problematic, needing to be given significance from without, and thus needing to *obey*: 'whoever is incapable of laying his will into things, lacking will and strength, at least lays some *meaning* into them, that is, the faith that there is a will in them already':[21] this is the will to truth. It characterizes the life of 'those who suffer from the impoverishment of life'[22] which 'instinctively' 'bestows honour upon servileness'.[23] With truth as the supreme value this servility is directed towards *the truth* of life, which thus applies universally and so to humanity as a whole. In this way, the pursuit of truth is revealed as a form of 'herd' thinking: 'the herd instinct . . . will allow value to the individual only from the point of view of the whole'.[24] The 'whole' at issue here, however, is 'humanity as such' in terms of which a universally valid goal is to be given to life. The 'will to truth' as the *organizing* principle of life emerges as a transmutation of herd life, where that form of life which needs to be given a meaning and so is essentially servile, achieves dominance (the *supreme* value of truth) in the context of the collapse of concrete social forms which had previously given the 'herd animal' its sense of value in terms of the group. The emergence of life lived in terms of truth is thus itself a response to a collapse of meaning, the nihilism that threatened when 'the old Athens was coming to an end'.[25] Deprived of a *concrete* social formation, the life needing a purpose now sought it in an *abstract* humanity and its standards. The need for a 'master' to give it a purpose is now fulfilled, in the absence of the concrete tradition of Athenian life, by reason:

> Moral judgements are torn from their conditionality, in which they have grown and alone possess any meaning, from their Greek and Greek political ground soil, to be de-naturalized . . . as liberated 'ideas' [they] became the objects of dialectics.[26]

And so one had to invent a 'timeless', non-historical world where they were at home. At the same time, however, this created the 'individual', the herd animal which no longer derives its value from a specific social form but as a particular case of a general 'humanity'. Such an individual, related to the standards of a universal humanity, appears first in the form of 'the abstractly perfect man . . . good, just, wise, a dialectician – . . . the scarecrow of the ancient philosopher: a plant removed from all soil'.[27] In this way, the form of human life which *needs* to be given a meaning from outside itself 'achieved victory with dialectics',[28] organizing life in terms of the 'will to truth' which privileges questioning, giving reasons, through which the abstract, universal standards for humanity as such may be apprehended and justified. But by that very truthfulness, it is now in the process of self-destruction, re-creating that loss of meaning for which it was itself a remedy.

It is important to stress here that what is to be 'overcome' for Nietzsche is the 'supreme value of truth' and not the notion of truth itself, provided we do not interpret this in the philosophical sense as a 'correspondence with reality', a corresponding we are in no position to determine. The will to truth produces knowledge, of which Nietzsche remarks: 'The entire apparatus of knowledge is an apparatus for abstraction and simplification – directed not at knowledge but at taking possession of things.'[29] Knowledge produces 'truths', propositions valid for all, because they are the result of employing general forms, universals. Prior to the project of producing such truths lies that of conceptualization through which we gain a conception of 'reality' at all. The notion of world is the result of a particular way in which humans have imposed form, that form which 'abstracts and simplifies' and which is instantiated in the general concepts through which there is a 'world' for us. The general form of the universal and the resultant ideas of 'truth' and 'knowledge' and of the logical relations between propositions, are the most general principles of this project. Nietzsche asks whether 'the axioms of logic' are

> adequate to reality or are they a means and measure for us to *create* reality, the concept 'reality' for ourselves? To affirm the former one would . . . have to have a previous knowledge of being – which is certainly not the case. The proposition therefore contains no criterion of truth, but an *imperative* concerning that which *should* count as true.[30]

The concept of 'reality' is produced by the human project of imposing *general* forms, so that 'Reason, logic, the categories, are formed out of a *need* to subsume, schematize, for the purpose of intelligibility and calculation: only if we see things coarsely, made equal, do they become calculable and usable.'[31] Such a human project is one directed towards living in a 'world', in 'reality', which is intelligible and permits us to gain a universally valid knowledge through which we can control that world, either as a basis for its manipulation or in rendering it conformable to our intelligence. The project is, we might say, directed towards domestication, to being at home in life. Knowledge enables us to remove what threatens us or to remove the appearance of threat through comprehension, and is thus *essential* for the maintenance of human life.

Furthermore, 'the assumption of similar cases' presupposes 'similar souls':[32] schematization in terms of general concepts involves the general concept of a humanity for which such concepts are valid. It is a humanity motivated by the desire for familiarization, for an absence of the threatening. Hence, Nietzsche speaks of it as a result of the instinct for 'self-preservation'. The primary values of such a humanity lie in the absence of threat and opposition, and so in 'happiness' and 'peace'. Such human life which needs to understand itself in terms of a *general* concept of humanity Nietzsche calls the 'herd', for whom the general has priority over the individual. Hence he speaks of 'The earthly kingdom of desires out of which logic grew – the herd instinct in the background.'[33] 'Truth' exists, but as a human product, the result of the imposition of its forms of a life directed towards self-preservation. Where truth becomes the *supreme* value, life itself becomes organized in terms of security, peace and happiness and so against the perspective of those cultures which had subordinated truth in the name or other values, whose character I will discuss shortly.

'Christian truthfulness must now draw its strongest conclusion, the one by which it shall do away with itself. This will be accomplished by Christianity asking itself 'what does all will to truth signify?'[34] It signifies, first, that life which gives the supreme value to truth is a problematic, servile, herd life. But this revelation, second, confronts us then with a *new* questions:

> The problem of the value of truth stepped before us – or was it we who stepped before this problem? . . . it has finally come

to seem to us that this problem has never before been posed – that we have been the first to see it, to fix our eyes on it, to hazard it.[35]

The questioning intrinsic to the value of truth now turns on that value itself: 'We asked after the value of this will. Granted we want truth: *why not rather* untruth? And uncertainty? Even ignorance?'[36] Philosophy has since Socrates 'wanted to furnish the rational ground of morality' but 'morality itself was taken as given'.[37] Operating within the will to truth, philosophy has tried to identify the goal of life and its justification, but in this way it has taken the project of subordinating life to truth as something unquestionable. With Nietzsche, truthfulness now directs itself towards this project itself, revealing it as a human project involved in the illusion of access to a suprahuman standpoint, and so raising the question of the value of truth itself. In this way, fundamental questioning, philosophy, undergoes a transmutation. The philosophy of 'philosophical labourers' such as Kant and Hegel takes 'former *assessments* of value, creations of value which have become dominant and are for a while called "truths"' and makes them 'clear, distinct, intelligible and manageable'. But 'actual philosophers' 'determine the wherefore and whither of mankind' reaching 'for the future with creative hand'.[38] Such a 'creating' had taken place with Socrates in initiating the supreme value of truth, and now must take place again where this value is itself questioned out of 'truthfulness'.

The question 'What is the value of truth?' cannot be raised from within the structure of the life lived in terms of the supreme value of truth itself. To raise it, we must *already* have moved outside such a life in order to see its character: problematic, servile, herd thinking. But that very move thus involves us in judging its value, and so reveals the values of the perspective from which truth can be judged:

> he who has really gazed ... down into the most world-denying of all possible modes of thought – beyond good and evil and no longer ... under the spell and illusion of morality – perhaps by that very act, and without really intending to, may have had his eyes opened to the opposite ideal; to the ideal of the most exuberant, most living and most world-affirming man.[39]

The pursuit of the truth as reflective questioning reveals ultimately that it is for us an 'inadmissable problem' and so shows us its character as a form of human life. To characterize this form of life is thus already to see it as one lived under an illusion and so untruthfully. To be truthful is to ask what function this illusion played: why it was believed, where this is not directed to the 'reasons' that way of life had but to why it had those reasons. In asking this, we have stepped beyond the perspective governed by 'the truth' into another from which the will to truth can be characterized. Such a characterization implies a different set of values by contrast with which the will to truth is determined in its specificity, the values of a non-problematic life, non-servile and non-herdlike, and so raises for us the question as to what these values are. What is the perspective of the 'most world-affirming man'?

Rather than needing to be given a purpose, he posits 'himself as a goal'[40] and through this goals for himself. His values are thus not a means towards a goal for life, but rather characterize the supreme value which he himself is: 'The highest virtue is uncommon and useless.'[41] Prior to the rise of Socratic rationalism, it had been precisely such lives which had given a supreme point to society itself, representing 'happiness, beauty, benevolence on earth'.[42] They are lives characterized by a purposelessness which is not a lack but a glorification of life: with them, life ceases to be directed towards a purpose external to it and becomes celebrated, affirmed. The forms of their social living are severed from essential connection with purpose and are raised to the level of art in elaborate custom and ritual, whilst their characteristic activities celebrate a rejection of all concern with values of utility in the pursuit of great deeds, exploits within which self-preservation is deliberately put at risk so that their freedom from such values can find expression: within their own society, for example, in the competitive games and in rivalries upon which they stake their lives, and outside it in war and conquest. Their values are those of 'Pride, pathos of distance, great responsibility, exuberance, splendid animality, the instincts that delight in war and conquest, the deification of passion, of revenge, of cunning, of anger, of voluptuousness, of adventure, of knowledge',[43] the last named presumably lying in the knowledge of their own freedom from imposed purpose. Their lives are not *for* something, in the way that the lives of the other strata of their societies find their rationale in preserving the group, whether through the maintenance of law or through the performance of necessary tasks: 'To be a public utility, a cog, a function, is a natural vocation: it is the kind of happiness of which the great majority are alone capable.'[44] And nor, of course, are the nobles' lives directed towards the achievement of, or moving towards, some goal for individual life: with them, life 'stays aloft' celebrating its triumph over the tyranny of imposed purpose and thus becomes its own goal. But the societies of which these are the exemplars of life-affirmation ultimately destroy themselves in 'fearful and ruthless external hostility': 'the city states tore one another to pieces'.[45] Such life-affirmation, celebrating a freedom from *externally* imposed purposes, from domination by others, and from the instinct for the preservation of individual or social life, is essentially *active* and finds its expression in external forms, of ritual, custom and the performance of great exploits. The destruction of such societies creates a vacuum of purpose for servile life, allowing it the opportunity to develop the will to truth as life's organizing principle.

It is in the context of the overcoming of the dominance of this will through itself that the revelation of the 'opposite ideal' takes place within Nietzsche's thought. It appears, that is, in contradistinction to life governed by truth within which the *individual* has been created. The issue *now* is what a life which was not directed towards a purpose but was its own source of value could be, where this is asked in the context of the self-overcoming of a servile humanity, in the world of 'we moderns' characterized by humanistic ethics, democratic politics, and a scientific relation to the non-human. The question, that is, is faced by *the individual* in the cause of a liberation from the hold of truth and so from the very self-understanding *as* an individual in relation to a general concept of humanity in terms of which the ideals of truth have been generated (universal validity of claims to knowledge and of ethical and political imperatives). Such a liberation is thus *from* the individual and so from the idea of a unitary self whose meaning lies in relation to a single goal or standard derived from the notion of an abstract humanity.

With the help of custom and the social strait-jacket man was . . . made culculable. However, if we place ourselves at the terminal point of this great process, where society and custom reveal their true aim, we shall find the ripest fruit of that tree to be the sovereign individual, equal only to himself, all moral custom left far behind. The autonomous, more than moral individual (the terms *autonomous* and moral are mutually exclusive) has developed his own independent, long-range will.[46]

In this way, Nietzsche can say both 'My idea: goals are lacking and these must be individuals!',[47] and 'My philosophy aims at an ordering of rank: not an individualistic morality.'[48] His thought aims at a transformation of life lived by 'individuals' understood in relation to a general humanity to a new form of life within which the idea of the unitary self would itself be overcome: the passage from 'the species across to the super-species'[49] from man to the overman. Such a life would lie in a process of 'constant becoming' and so without direction towards an end, without finality, in which a certain order is imposed on life only to be itself overcome where it threatens to dominate, where it ceases to be part of the project of 'staying aloft'. This constitutes the 'idea that life could be an experiment for the seeker for knowledge',[50] where this knowledge is of freedom: 'How is freedom measured, in individuals as in nations? By the resistance which has to be overcome, by the effort it costs to stay aloft'.[51] Such a life is one of constant creativity of life itself: 'We . . . want to *become those we are* – human beings who are new, unique, incomparable, who give themselves laws, who create themselves.'[52] Life itself would thus become 'art', 'Art as the redemption of the man of knowledge . . . of the man of action . . . of the sufferer.'[53] Art is 'redemption' because the human being who lives life as art, giving life its own law and overcoming it, affirms life in its totality, being subject to nothing beyond its own creative process. 'The two futures of mankind: 1) constant growth of mediocrity, 2) conscious distinction, self-shaping.'[54] The will to truth is overcome by what it itself reveals: it has been a 'creative' project, the imposition on life of a form produced by a particular *kind* of life, the servile, which, however, could not understand its own project *as* a 'creation'. Truthfulness thus reveals this project as a *degenerate* kind of art. The will to truth overcomes itself in the perception that 'art . . . [is] *worth more* than truth'.[55]

But the superspecies is not yet. As a life completely self-sufficient, it needs no *justification*. Nietzsche's thought occupies a transitional place, where truth is overcome by truthfulness and the superspecies is seen *as* the goal. What is necessary now is the undermining of the hold of the value of truth, an active nihilism:

> Overcoming of philosophers through the destruction of the world of being: intermediary period of nihilism: before there is yet present the strength to reverse values and to deify becoming and the apparent world as the only world and to call them good.[56]

This line of thought within Nietzsche's *own* constitutes a *justification* of these values: it is *itself* a product of an inquiry into 'truth', a value whose predominance is to be overcome. The truth about values is that there are only different evaluations of life on the part of life, the difference lying in whether these evaluations affirm this, and so affirm life as creativity, or, by their very form, deny it, and so seek to live in illusion. But this measure of values cannot be lived by the one who pursues it since life which truly 'believed' in itself would need *no justification* and so no appeal to 'truth'. If we pursue truth, we see the illusions of the appeal to God or to the 'pure, will-less, painless, timeless . . . knower' of 'pure reason' and 'absolute knowledge'[57] and the truth of Nietzsche's thought. But this itself shows that to live in this 'truthfulness' can only be a preparatory stage, engaged in undermining the claims to truth of the evaluations which the history of truth has produced, clearing the ground for a form of life which would need no appeal to truth to justify itself and which would value truth merely as an instrument for the preservation of life and control of the environment.

> Strong ages and peoples do not reflect on their rights, on the principles on which they act, on their instincts and reasons. Becoming conscious is a sign that real morality, that is instinctive certainty in actions, is going to the devil.[58]

The need for justification is itself the mark of the dependent life, unable to believe in itself. Yet Nietzsche's own thought constitutes a justification for action, albeit directed against the universal claims of herd thought. As such, it marks the extreme point of the form of life which needs justification and so truth, where this is finally turned against itself to provide the conditions under which individuals beyond justification could arise. Nietzsche's thought constitutes the 'self-overcoming of morality through truthfulness'.[59]

'Our age knows'[60] and this knowledge opens up new possibilities and ultimately that of a new birth of Dionysian existence. Prior to this, however, the hold of herd values on those who can hear must be broken and the will liberated: Nietzsche looks towards the breeding of humanity and the destruction of degenerate elements which 'will again make possible on earth that *super-fluity of life* out of which the Dionysian condition must again proceed'.[61] We are not now, even if we feel the force of Nietzsche's thought, such as *can* will in such a fashion, since to feel that force is itself the mark of our motivation by truth. Rather, we can only act to undermine the claims made on behalf of herd values and so prepare the way for a humanity which will be so able. Our knowledge leads to our destructive activity: we are to be the lion of Zarathustra's parable which 'cannot create new values but creates freedom for new creation'.[62] After the lion, though, comes the Child, 'a new beginning, a sacred Yes. The spirit wills its *own* will, the spirit sundered from the world', that is, *the* world understood in terms of the value of truth, 'now wins its *own* world'.[63] But this will not be a return to a previous Dionysian existence. This possibility has only emerged through a deepening self-examination of man, of which the dominance of the herd value of truth has been an essential part and within which the 'individual' has itself been created. The noble cultures of the past lacked the results of this examination and so affirmed life in the form of external *action*. And lacking the knowledge produced by the will to truth, they did not know, as we do, that the higher human beings create their own values, are themselves, as the embodiment of the principle of life, the source of value. 'Only we [higher beings] have created the world that concerns man – But precisely this knowledge we lack.'[64] Rather, such higher human beings in the past worshipped themselves in the form of gods, not recognizing this self-projection for what it was and so interpreting themselves merely as the recipients of the gods' favours.[65] Nietzsche does not look forward to humans who would possess this knowledge, since we do so already. That we do, however, means that we cannot live 'the Dionysian condition'. Future Dionysian human beings would be un-encumbered by such knowledge, and so both liberated from the past's projection of itself upon a god, and from the 'individual' of post-Socratic herd thought: they would be free as instinctive and autonomous creators of value. 'One could conceive of such a pleasure and power of self-determination, such a freedom of the will that the spirit would take leave of all faith and every wish for certainty ... such a spirit would be the *free spirit* par excellence.'[66] Without gods or a dependence on knowledge of man as self-creating which only takes place through the over-coming of the herd individual, a product of the pursuit of truth, such free spirits would be a truly instinctive Dionysian existence of a radical, new kind. 'Man', the human understood according to the universal standard for humanity of herd values, would be overcome, and the passage made 'from the species to the superspecies'. But such overcoming must first be undertaken in the destruction of the hold of herd values. Nietzsche thus welcomes 'all signs that a virile warlike age is about to begin, which will prepare the way for one yet higher'. The higher age is the new Dionysian: the warlike one of 'preparatory human beings who are bent on seeking in all things for what in them must be overcome', that is, the imprint of herd values.[67] In engaging in such war, we can begin to become what we are, human beings who *know* they determine their own values and who can, therefore, look towards the prospect of a higher form of human life which would genuinely be that of 'the free spirit *par excellence*'.

## III

We can immediately see what the Nietzschean response to the analytical perspective with which we began would be. It takes happiness as the end of human life. Happiness, as the un-hindered pursuit of chosen activities and relationships within self-determined limits which demarcate the degree to which they are to be pursued and what it is to count as their satis-factory performance, is taken to be the universally valid end for human life, and only as such is it able to give reasons for one's actions both in relation to oneself and others. Such a view we know is characteristic of the weak in will. Those unable to regard themselves as the source of value need to believe in an external standard, such a truth. The determiners of their own values seek resistance, those who lack such a power desire a state of peace, absence of resistance, and need to regard this as 'truth'. The justification for this characterization emerges, as we have seen, from the problem of the status of the 'end' of life propounded by philosophy. What is it which makes happiness 'the end'? Either we have access to a position beyond life from which the truth about life could be seen, or we must accept that all valuations on life are by life itself. As living beings we can have no access to a position from which life in its totality can be judged. But then that *perspective* on life which declares its view as 'the truth', and so from which flows universally valid reasons and thus the claim of obligation to others on the individual, is involved in illusion, and thereby revealed as the view on life of a life which *needs* an external standard, a 'truth' to obey. 'Happiness' appears, not as 'the truth', but rather as the end for a life which cannot create its own values in the celebration of life as creativity itself.

Nor need we doubt how Nietzsche would assess Kierkegaard. For Kierkegaard, life cannot be its own measure and so must be related to what is essentially beyond life, an 'eternal happiness' and the absolute measure, God, for its meaning. This is characteristic for Nietzsche of the Church's reinterpretation of the message of Jesus. He sees Jesus as prescribing a way of life which is 'the opposite of all contending, of all feeling oneself in struggle', 'the incapacity for resistance here becomes morality ("resist not evil")'.[68] Through this one attains an unshakeable peace, impervious to the intrusions of others and external events. This peace is 'the kingdom of God' within us[69] and is, therefore, something attainable within the Christian life. That it should be the highest value, however, proceeds from feeling 'all resisting, all need for resistance, as ... harmful' and knowing 'blessedness (pleasure) only in no longer resisting anyone or anything'.[70] Nevertheless, this is 'a very proud life', one which aims at and achieves 'the completest spiritual-intellectual independence',[71] and to that extent is a manifestation of a certain degree of self-affirmation, even if it is the power of a life which desires such independence and so sees in the fear of resistance 'a sufficient motive for letting everything go'.[72] The Church, however, takes this recipe for human bliss and converts it into a doctrine for those incapable of such resistance to resistance, teaching this happiness as a reward beyond life for those who live morally, eschewing intrusion on others, helping those in need, and so on. It becomes a doctrine for those incapable of any sort of self-affirmation and so a 'faith', incorporating the values of those who value above all else an absence of opposition in the appropriate form of an external 'truth'. If they live a life in relation to others of peace and compassion, they will attain in the afterlife what is unavailable to them here below, a perfect internal peace. Nietzsche would have regarded Kierkegaard as expounding a faith whose values are those of the weakest in life, so that in shifting

> the centre of gravity of life *out* of life into the 'Beyond' – into nothingness – one has deprived life as such of its centre of gravity . . . So to live that there is no longer any *meaning* in living: that now becomes the 'meaning' of life.[73]

Kierkegaard articulates the faith of those who say 'No' to life, being incapable of even the affirmation contained in Jesus' 'kingdom of God within you'. And in that sense, it is the lowest, most life denying, of life evaluations, lower even than those who look towards, as in the analytical perspective, a contentment within their lives.

Can there be an adequate Kierkegaardian response to this? Let me begin by suggesting how Kierkegaard might have regarded Nietzsche's project. He would, I think, have seen it as a species of 'reflective aestheticism', in certain important respects close to that portrayed in the writings of 'A' in the first volume of *Either/Or.* The aesthetic, as we have seen, is initially that unreflective and immediate view of life which sees its significance as lying in what happens to the individual: its categories are fortune, misfortune, fate. What happens in this external sense is significant, of course, in relation to the desires the individual has, in that they bring their satisfaction or its opposite: hence, the aesthetic individual sees pleasure as the goal of life. But when and if the individual reflects about his life, this immediate and passionate direction towards external goals and situations is broken. Now it appears he must determine which desires to act upon, and this moment disrupts the unconscious orientation towards pleasure. For then, it appears, as A writes, 'If you marry, you will regret it; if you do not marry, you will regret it; if you marry or do not marry, you will regret both; whether you marry or do not marry, you will regret both'.[74] To decide to follow one desire, involves the impossibility of following another, and so a regret at a lost presentiment of pleasure. The prospect of unalloyed pleasure, characteristic of unreflective life, is lost. But one cannot do nothing. Regret is attendant upon decision: so the secret of the reflective aesthetic life is to avoid decision, whilst still acting. This is possible, A believes, by accentuating the *arbitrary*. One's desires and what happens are both to be treated as a field of possibility in which one will determine *oneself* what has significance:

> The whole secret lies in arbitrariness. One does not enjoy the immediate but something quite different which he arbitrarily imports into it. You go to see the middle of a play, you read the third part of a book. By this means you insure yourself a very different kind of enjoyment from that which the author has been so kind as to plan for you. You enjoy something entirely accidental; you consider the whole of existence from this standpoint.[75]

In this way, what you enjoy is not what happens, which can only bring pleasure to the unreflective individual, but rather *having your own way*: 'pleasure consists not in what I enjoy, but in having my own way'.[76] This is, in fact, the hidden nature of the unreflective individual, since he finds pleasure in what happens because it satisfies a desire with which he has temporarily *identified himself*. He has had, courtesy of the world, his own way. But reflection, in destroying this immediate pursuit of external objects, seems to suggest that now pleasure can only be found in the bare 'having of one's own way' itself, which must therefore be *explicitly imposed* on all facticity, both on what the individual finds himself with in the way of desires and on what occurs to him. This project can only be carried out, A believes, by arbitrarily deciding on what is to have significance, not letting this be determined by one's desires themselves. It is thus the attempt by the individual to *create* the significance of their own life, to live life as art, to live 'poetically'.[77] In this way, one is to take pleasure in the exercise of one's freedom, revealed in the reflective moment through which one is distanced from one's desires and events in the world, a distance which makes the pleasure of the unreflective life impossible.

In treating one's given nature as a field of possibility whose significance is to be arbitrarily determined, the unity of the self is disrupted. One's life deliberately lacks coherence, so that 'one ought to be a mystery, not only to others, but also to one's self'.[78] As Judge William says in his response to A: 'Everything that is established by divine and human law you despise, and to liberate yourself from it you grasp at the accidental . . . You want to experiment, and you contemplate everything from this point of view.'[79] And yet, as A's remarks reveal, such an attempt at a life of reflective pleasure is impossible to carry out: pleasure is essentially something which may or may not come, and so cannot lie 'in having my own way' as a *deliberate* project. A's attempts at the arbitrary imposition of significance cannot guarantee their own success, so that they are marked continually by the irruption of a sense of pointlessness and so of dissatisfaction: 'My view of life is utterly meaningless . . . my eyes are sated and weary of everything, and yet I hunger.'[80] Reflection removes the possibility of the assumption A tries to maintain: 'I assume that it is the end and aim of everyman to enjoy himself':[81] only a man who has not arrived at the reflection upon his assumptions can pursue that aim with the possibility of success.

A Kierkegaardian reading of Nietzsche might then plausibly interpret him as expounding a form of reflective aestheticism where the appeal to pleasure is indeed rejected as characteristic of the unreflective life, leaving the will 'to have my own way' revealed in its nakedness. Thus, whereas A wishes to enjoy freedom, Nietzsche projects a life which 'stays aloft', free of submission to external law or internal habit. A, as Judge William says, seeks 'to enjoy the particular' and so places 'the particular outside the universal' where the determination of the significance of his actions lies solely with himself.[82] Nietzsche wishes to free the individual from the imposition of law derived from the universal notion of humanity so that he gives himself his own law. Such giving, in order to celebrate 'staying aloft', requires both an imposition of order and the strength to overturn it where it threatens to become a fixed habit, just as A remarks that 'one ought to devote oneself to pleasure with a certain suspicion' so that 'when you begin to notice that a certain pleasure or experience is acquiring too strong a hold upon the mind' you can stop, thus developing 'a distaste for continuing the experience too long',[83] where it threatens to control the individual rather than be engaged with through one's freedom. Both strategies deprive life of unity, so that A has, according to Judge William, no self, 'in fact you are nothing'[84] whilst Nietzsche looks forward to a future of mankind as 'self-shaping', 'constant becoming', within which the idea of a unitary self would be overcome. A, Judge William says, 'wants to experiment' and contemplates 'everything from this point of view', whilst for Nietzsche life is to be an experiment, the production of the knowledge of the degree of one's freedom.

Nietzsche, Kierkegaard might say, sees 'having my own way' as the general character of *all* views of life, so that the essential distinction lies in whether they try to avoid this recognition by an appeal to 'truth' and so have the nature of illusion or clear-sightedly accept it. But, it may be rejoined, if any view of life is one on life by life itself, then this applies equally to a religious understanding of human existence. And in that case, how are we to avoid the conclusion that the ultimate measure for life must be life's own creativity, rid of the illusion of an external standard and which sees the religious understanding as embodying the values of a life unable to celebrate itself? Kierkegaard would have agreed with the first part of this: the religious understanding of life is indeed one formed by human beings about their own lives. And he could immediately object to Nietzsche's characterization of this. Nietzsche requires further that this understanding be characterized in terms of 'weakness', that is as produced by a *desire* for the absence of what characterizes the values of the strong: opposition, resistance and the necessity of the imposition of one's own will. For Nietzsche, the religious view of life values a state of absolute peace, uninterrupted by the intrusions of others or the necessity of exercising one's own will whether this is looked for in this life or in one to come. It sees life's end as the satisfaction of this dominant desire, even if this should be unattainable in this life. But this is hardly adequate to Kierkegaard's account of religious existence which emphasizes that an end for one's life as a *whole* cannot lie in the satisfaction or fulfilment of some *part* of it, and so not in the satisfaction of such a desire. The measure in terms of which such an end is determined cannot, therefore, be such as to produce this result.

But Nietzsche's characterization of the religious understanding is a product of the underlying structure of his thought, to which Kierkegaard would therefore object. I have suggested that the point of Nietzsche's discussion of truth and reason is not to deny their adequacy to reality, which would assume a position beyond being in terms of which such adequacy could be assessed, but rather to see them as constitutive of what we call 'reality' and yet at the same time as the result of a certain human project. 'Reality' is indeed articulated in terms of the categories of reason, and so in terms of universals and their application, but the placing of a relation to reality as the supreme human value expresses a particular form of human life, one which needs to see *itself* as an instance of a general humanity. It is incapable of justifying this valuation in the appropriate way, *as* a form of life, and so appeals to a position beyond life, to Reason or God. The human project of the will to create has, however, such justification, whilst at the same time rejecting the need for any justification whatever. The essential contrast for Nietzsche is between life which needs some general idea of what is appropriate for humanity as such, in terms of which it could justify itself, and one which does not but 'determines its own values'. Whereas the former sees itself as an instance of a general concept the latter is essentially individual, producing its own significance through the *constant* imposition of itself on what is given, whether by circumstance or its own past. The weak in will impose a *general* form on their lives, the strong the form of *themselves.*

Now Kierkegaard too sees reason and understanding as characteristics of human life, whose validity of application within a certain limit he has no desire to question. But it is not that they are valid for a kind of life which needs to understand itself in terms of a general concept but not for one which has no such need, but rather that they are inadequate in relation to human existence itself, where this is seen from the primary viewpoint of the existing individual himself: 'It is not denied that objective thought has validity; but in connection with all thinking where subjectivity must be accentuated, it is a misunderstanding.'[85] Indeed, objective thought is valid in relation to all reality save the individual's own, since such reality, unlike the individual's own, can be known 'only by thinking it'.[86] Such thought is essentially conceptual, and the cognitive subject 'moves in the sphere of the possible'[87] for a 'conceived reality is a possibility'.[88] Thus, if I think about something that another has done, I conceive it as an *instance* of a kind of action, and so of what is possible, just as my thought of the non-human essentially sees the particular as an instance of a general concept. But my relation to my own existence is quite different: it is not for me an instance of a general concept of human existence. To conceive the particular as an instance of the general and so as possibility, as what it is possible to think, is to operate under the assumption of being *sub specie aeterni*,[89] since what is possible conceptually is not Kierkegaard thinks temporally delimited. But the existing individual who engages in such thought is not identical with the cognitive subject: 'The real subject is not the cognitive subject, since in knowing he moves in the sphere of the possible; the real subject is the ethically existing subject',[90] for whom engaging in such cognitive activity is itself a 'possibility'. Here 'possibility' does not mean conceptually, as an instance of what is generally conceivable, but rather that a question arises as to whether we *will* engage in it here and now or not. Is it possible for me here and now, that is, is it something I should embark on in the light of my relation to my existence as a whole, in terms of the 'how' of my life? This latter relation is not one of an instance to a generality, but that living relation through which I can undertake what is conceivable, *actualize* it in my own activity. But this applies, therefore to the *intellectual reflection* with which Nietzsche engages. It is impossible

> to think about existence in existence without passion . . . To think about existential problems in such a way as to leave out the passion, is tantamount to not thinking about them at all, since it is to forget the point, which is that the thinker is himself an existing individual.'[91]

It is here that the fundamental difference between the thought of Nietzsche and Kierkegaard appears. Their objections to the metaphysical tradition share a common form, being directed not towards questioning whether it has apprehended 'the truth' in order to provide a rectification, but rather towards questioning its implied claim to *access* to a position from which such truth would be an intelligible objective. Thus, as we have seen, Nietzsche claims that value judgements 'concerning life, for and against, can in the last resort never be true' for 'the value of life cannot be estimated. Not by a living man, because he is party to the dispute, indeed its object, and not the judge of it.' When 'we speak of values we do so under the inspiration and from the perspective of life: life itself evaluates through us when we establish values'.[92] And it may appear that a parallel argument occurs in Kierkegaard: 'if an existing individual were really able to transcend himself, the truth would be for him something final and complete; but where is the point at which he is outside himself?'[93]

Yet it is important to mark the differences in the conclusions each draws, which mark the differences between the senses which these criticisms have. For Nietzsche, what this shows is that any view on life is by life itself, so that the new questioning arises, not of the truth of such a view, but rather of the form of life which produces it. The form of life which needs to regard its perspective not as such but as the truth thereby reveals itself as slavish and herd-like, and this revelation at the same time opens our eyes to another possibility, of a non-slavish and non-herd existence. Nietzsche's criticisms, as a putting of the supreme value of truth in question through being 'truthful' about it, is thus a further, deeper development of the intellectual reflection which characterizes that tradition itself. But it would be just this to which Kierkegaard would object.

What Kierkegaard wants to remind us of is that such 'fundamental thought' is carried out by an existing individual involved in their *own* life: as he says of Hegel, but it would apply to the philosophical project as such, 'let us then ask . . . "Who is to write or complete such a system?" Surely a human being . . . an existing individual.'[94] Questioning about life can only be raised by an I and therefore is *first* a questioning by the individual of their *own* life. The problem which such questioning claims to articulate must therefore have the character of the problems an individual can have with their own life. Whereas Nietzsche wishes to reveal the 'objective' metaphysical claims as the product of a form of *human existence*, and thus in terms of a *generality*, Kierkegaard reminds us that *all* such forms of reflective intellectual response, including therefore Nietzsche's, to the question at issue, fail to respect the primacy of the *first-person* position from which alone any such intellectual activity may proceed. A 'problem' with life's significance is always first one for an I with their own life, within which context it manifests itself not as intellectual but as despair. Nietzsche's ascent to the general, to a reflection upon metaphysics as the product of the will-to-truth so as to reveal a new possibility for life, *repeats* the characteristic philosophical move. Such a move divorces the individual thinker, the I, *from* the problem in order that an intellectual resolution be revealed which will then encompass the individual as a *case* of a form of life. The I speaking in the first person is lost, but with that the very *sense* of the problem to which the intellectual pursuit is claimed to be directed. Kierkegaard wishes to remind us that behind all this theoretical discourse lies the one who speaks, an I, who can only speak about the significance of life in such a way that it *involves* himself: either the problem is indeed one the I has with their own life, in which case it has to be characterized as despair and its resolution as a dissolution in the taking on of a new 'how' of life which answers to the *character* of the despair, or it is expressed as an intellectual problem which thereby already reveals a particular relation of the I to his life, one which involves the confident assertion of the primacy of his intellectual reflective powers in relation to the question, and so *fails* to *pose* it in the appropriate existential form, that of the despair of the I over the significance of his life in its *totality.*

It is, of course, quite possible, indeed, Kierkegaard thinks, it is the general case, to think existentially in a quasi-objective manner, which occurs when we regard our lives as if they were directed towards some end or measured by some concrete standard which answers to the question which our lives are, thus precluding the possibility of an absolute despair, and determine our actions accordingly. Such passion is therefore not absolute, relating to our lives as a *whole,* since for the existing individual, the question of their *own* life in its totality can only manifest itself *as* such despair. To exist purely as the existing individual is to relate to the measure for one's life as a whole and thus to an *absence* from that life and so to one's future always as future. Now this indeed precludes relating to one's future as an imagined past future within which one's life would achieve completion, which is the character of the weak in will's interpretation of life for Nietzsche. But Kierkegaard's criticism of Nietzsche would be that it also precludes the interpretation of life in terms of the will to create. Nietzsche characterizes this as life which rejects the idea of a general measure and which gains its significance through the *process* of self-creation itself. But for Kierkegaard the constant imposition of oneself on what is given remains a conceptually possible project for which the question arises existentially for the individual as to whether it could answer to an absolute despair, the only way the question to which this project is a response can appear for an I. The very characterization of this life in terms of the rejection of measure merely reveals it as an attempt to deny the existential relation of the individual to his own existence, that the question of the significance of life is one the I has with his *own* life. And in terms of that, we can see that no immanent character of life, such as the process of self-creation must be, can be adequate. Life existentially understood cannot give itself its own significance, since any such significance can itself be the object of despair for the I. Nietzsche replaces the finality of the will to truth's interpretation of life by the process of the will to create. But such a process is, from the viewpoint of the existing individual's relation to his own existence, a character his life could exhibit, albeit constantly, and so is subject itself to the question of *its* significance in terms of what could give meaning to life as a *whole*. It is this which requires the recognition of the essential *absence* of an end and a measure for human existence in that existence itself. To recognize such an absence is not to grasp anything concrete which could offer renewed scope for the exercise of our powers: it is essentially an absence. To believe that life is meaningful, and so to transcend the absolute despair which *as* despair marks an attachment to a human source of value which is at the same time seen as impossible, and so to live it without looking for any satisfaction of human nature, however understood, is to recognize the measure that is essentially absent and alone can constitute a measure for human life as a whole. As we have seen, we can only express the recognition of such a measure in the exercise of renunciation, dying away from the world. For only to the absent measure, God, can I give myself in my entirety, whatever concrete capacities or conditions I find myself with, and so *always*, throughout my whole life. Only a *negative* measure is adequate to the problem of the measure for human existence. Such turning away from temporal determinants of value constitutes the 'infinite resignation' which the recognition of the measure as absent requires, and which is all we are capable of. It is true that in terms of the measure an end remains, that 'eternal happiness' of which Kierkegaard speaks, for which everything must be ventured, but it is an end which can be related to only as essentially absent. As soon as one thinks about it as something that could be present, and so as a reward, one ceases to venture everything and so ceases to have a relation to it. Such an end is not the satisfaction of human capacities, since if it is to be granted all such satisfaction must be given up as a goal.

What neither the Nietzschean nor the analytical views conceive is, as Simone Weil says, that 'The true road exists. But it is open only to those who, recognizing themselves to be incapable of finding it, give up looking for it, and yet do not cease to desire it to the exclusion of everything else.'[95] Even if one affirms one's own life, and even if this involves one in affirming all of life, this still leaves the question as to the value of such affirmation. The religious view is indeed the result of life's reflection on itself, namely, that it cannot give value to itself: it is not, therefore, an 'evaluation' which would presuppose access to a source of value and which *as* access could only result in an immanent determination.

'Christianity' says Kierkegaard, 'is not a doctrine, but an existential communication.'[96] That is, it is a communication directed towards *intervening* in the relation the individual has to her own life, a relation which is already underway. It does so by showing us a life lived in absence of self and thereby intimates what would be required for *us* to live a life directed towards a measure for it in its totality. It thus confronts us with the question as to whether we will have such a measure or not. It does not attempt to argue us into a position, since what we can see as giving us reason depends on the relation we *already* have to our lives: rather, through showing us such a life, it provokes us to a passionate response, whether of resistance or despair over our present relation. Christianity 'proposes to endow each self with an eternal happiness provided a proper relationship is established'[97] to this end. Since it is one for human life as such, its goodness cannot consist in its satisfying or fulfilling some power or capacity man has. It is an end characterized by *absolute* goodness, and one can only establish a relation to such an end by recognizing 'that the individual can do absolutely nothing of himself, but is as nothing before God',[98] before the conception of absolute Goodness. Establishing such a relation requires a transformation of one's attachment from relative ends to the absolute end, an 'infinite resignation' within which one recognizes in terms of one's *own* powers the claim of the infinite, that an absolute good can only be recognized by living without seeking a finite reward whose character *as* reward is dictated by one's given human nature. The movement of infinite resignation is one 'which I can train myself to make, for whenever any finiteness would get mastery over me, I starve myself until I can make this movement'.[99] But this is the limit of my powers, since 'the individual cannot make himself over'.[100] 'I am able by my own strength to renounce everything . . . But by my own strength I am not able to get the least of things which belong to finiteness, for I am constantly using my strength to renounce everything.'[101] What I cannot do is to make myself anew, to live in the absence of self, so that living in terms of the infinite characterizes my *whole* life; that is, so that my relation to the absolute good is no longer 'the pain of resignation', but the 'joy by virtue of the absurd'.[102]

Such 'infinite resignation' transforms our given human nature away from temporal ends towards the non-temporal. But as such a movement, it presupposes the resistance of our given nature to this transformation. Hence, Kierkegaard says, religious existence, the explicit submission of one's whole life to the conception of absolute goodness, is 'essentially suffering'.[103] That one's whole self should be totally transformed, that one's whole life should be lived not in 'infinite resignation' but through an absolute relation to absolute goodness itself, is not something within our power. Since 'it is a question of being delivered from self' Simone Weil writes, 'Any attempt to gain this deliverance by means of our own energy would be like the efforts of a cow which pulls at its hobble and so falls onto its knees.'[104] It is this which is indicated by the religious conception of 'being born again': 'It is a different being that has been engendered by God, a different "I", which is hardly "I" because it is the Son of God.'[105] To believe in this is what Simone Weil and Kierkegaard call 'faith'. 'Faith' for Kierkegaard is what characterizes Christianity or religiousness B as against the universal form of religious consciousness, religion A. Within the latter, the individual comes to understand what is required of life if it is to be related to the absolute measure, God, that it be lived in the exercise of infinite resignation, and so confronting the paradox of life, that it cannot be the ground for its own meaning. Here the individual 'comes to know the difference [between himself and God], . . . comes to know it absolutely and comes to know the absolute difference, and this is the first paradox',[106] a paradox revealed through human reflection on life. But the 'absolute paradox' which is the content of faith is that 'he is now to become like the god' (Ibid.) which can 'be believed altogether against the understanding. If anyone imagines that he understands it, he can be sure that he misunderstands it.'[107] Faith is the fulfilment of man's recognition of his nothingness before God, since it involves believing in the actual total transformation of the individual by God, and so in 'the Deity in time'.[108] To accept this is to believe that 'I shall get [the love which is the content of my life] in virtue of the absurd, in virtue of the fact that with God all things are possible.'[109] Such a belief is not, however, an exercise of our capacity for knowing, but is the *expression of the transformation* of the individual itself, which is why it cannot be 'understood'. 'The Christian language uses the same words we men use . . . [but] it uses words inversely . . . For example, Christianity says that to lose the earthly is a gain, to possess it a loss.'[110] The 'knight of faith' *inhabits* this Christian language, and so the life of infinite resignation is transformed to living 'joyfully and happily every instant by virtue of the absurd'.[111] Because faith is the expression of this existential transformation of the individual by God, it is itself said to be given by God,[112] and to be thinkable only by one newborn. We can describe the 'movements of faith',[113] in the sense of articulating the nature of such an existential transformation, but faith as the belief in its *actuality* is unavailable outside the transformation itself. Whether faith exists or not is itself a matter of faith.

Humanity cannot form the ground for the determination of its own goodness. In so far as our conception of goodness encompasses human life as a whole, we know that all temporal goods and their temporal grounds in human nature are falsely so called. To turn from such goods as goods is the movement of 'infinite resignation', and it is the most we can do of our own power. It is not done out of a concrete conception of a higher good, but simply out of the recognition that nothing temporal or ideal having its ground in human life itself, can be adequate to the problem which existence is for an I.

My reason for turning away from them is that I judge them to be false by comparison with the idea of the good . . . And what is this good? I have no idea – . . . It is that whose name alone, if I attach my thought to it, gives me the certainty that the things of this world are not goods.[114]

It is a 'Negatively determined concept'.

To recognize the inadequacy of temporal and ideal goods through infinite resignation is to recognize that an 'eternal happiness' constitutes the end for human life as a whole, and which precisely as such cannot be taken as an end which can be determined and achieved by man's own powers. It is because of this that reasons cannot be provided in terms of those powers why the individual should take it as his end:

When a man so lives that he recognizes no higher standard for his life than that provided by the understanding, his whole life is relativity, labour for a relative end; he undertakes nothing unless the understanding, by the aid of probability, can somehow make clear to him the profit and loss and give answer to the question why and wherefore.[115]

The understanding appeals to ends already recognized as goods by human capacities, and so not to an *absolute* end for life as a whole. Concerning that, no 'why or wherefore' in this sense can be given, and it therefore appears mad to the understanding. It requires that we give up the presumption to determine what is good ourselves, so that as 'far as venturing everything is concerned, I have no "why" at all':[116] rather, any 'why' is now to be determined in terms of such an end.

Nevertheless, we can be given reason to take this as our end in the sense that it can be shown to constitute the only resolution to the question of the meaning of life in its totality for the I. Whether we see this as a reason is then a matter of whether we will to have an end for our whole lives or not. Here, as with the move from the aesthetic to the ethical, there is a leap, a radical break with the previous form of existence, which, as there, requires an increased commitment and so is possible for us to do. Just as it is possible for us to embark on the imposition of ethical choice upon our lives, so it is possible to engage in the task of infinite resignation, 'the expression existentially of the principle that the individual can do absolutely nothing of himself, but is as nothing before God'.[117] Faith, however, since it is the expression of the total transformation of the individual from resignation to living 'joyfully and happily every instant by virtue of the absurd' involves a leap, but one which does not involve commitment and so the exercise of human powers. Such a transformation is not something we can do: 'I can indeed by myself despair of everything, but when I do this, I cannot by myself come back. In this moment of decision it is that the individual needs divine assistance.'[118] The leap of faith is made only through grace: if, of course, it is made at all.

In relation to God as the measure, human life acquires a significance at variance with that which can be conferred by any concrete measure suggested by human capacities. Within the latter perspective, that we have obligations to others, what others they are, and what those obligations consist in derives from the measure in terms of which we set our own end. In so far as the measure is satisfaction and our end a personal happiness, we can be held to have reasons to act in ways already mentioned to all who can be taken to have the same measure and end. That this is taken to be human beings as such is a result of viewing self-satisfaction as an end dictated by human nature. But no such end is given in human nature as such, and even if all humans naturally desired such an end this would not show that it was the end for human life. We must adopt such an end, and can only do so in the light of the problem which human existence is. Within the measure of happiness, our obligations are relative to the pursuit by others of the end which we ourselves pursue. If that end were the self-overcoming which Nietzsche describes, or the intellectual end Plato identifies, what we have reason to do in relation to others becomes quite different and involves making a radical distinction between those who are capable of pursuing the end and those who are not. Individual lives have the significance they do within the analytical perspective because it is taken for granted that the end for human life is an individual satisfaction. Nor can such significance be claimed by taking as the measure man's capacity to pursue an end as such, since this would attempt to reduce all such concrete ends to the same level of significance. But, as the examples of Plato and Nietzsche show, it is possible to have such an end which creates a hierarchy among forms of human existence and which therefore rejects such a levelling process.

Within the idea of the pursuit of an end determined by human capacities there is no way of justifying treating all ends as having the same significance. Religiously conceived, of course, they all do have the same value, namely none. The religious measure can reduce all ends suggested by human powers to the same level since the end it proposes for human life is not the fulfilment of human ability. In requiring the giving up of all such presumption to set ends, it places all human life before a measure and in face of an end which gives an equal value to every individual. And it does so by being the only response which is adequate to the problem of the meaning of human life. In terms of that measure and that end, individual human life attains a value which is not relative to human capacities and which does not depend, as all human valuing does, ultimately on the *assertion* of individuals as to where the end of human life lies.

That it lies in the transformation of the individual by absolute goodness, which is beyond the capacity of human beings to accomplish, means that we cannot relate to it as an end we propose to ourselves and towards which we can take the appropriate means. All individuals are in the same relation to such an end, namely, that it is beyond their power to accomplish. We recognize such an end in our own case through the practice of infinite resignation, the recognition that our own capacities and what happens to us are alike incapable of conferring value on our lives. And we recognize this end as applying to all others in the recognition of a value which their lives have which is given to them neither by us nor by themselves. It is a value which, not being relative to any aspect of human existence, is truly unconditional.

> To love an ordinary human being unconditionally one needs to have perceived in him an unconditional good. There is no unconditional good in any man who has not reached the state of mystical union, except the possibility of reaching it.[119]

Since such possibility does not depend on human capacity, it is present in the case of all human individuals. It is in terms of this unconditional value of human life that obligations can be understood. Whereas the obligations conceived by the analytical view derive from an end which the individual who can be said to have them pursues, and so are relative to that pursuit, these obligations are unconditional. They do not depend on what ends the individual pursues: all individuals have such obligations to all others. Yet they cannot be understood, as are the obligations of the analytical interpretation, as specifying actions which are means towards the achievement by others of the end concerned. For man can take no means towards his 'eternal destiny'.[120] That destiny requires us to recognize the unconditional value of all human life, and it is this which gives significance to 'man's earthly needs', my own as well as those of all others.[121] 'To love one's neighbour as oneself implies that one reads in every human being the same combination of nature and supernatural vocation.'[122] The hunger, cold, insecurity, and so forth of others can have the same significance as my own for me only in so far as I recognize for all an end and a measure which do not depend in any way upon myself and to which I, in the totality of my life, am also subject. That such relations to others manifest themselves in the form of obligation marks the same resistance that characterizes my own relation to my own life in terms of infinite resignation. The 'ought' in this way applies to the individual in so far as his self has not been totally transformed by absolute goodness: in that transformation 'When one has come to the end of evil there is no longer any place for duty.'[123] But as such an individual would recognize the unconditional value of all human beings without the contrary promptings of his unreformed nature, this would not prevent 'there being a conformity between behaviour and duty'.[124]

I can only recognize true obligation, an ought which applies to me unconditionally, in so far as I regard myself as subject to a measure which applies to me without conditions. And such a measure, just because of this, applies to all others too. There can be such a measure only if I give up the ambition of determining a measure for myself in terms of conditions that I and others may satisfy. But that requires giving up the idea that human life can be its own measure and set its own end. What is required is 'To empty ourselves of false divinity, to deny ourselves, to give up being the centre of the world'.[125]

# Chapter 4

# God and Heidegger's later thought

One of the essential characteristics of the age in which we live, according to the later Heidegger, is 'the loss of the gods'.[1] This is not, however, merely one of the manifestations of the way in which we now understand and relate to what is as it is, as might be said, for example, of the impetus towards 'automation' and 'systematic improvement',[2] but rather concerns the very nature of the way in which we find ourselves 'in the midst of beings as a whole'. 'The default of God means that no god any longer gathers men and things unto himself, visibly and unequivocally, and by such gathering disposes the world's history and man's sojourn in it.'[3] It means that the default of God is not experienced *as* a default, and through this 'there fails to appear for the world the ground that grounds it'. We live in the age 'for which the ground fails to come'.[4] Philosophy as metaphysics has been since Plato the thought of such a ground, which as the ground of all that is, is at the same time an interpretation of God, the ultimate measure for man and what is. Our age is no longer metaphysical: philosophy 'turns into the empirical science of man, of all of what can become for man the experiential object of his technology'.[5] In *An Introduction to Metaphysics* Heidegger had characterized this aspect of our contemporary existence as 'spiritlessness', 'the rejection of all original inquiry into grounds and men's bond with grounds'.[6] The way in which we now relate to ourselves and to what is, is one which drives us, not towards, as during the epochs of metaphysics, establishing a ground for ourselves and what is, but away from such a concern and solely towards 'the manipulable arrangement of a scientific-technical world and of the social order proper to this world'.[7] It is because of this that Being, the name which within metaphysics indicated the ground which it sought, has become for us 'a mere word', its meaning 'an evanescent vapour'.[8] And with that too, 'God' has become a 'mere word' which lives on in the 'religious experience' of individuals,[9] divorced from any central role in the understanding of man's nature and the Being of what is. Nevertheless, this predicament, precisely in revealing metaphysics *as* a tradition, opens up the possibility of a new form of thinking which may herald a non-metaphysical and non-technological way in which humans may exist. This possibility is, at the same time, that of a non-metaphysical apprehension of 'what the word "God" is to signify'.[10] But this is not just a new form of human existing and a new understanding of God: 'The god-less thinking which must abandon the god of philosophy . . . is . . . perhaps closer to the divine God . . . more open to Him than [metaphysics] would like to admit.'[11] For that thinking would not think God through a thinking of the Being of beings, as the ground of an intelligible totality, but through a thinking of Being itself. It is only such thinking which prepares the way for 'the divine God' to manifest Himself to humans, that God who could be *as* the 'All-High'. It is precisely towards a recognition of the absence of such a God, an absence due to the failure of Being to address man as such in metaphysics and technology, that Heidegger's thought summons us. In an address given on the occasion of his eightieth birthday, Heidegger posed the question with which our age addresses us as 'Is our "dwelling" a sojourning within a withholdment of the All-High?':[12] that is, do we, in the age of Technology, understand ourselves in the light of the default of God so that we may be prompted towards a thinking which could make possible the manifestation of 'the divine God'? 'Only a god can save us' Heidegger famously remarked in his interview with *Der Spiegel*.[13] But this god for Heidegger, encountered from out of the thinking of Being and not from metaphysics, would *be* 'the divine God', the 'All-High' in His Being as such. This would not be for man one further interpretation of God: 'Man measures himself against the godhead: only in so far as man takes the measure of his dwelling in this way is he able to *be* commensurately with his nature.'[14] It would be to understand God as the measure for man and hence as the All-High, rather than as the ground at which man himself arrives. It would be to think God *as* God, to let God be God, the God who can be God for man in his 'nature'.

It is this aspect of Heidegger's thought which leads Derrida to see it as a further manifestation of metaphysics, a further twist in man's desire for a ground.[15] I shall discuss Derrida's treatment of the question of Being in the next chapter. Through a somewhat fuller sketch of Heidegger's position in his later writings, I should like now to bring out the centrality of the issue of God for him, and then to raise the question of whether God so understood *could* constitute the 'All-High' for man. Such a question raises the issue of whether Heidegger's thought is not 'metaphysical' in a sense which would encompass, I think, Derrida's too.

## I

'The guiding question of Western philosophy is "what is being?" . . . what is meant is the whole, being taken as a whole from the outset, being taken *as* such unity'.[16] Metaphysics asks after the Being of beings. That is, it addresses what *is*, and asks after its nature: in Wittgenstein's phrase, 'all being'. The metaphysical question asks, therefore, about the possibility of truth: what is it about what is that enables there to be truth? The posing of this question required, as we will see, the unconcealing of 'the being as such', of the realm of 'all being', the correlate of the proposition which can be true or false. Greek metaphysics responds to this revelation of 'the being as such' by thinking its nature as what manifests itself of itself to us, as what can be apprehended by our intellect. What is can only be understood as being in so far as it manifests itself as participating in intelligibility and so exhibits a principle in terms of which the intelligible and that which participates in it can be understood. Such a principle is the idea of the Good or Aristotle's God, thought thinking itself, which shows itself to *our* intellect. In terms of this we can then understand things within the world as they participate in the purely intelligible and which thereby reveals them in their truth. Man is as a being not merely in having an essence, but in apprehending the truth of all else: in knowing the truth he participates in the divine, the principle of harmony between the intelligible and what is in time. The Being of what is, its nature as being, which makes possible our thinking truly or falsely about it, lies in its intelligibility, which itself involves the principle of the unity of the intelligible and what is in time and which, manifesting itself *within* our own intelligence, makes possible our possession of *logos*. The wonder of Greek metaphysics is directed towards this: that reality is intelligible. This wonder is, as wonder, directed towards the principle of intelligibility which man both participates in and can apprehend through his own intellectual power.

That there should be the truth of truth available to our intelligence in terms of which what is can be thought of as being does not address Greek metaphysics as a question. The Greeks respond, rather, to an intelligibility which gives itself and to which we should subordinate our intellect. For that question to address man, this self-giving must give way so that man is thrown into an uncertainty as to how he can know that what shows itself to his intelligence is the truth of what is, so that he can be sure of his own truth. The Medieval Christian interpretation responds to this question by an understanding of what is, not as showing the principle of its truth to us of itself, but as created in order to lead man to its creator. The 'certitude of the salvation of the individual is the standard for all truth'.[17] Man's relation to such a creator God can only be that of faith, 'that kind of certainty which is safe even in the uncertainty of itself, of what it believes in',[18] since God is beyond the order of what can be manifested to us, as its guarantor, its end. Man can exercise his *lumen naturale* itself only as 'a certainty native' to him, since he can trust what he apprehends as being truth only through the certainty of faith that things have been created so as to reveal their truth in this way to him. God, as creator, and so the ground of all truth, is now the highest being, 'that real being whose reality binds and directs all human activity in its plans and ideas'.[19] God is *causa sui*[20] and as such the cause of all that is. We apprehend such a God by asking why there is the being, why there is truth about what is, by asking after its cause. Such a cause as cause of all else must be *causa sui* and so impenetrable in itself to the human intellect, which can know something only by knowing its causes. We can only know God as the unknowable cause of all that is as it is. But the end of man lies in the best activity of his highest power, the intellect, through which he apprehends things as they are. This power can only achieve fulfilment in the direct apprehension of God, which is, nevertheless, impossible for us to conceive. 'This contemplation is perfect, and shall be in the fatherland, and is possible to man according to the supposition of faith.'[21] The fulfilment of man's essence, his apprehension of what is as it is, is something which, unrealizable in this life, can only be believed in with a certainty unshakeable by what occurs in that life: it becomes 'salvation'.

> What is new about the modern period as opposed to the Christian medieval age consists in the fact that man, independently and by his own effort, contrives to become certain and sure of his human being in the midst of beings as a whole.[22]

The truth of what is is now to be determined by that of which man, independently and for himself, can be certain. For man to respond in this way, the medieval understanding must have become questionable, have come to confront man with the question as to how he could know what was believed in by faith, thus submitting all that depended on this, namely everything, to the question of his own certainty. 'The question of "method" . . . about attaining and grounding a certainty secured by man himself – came to the fore.'[23] What man is most certain of is himself, only of what can be referred to that ground can man be certain. 'Man becomes the measure and the centre of beings.'[24] What things really are is now something man can be certain of through himself. Nature becomes an object, in principle knowable completely by man because it is in accordance with a plan he himself projects. It becomes the manifestation of mathematical laws, an unchanging structure surveyable in principle completely by man's intellect. Man himself, as the ground of the reality of what is, knows himself as the source of law, and so of law for himself. Only then can the question arise as to whether this law is to be derived from a conception of man as a rational being, or as the bearer of the progressive emergence of universal rationality, or from the notion of self-reliant nations, the proletariat of all lands, and so forth.[25] The 'new freedom consists in the fact that man himself legislates, chooses what is binding and binds himself to it'.[26] Man reveals his own truth in giving law to himself, and reveals that of all else through the revelation of its lawfulness. God, as the highest being, must now be subject to the determination of man's certainty: proofs are demanded to establish his existence as a being, which must, nevertheless, fail *as* proofs. The very demand for proofs submits

God to the measure of man's certainty, which, however, under the supposition of God, cannot be the measure of what is true. Any god which emerged from such a proof could not be God as the All-High, the measure for man and what is. The demand for proofs merely marks

> the fact that . . . [Christianity] has continued to be that *against which* the new freedom . . . must be distinguished. Liberation *from* the revealed certitude of the salvation of individual immortal souls is itself liberation *to* a certitude in which man can by himself be sure of his own definition and task.[27]

When man becomes the measure and the ground of the truth of what is, God, as the name of the non-human measure, is only as the superceded opposition. Faith can only now exist as a matter of individual belief, essentially divorced from the ways in which what is is now interpreted: 'Christianity is bereft of the power it had during the Middle Ages to *shape history*.'[28]

The concepts of metaphysics are, however, no longer adequate to articulate the contemporary mutation in the understanding of what is. Metaphysics thinks the Being of being; that is, it thinks of what is as having a truth which man may apprehend, even if only in 'the fatherland'. But now 'our whole human existence everywhere sees itself challenged to devote itself to the planning and calculating of everything . . . beings . . . make a claim on us with respect to their aptness to be planned and calculated'.[29] Knowledge of the natural world is no longer the apprehension of its lawfulness in the direction of grasping its truth, but rather has become 'research', ongoing activity without a terminus, directed towards ever increasing calculability and predictability. We can no longer think of a truth of being which can be apprehended by man: rather we merely have the present state of research which provokes ever new efforts at increased ordering. The real is revealed as 'standing-reserve', standing there 'just so that it may be on call for a further ordering'.[30] What is is now what man can order, calculate and predict, so that he now 'exalts himself to the posture of lord of the earth':[31] 'it seems as though man everywhere and always encounters only himself'.[32] But these ever new possibilities of ordering are not referred to an *end* of man, some determinate truth of man in terms of which such possibilities could be employed. There appears no such truth of man any more than of the non-human. Man too finds himself a 'standing-reserve' of 'energies' to be converted into producing, consuming and ordering the ever emerging possibilities revealed in technology. Far from being 'lord of the earth', man himself is 'challenged', in the grip of something beyond himself, the recognition of which is, however, precluded by the very imperiousness of the challenge. Philosophy, which as metaphysics had articulated the fundamental conceptions of man and of what is, providing their grounds, turns into the empirical sciences of man, and 'Being' becomes 'a mere word'.

But this very break with metaphysics discloses a quite different possibility. It reveals the *tradition* of metaphysics *as* a tradition through the very inapplicability of metaphysical conceptions as a whole to the present situation. Essence is no longer idea.[33] Yet metaphysics as a form of human existing did not understand itself as a tradition. Its avowed intention was to reveal the Being of being, the nature of reality as it timelessly is. We come to see it as a tradition when we see its project, in its various forms, as a response to an ever increasing *loss* of a sense of tradition, of man's historicality. It is revealed as a tradition, as a form of man's historicality, characterized by an increasing flight from that very historicality.

Metaphysics begins by articulating the Being of what is as a determinate intelligible whole apprehensible by man's intellect. The truth is unchanging, and man's access to it has no essential reference to his historical situation. This understanding, however, becomes questionable, prompting an uncertainty about the truth of what man's intellect can apprehend in the withdrawal of contemplation. This uncertainty finds resolution in faith in a creator God. This, in turn, becomes questionable, throwing faith into uncertainty and driving man to depend on the certainty he has of himself. He becomes the ground for the determination of the nature of what is and of his own Being. But in the present age, the questionableness afflicts the very ideas of truth and Being themselves, prompting their replacement with those of calculability, predictability, and capacity for being ordered. Each formation responds to a particular kind of questionableness which comes to characterize the previous interpretation. The solutions of metaphysics are responses to the provocation, the question which the past poses. But they do not understand themselves as dependent upon the question, but rather as articulating *the* truth which is, quite independently of what has been thought. Their responses have the form they do because the general character of the question posed by the past has been that of progressively concealing that very historicality without which there would be no tradition of metaphysics at all.

But such a provocation could only be given to thought if that historicality had been in some way revealed so that it could be progressively hidden. Metaphysics begins as a response to a withdrawal. What withdraws was initially in a certain way articulated in the arising of philosophy. That philosophy was not metaphysical, thinking the nature of an unchanging reality, the Being of being. Metaphysics thinks of what *already is* and asks after its nature, its form of completeness. It depends, therefore, upon the revelation and conceptualization of the realm of what already is. What is already manifest to us is so within the realm of the familiar, that realm within which what is already can be encountered unobtrusively, in a way which does not provoke a question as to what it is. Early Greek philosophy begins with the revelation of the realm of the familiar *as* familiar, and this can only take place through the irruption into it of the unfamiliar, the strange, that which cannot be familiarized. 'In the beginning of its history Being opens itself out as emerging (physis) and unconcealment (aletheia).'[34] Physis, said Heraclitus, loves to hide. Being as *physis* manifests itself to man *as* hiddenness, as concealed. Greek pre-metaphysical existence is characterized, says Heidegger, by the fundamental passion of the struggle for Being itself:[35] the familiar is only preserved and guarded so that man may venture out in order to bring about the manifesting of *physis*. He struggles with the familiar in order to preserve its strangeness. *Physis* manifests itself in this alienness which is covered over by familiarity. Man is, in his Being, the happening of strangeness. Man is the mortal: he does not just die, but must *be* until death, which is no event in life, occurs. That he must always *be* so long as he is means that there can be no determinate state within life which brings it to fulfilment, as satisfying his nature. Man is the being who is 'without issue'. He is *as* such a being, therefore, precisely in preventing the illusion of there being such issue, the subsiding into the familiar, the secure, the certain. The *creative* man is man in his Being, setting forth into the unsaid, unthought, unhappened in order to make these said, thought and happen: that is, to *preserve* the *unsaid* in the said, the *unthought* in the thought, the *unhappened* in the happened, to keep these open, preserve their strangeness. 'Man cultivates and guards the familiar only in order to break out of it and to let what overpowers it break in.'[36] Such a form of human existing is essentially *historical*: 'History as happening is an acting and being acted upon which pass through the present, which are determined from out of the future and which take over the past.'[37]

Lacking issue, as the mortal, man is in his Being an exile from home, the realm of the familiar: and it is only in its conflict with strangeness, the overpowering power of the unhomely, that the realm of the familiar is revealed as such. Man is who he is when he struggles with what already is in order to bring it into its Being, when he 'projects something new, not yet present, when he creates original poetry, when he builds poetically'.[38] Only so is the *unheimlich*, the overpowering, what cannot be mastered, disclosed as such, and with that the realm of the familiar. Unconcealment takes place, which is 'nothing other than the *happening* of the *unfamiliar*'.[39] Being human is the happening of man where, through acts of power, the *overpowering* is made manifest, where the strangeness which summons human effort and so is beyond its mastery, is unconcealed and preserved against the concealment of familiarity. Truth as *aletheia* is unconcealment, the manifesting of essential strangeness, the revelation of concealment. To bring something into its truth is to reveal it in its alienness over against the familiar. Being as *physis*, the overpowering power, 'loves to hide', to conceal itself in familiarity: it becomes unconcealed *as* the overpowering power, as what *cannot* be mastered, made familiar, when man breaks out of the homely. The world as the realm of the familiar is experienced as such only through the irruption of the strange: there world comes into *Being*. 'Where the struggle of creative men ceases', there 'world turns away'[40] so that what is is found merely ready made, as already there, as what *is* in a determinate and given way. It is precisely the revelation of what is in this form, as the familiar, by the manifesting of Being as *physis* which makes the tradition of metaphysics, the thought of the Being of what is, the Being, possible. It is only when this, what already is, addresses us in its questionableness that it can be thought as a whole, and that happens with the concealing of Being as *physis*. Being as *physis* is what provokes action, speech and thought: the essential strangeness of what is, the provocation, the question posed by what is already, one's past. Metaphysics is a response to the progressive withdrawal of that question, to the concealing of historicality.

Although the early Greeks articulated their experience of Being as *physis*, they did not understand it as the happening of history. Nor could they, for that requires the necessary contrast with metaphysics, with the unhistorical understanding of man and what is. This is the possibility opened up for us with the revelation of metaphysics as a tradition. What it is now possible for us to think explicitly is 'the clearing itself', as occurrence.[41] The clearing is *aletheia*, unconcealment,[42] to which belongs essentially self-concealment.[43] 'What withdraws from us draws us along by its very withdrawal . . . drawn into what withdraws, pulled toward it and thus pointing into the withdrawal, man first *is* man.'[44] The clearing, *aletheia*, is that happening within which the familiar is revealed as such through the manifesting of the strange *as* strange, of the 'overpowering', of what *cannot* be overcome since it is presupposed in any mastering, any making familiar, as such. This happening is what Heidegger calls history in the fundamental sense: where what already is, our past, is revealed in its familiarity by the emergence of the questionableness of that very past. Man is always historical. Metaphysics is that form of human historicality which has resulted from the withdrawal of withdrawal, from the concealment of the unthought, the essentially unmasterable in thought, *as* what provokes thought: hence, the response of such human historicality in searching for a ground, for *the* truth, for a final answer to the question posed by the past. The possibility that now emerges for us is that man may live historically in an explicit manner. This would be for man to *be as* a mortal, always having to be without issue. To be a human being means, says Heidegger, to be on the earth, the past as the *source* of possibility which as such is fundamentally concealed, under the sky, the realm of the familiar,[45] before the divinities, the unknown as measure: 'The measure consists in the way in which the god who remains unknown is revealed as such by the sky.'[46] To be in this way, Heidegger calls 'dwelling': 'Dwelling has never been thought as the basic character of human being; it recedes behind the manifold ways in which dwelling is accomplished',[47] behind the ways in which man has existed metaphysically, in that form of human historicality which has resulted from the withdrawal of historicality. But the possibility of existing historically, as befits a mortal, is one we can conceive only in outline, since it is revealed to us as a possibility only in the claim of the age of Technology, in a world formed on a fundamentally opposed basis, the provocation to a non-ending project of calculability and ordering. The god can only manifest himself as such, we can only be claimed by the unknown as the measure, from out of the holy, our heritage as what commands preserving and which can direct us to the unknown as measure. It is towards cultivation of that, the preparation of the realm within which the unknown could manifest itself as the measure, that Heidegger directs us as the contemporary task. Whether and how the unknown may claim us as measure cannot be foretold. All that is possible now is to articulate it as a possibility.

Such a god is not that of Christianity, which involves for Heidegger a metaphysically based interpretation of divinity. Christianity is faith which is 'ultimately protected in the sense that it enjoys confidence',[48] that certainty characterized by medieval philosophy in the creator god who guarantees the understanding of what is as creation. Such an understanding of what is, as formed so as to lead man to God, is superceded by the interpretation of man as subject, as the ground of what is, in the modern age. It becomes that against which the 'new freedom' of that age distinguishes itself. 'Its interpretation of what is no longer having a binding claim on man' it can remain only as a matter of individual religious experience, divorced from its capacity to 'shape history'. God as the unknown, the measure for man as mortal, as living without issue and so without an interpretation of what is in terms of *the* truth and the Being of beings, can only manifest himself when man comes to live historically in an explicit manner, in the constant renewal of tradition. Since our tradition has been formed as a flight from our historicality, such a way of existing can only be glimpsed as a distant possibility, one whose outlines we can only dimly perceive and for whose emergence we can only prepare ourselves. God, in the age of technology, is absent: all we can do is to recognize the default as default and to think the possibility which this opens up.

## II

Kierkegaard sums up his criticism of Hegel succinctly when he declares: 'the Hegelian philosophy, by failing to define its relation to the existing individual and by ignoring the ethical, confounds existence'.[49] By confounding existence, it can only profoundly misrepresent God, for 'the ethical demand is that [the existing individual] become infinitely interested in existing'[50] and 'God is not an externality but the infinite itself.'[51] We understand God when we understand the God-relationship as constituting the existence of an individual characterized by 'the passion of the infinite',[52] an existence which can truly be said to have a relationship to God *as* God: 'He who does not involve himself with God in the mode of absolute devotion does not become involved with God.'[53] Can we say of Heidegger too that he 'confounds existence' and so fails to apprehend what it is to relate to God as God? This might seem an unlikely prospect. Isn't Heidegger's account, at least as represented above, concerned to reveal what it would be to relate to God as the All-High, rather than as the *causa sui* of metaphysics? And isn't such a relation precisely one where man is understood as mortal, and so as 'existing', as always having 'to be its Being',[54] as opposed to metaphysical understandings of human being as subject, a created being, and so forth? And hasn't Heidegger, above all, absorbed Kierkegaard's criticisms of Hegel in developing his understanding of human being against such metaphysical interpretations, a Kierkegaard who 'seized upon the problem of existence as an existentiell problem, and thought it through in penetrating fashion',[55] although hampered by his adherence to certain fundamental metaphysical conceptions? Yet, for all that, I think Kierkegaard's central criticism of Hegel applies just as much to Heidegger.

A constant theme underlying Heidegger's work, early and late, is that of the human being as a being which is as the constant taking over of what it has been, of its own past. Dasein in the earlier works is, as the Being of human being, Temporality, the mode of appropriation of world, the realm of the familiar, within which any other kind of being can have its own Being, its own temporal mode. Inauthentically, Dasein takes over its world as determinate, as something already finished. Authentically, it appropriates its world in terms of its own nature, explicitly as temporality, holding the past open as possibility into an open future. Man is *in* his Being as creative, in bringing forth the genuinely new which is not mere novelty but has a binding claim on men as a revelation of a new possibility of their own heritage. I don't think this fundamental apprehension changes in Heidegger's later thought. What comes to the fore there, however, is the determination of the situation within which this can be conceived as a possible way for man to exist: namely, that situation within which Being has become 'a mere word' and thereby reveals that our tradition has been formed on a quite opposite basis. Hence the possibility can only appear as an intimation of how man could come to exist, one that requires us now to prepare the ground by its articulation through divesting man and Being of 'those qualities with which metaphysics has endowed them'.[56] Man as the mortal, always 'without issue', is man who would be in his Being, in his explicit temporalizing, as creative, manifesting the realm of the familiar as such through the revelation of the strange. The God as the unknown is the All-High for the mortal, for the human being understanding himself as essentially without issue, having always to take over his past as possibility into an open future.

For Heidegger, 'man essentially occurs only in his essence where he is claimed by Being'.[57] He is claimed by Being in different ways: the withdrawal of Being in favour of the Being of beings, which precipitates the conceptions of *the* truth and *the* being we find in metaphysics, is the way he has been claimed for almost 2,500 years, and which has now undergone a mutation. That mutation makes possible that man may come to exist explicitly in Being, *as* historical. But it is only in so far as man is claimed by Being, exists within a claim made on him by his past which opens up his future, that any particular way of relating to himself or other beings can be *binding* on him, can be experienced as revealing these to him in their truth.

> Only so far as man, ek-sisting into the truth of Being, belongs to Being, can there come from Being itself the assignment of those directions that must become law and rule for man. Otherwise all law remains merely something fabricated by human reason. The truth of Being offers a hold for all conduct. 'Hold' . . . means protective heed.[58]

Man has existed under a particular claim of Being, a particular demand to interpret the way man and what is truly are, in the epochs of metaphysics, and does so now: the claim changes, but only if there is such a claim can we have what obligates and binds our conduct and thought. Man always relates to himself and to what he is not through some interpretation of the way they really are, formed in response to the claim made on him by previous interpretation, by his heritage. And that applies, of course, to God too: 'the god also is – when he is – a being and stands as a being within Being'.[59] 'Man does not decide whether and how beings appear, whether and how God and the gods or history and nature come forward into the lighting of Being, come to presence and depart.'[60] A god *is* in his binding of us, in claiming us. Whether this occurs or not does not depend upon us or upon the god, but rather upon the way in which we are claimed by the tradition of the interpretation of what is. That claim now, to render what has been ever more calculable and predictable, is one which allows the God to presence only as absent, His claim on us merely to recognize that default *as* default. If man has always 'to be his Being', then this means that he must always be as the claim of Being. God's claim on us, and its particular form, depends on the nature of the claim of Being at any time, so that it may happen, as it now has, that His claim on us has departed. We can have no direct relation to the All-High. Whether or not God claims us, and how, is something that we can only know by determining the nature of the present claim of Being, by determining what the claim of our time is on us. For Heidegger, no less than for Hegel, ethics and the claim of God depend for us on discovering 'what it is the age demands'.

But that would have struck Kierkegaard again as *comical*. Of course, Heidegger's thought, like that of Nietzsche, puts metaphysics in question. The grounding concepts of the metaphysical project, absolute truth and its correlative, timeless being, and that of the autonomous individual, are revealed *themselves* as constitutive of a particular *historical* project, one which must have foundered, in nihilism or the advent of the age of Technology, in order for this revelation to be available to the thinker. Such revelation is at once both destructive, in undermining the hold on us of the forms of thought through which we think of ourselves and the non-human, and at the same time constructive, in allowing a new claim, that of self-creativity or of a truly historical existence, to manifest itself to us. This claim is experienced out of the process of reflection through which the pursuit of truth undoes itself, thus holding out a prospect to us which we cannot occupy: it places us, rather, under the necessity of a strategic thinking through which we liberate our forms of thought from the hold of the fundamental metaphysical concepts, through 'philosophizing with a hammer' or the 'destruction' of the metaphysical interpretation of the human and of being. Such thinking is situated as being both within metaphysical forms of thought, those we have inherited, and yet without, since we can no longer believe in them.

Nevertheless, there is a fundamental continuity here with the metaphysical project, since it is never doubted that an intellectual inquiry is necessary in order to see what is required of us, one no longer directed towards apprehending the absolute truth of metaphysics, of course, but rather at diagnosing our historical situation and its demands at the moment where the pursuit of truth undermines itself. But it is just this presupposition that appears comical to Kierkegaard: 'to let the ethical become something which it needs a prophet to discover, a man with a world-historical outlook upon world-history – that is indeed a rare and ingeniously comical conceit'.[61] As we have seen, the comical aspect of Hegel is the product of a 'double confusion':[62] 'first, by overleaping the ethical, and then proposing a world-historical something as the ethical task for individuals'. Such a position 'overleaps the ethical' in that the very *posing* of the question in its philosophical form is *already* subject to ethical criticism.

> What, specifically, is the ethical? Well, if I put the question in this manner, I am asking unethically about the ethical. I am putting the question just as the whole confusion of the modern age does, then I cannot put a stop to it.[63]

I cannot put a stop to it because to do so requires a decision, and decision, resolution, commitment do not follow from the process of intellectual inquiry itself. But for the *individual*, and the philosopher is at least that, the 'problem' of the significance of her *own* life is precisely to be understood in terms of the latter notions. Such a 'problem' manifests itself not as an intellectual doubt but as *despair* to the varying degrees made

possible by the individual's aesthetic, ethical or religious relation to the contents of her life. The intellectual construction,
since it claims to ask about the significance of human life as
such, would, as an *individual's* questioning, presuppose that the
individual questioned the value of her own life in its *totality*. To
do this seriously would be to despair in a quite radical way which
would encompass her intellectual pursuits as all other contents
of her life: it would not take the form of intellectual puzzlement. And its 'resolution' again would have the character of a
redirected or enlarged commitment not of knowledge. To pose
the question in its philosophical form is to ask 'unethically'
since an intellectual problem requires a disinterested inquiry in
which the relation of the individual herself to the inquiry is
irrelevant: whether she is in it for the money, fame, advance-
ment, interest as the exercise of her abilities, or to the glory of
God is neither here nor there, what matters is the proposed
finding and its justification. But the ethical question as asked by
the individual is necessarily one about her own life: it is one
which emerges out of just such a relation as a problem with it. 'A
contemplative spirit, and this is what the objective spirit is, feels
nowhere any infinite need of a decision. This is the falsum that
is inherent in all objectivity':[64] but the very nature of the
problem experienced by the individual with her own life is
precisely what requires decision or commitment for its resolution or, better, dissolution.

But to take the Hegelian route or the post-metaphysical one
of diagnosing one's historical situation as the proposed resolution to the problem is to compound the confusion. For the
problem of human existence concerns subjectivity, the relationship of the subject to *whatever* content her life may have, and so
the historical situation of the individual is irrelevant to the
nature of the problem she faces.

> Whatever the one generation may learn from the other, that
> which is genuinely human no generation learns from the
> foregoing. In this respect every generation begins primitively,
> has no different task from that of the previous generation.
> This authentically human factor is passion.'[65]

That task which is always the same is that of life itself: 'Life
constitutes the task. To be finished with life before life has
finished with one is precisely not to have finished the task.'[66]

To recognize life as the task is to recognize that the problem of existence is that of living in terms of a passion commensurate with the conception of one's life *as a whole*. The task is thus to live one's life *as* a whole at every moment of that life. The 'authentically human factor' is the passion which characterizes the way this task is undertaken. One may, for example, try to live one's life as a whole by subordinating the rest of one's life to some particular project to which one finds oneself naturally inclined: the development of some talent, or raising a family, say. To resolve the task in this 'aesthetic' way is to allow significance to be given to other activities by some further one which is privileged as satisfying some given proclivity of the individual. In this way one's relation to what one engages in remains *conditional*, for even the privileged activity has the significance it does only so long as it satisfies some given tendency one has. Nevertheless, such a given disposition may be taken away without the task of living one's life being thereby rescinded. The aesthetic individual, even in this developed form, does not truly have a relation to his life *as* a whole, but rather to the rest of his life in terms of some given part. He is, then, only half-hearted about the task of living his life as such a whole. The resolution of this task, since it lasts as long as one lives, cannot lie in anything given *within* that life. Hence, one only begins to express a true concern with that task through undertaking *unconditional* commitment, where the significance of one's engagement in one's activities and relations is not conditional on some outcome for oneself and which requires ultimately, therefore, a wholesale turning away from the human determination of what is good. Religious existence is precisely that form which is directed towards making unconditional commitment the characteristic of *oneself*, so that one's whole life is addressed at every moment since one looks for no reward within it, whilst recognizing that to look for a reward beyond it *is* to have such a present reward. One must live simply not looking for reward at all, 'by cutting off every resultant in the finite world'.[67] Only in this way can one live one's life as a task, having a relation to one's life as a whole in all that one does or that may occur. This is to live in terms of *the* Good, the good for one's whole life, an 'eternal happiness'. It is what Kierkegaard calls the God-relationship, for the goodness of such a good, one for our life *as* a whole, alone can be related to 'in the mode of absolute devotion'.

God is indeed 'the Unknown',[68] precisely because to think one should relate to God through knowledge is to fail to recognize the *absolute* inadequacy of the human to be the source on its own value: it is to reserve one's capacity for knowledge from this revelation.[69] Yet to 'relate to God' is precisely to live the recognition of this inadequacy. 'That is why discourse concerning this good [our end as an eternal happiness which we understand in terms of the conception of our nothingness before God] may be so brief, for there is only one thing to say: venture everything.'[70] One only has a relation to God, to what can give significance to one's whole life, to the very fact that one exists, by venturing everything, by giving up the presumption, in *either* assertion *or* despair, of the human to determine its own significance. Such a relation can only be embarked upon by engaging in the process of 'dying away from immediacy' which is 'absolutely committed to relative ends', ones determined by one's given proclivities. Only so can one express existentially 'the principle that the individual can do absolutely nothing of himself, but is as nothing before God'.[71]

Metaphysical and post-metaphysical forms of thought, which attempt to determine what the task for man is by inquiry into what would fulfil man's 'nature' or his historical situatedness, remain, for Kierkegaard, at the level of the aesthetic, since they refuse to give up the presumption of the human to determine its significance and so cannot relate to life as a whole. In doing this, they 'confuse existence', for they remain in illusion as to the task which human life is. That task is one faced by an I in relation to her *own* life and here, 'every generation begins primitively, has no different task from that of every previous generation.' There 'can be no abstract thought of one's existence':[72] no *conception* of the Being of human being can be anything but an *evasion* in confronting the task which one's life is. The relation to God as the recognition of the inadequacy of the I to the question which her life is for them, cannot be absent, conceptually unavailable, since the condition for this relation is given with the *first person*, and that for its claim on us is given by the existential dialectic through which the I can come to despair over her imposition of significance on her life. 'One thing continually escapes Hegel – what it is to live.'[73] Kierkegaard would have said the same of Heidegger.

The 'human standpoint' in relation to this task of life

Kierkegaard identifies with what he calls 'relative' or 'conditional' willing. Within such willing, situations, actions, and so on, are considered 'good' in relation to the satisfaction or fulfilment of human capacities and dispositions, so that if an end for life as such is proposed from within this perspective, it will lie in the fulfilment of some capacity which that life contains. Such resolutions can take various forms: following a traditional form of life, happiness as living without hindrance within self-determined limits, the pursuit of some unlimited end like wealth or power, the achievement of glory through the commission of great exploits and becoming thereby an example to others of what may be achieved, and so on. The only restriction upon what may be taken as the meaning of life here is that the solution should be able to encompass a life-span, and cannot therefore be restricted to the achievement of some particular goal. As we have seen, Kierkegaard categorizes such solutions as either 'aesthetical' or ethical, the former being the resolution of life as lying in certain conditions happening to come about, the satisfaction of my desires, say, or my achieving a fame which will live in the race's memory, whilst the latter sees it as lying in the imposition of myself upon the facticities of my life.

Such resolutions are, as Plato saw, essentially manifold and none, therefore, can claim a justified priority over any other. The philosophical move is made when the question of the truth about the meaning of life is raised, and so that of the measure in terms on which this manifold can be judged. It is tempting to think that this can only be resolved through some concrete understanding of what that measure is which we can then use in order to live meaningfully. The measure for life as a whole or at this historical juncture is to be apprehensible by man, and so to lie within the reach of his capacities, and apprehended, it is to be *used* by man to govern his life and thus constitute his 'free appropriation of himself'. But such self-appropriation, the measure for life lying within the reach of man's capacities and which can, therefore, be employed for the organization of life, is precisely what characterizes for Kierkegaard the 'human standpoint' and which finds its embodiment in the manifold resolutions of life's problem that relative willing displays. The philosophical move, therefore, is one within relative willing itself. Of course, the philosophical response attempts to go beyond these non-philosophical solutions by producing a measure which can be *justified* in terms of life itself: its measure is proposed in order that it should comprehend the *whole* of life or situate ourselves in relation to such a received ambition. Plato's idea of the Good or Hegel's Spirit as the process whereby the given is raised to its universal form are conceptions of such wholeness, whilst Heidegger's Being as Time, the temporal relation of past as possibility, the openness of the future and the present as the locus for the emergence of the new which grants validity to anything for its time and thus enables us to speak of the 'history of Being', is the conception of the very 'condition' which enabled such conceptions to emerge. The justified measure is to be gained by a reflection upon the wholeness of life, and the capacity through which this reflection is carried out, that of *nous*, thought, or Heideggerian Thinking, assumes a privileged and ruling position in relation to human existence in its articulation of the measure through which life can achieve governance of itself or an appropriate situating of itself in relation to this metaphysical form of life.

But, as we have seen, Kierkegaard argues that the very nature of the problem of life *precludes* such a resolution. Since that problem which can only manifest itself in the *first person* concerns what could give meaning to our whole lives, it requires the submission of *all* aspects of one's life to it. It is this which precludes the idea of life's self-governance or its post-metaphysical transformations. Reflection upon human life by an I can only show the impossibility of such immanent resolutions and so what is required if one's life is to be related to in its totality: the existential expresssion of 'nothingness before God'.

For Kierkegaard, therefore, the ambition underlying these projects is futile. There can be no measure for human life as a whole within that life. The problem of what can give meaning to the whole of life cannot be resolved through a reflective apprehension of a standard which man can then use to organize his life in a meaningful way. That would be to resolve the problem in terms of some proposed capacity which man has. But as a capacity *within* life, the question of the meaning of life as a whole for an I applies equally to it. That question, through its all-encompassing nature, means that no resolution to it *can* be arrived at in terms of the fulfilment of a human capacity, even where this is proposed through a reflection upon a concrete standard for the whole of life or for our lives where this very wholeness has become questionable. Self-reflection can only show us that no such conception of the wholeness of life *can* answer the problem of existence and hence no conception of our being situated between metaphysics and the possibility of non-metaphysical life. Man's 'free appropriation of himself' is a philosophical dream, the result of subliming the logic of the varied forms of relative willing within which human beings assert a human answer to the problem of life.

Religion alone, Kierkegaard argues, proclaims the kind of authority desired here, one to command life as such, but only on the condition that man gives up the presumption to be an authority to himself. Metaphysics and post-metaphysical forms of thought, even where they explicitly deny this, attempt to make a religion of humanity, to give to human nature an authority over itself. But this is impossible. If we ask what the meaning of life as a whole is in the sense of the measure which determines what can count for us as meaningful life in its totality, the answer is 'God'. This is not a discovery, as if we could understand what God is and then find out that this God is also the measure for life. It is rather a definition: the God-relation is what constitutes the relationship of an I to her life as a whole. The meaning of our lives as a whole would be what we could give ourselves totally to: and that can only be what we cannot conceive, since this is not to be a conception in terms of which we can make our lives and render them of our own powers meaningful. 'God is for man a nameless and formless constant.'[74] To live through such a measure would be to give ourselves completely and so to refuse to recognize any human determinant of goodness: and that means, therefore, to look for no reward assessed as such in terms of human determination. However, we cannot *do* this: we cannot make ourselves such that we live our lives wholly as such giving since the very conception of such self-formation presupposes that we are already oriented towards human goods. What we can do, in the light of such a recognition of our inadequacy and so directed towards such a life, is restricted to the negative effort of resisting our propensity to project goodness upon the world and so to affirm ourselves. 'God is worshipped not by moods but by action . . . particularly of action in the direction of asceticism';[75] 'If that which is highest can only be expressed in our speech through negation, so likewise we can only imitate it in a negative fashion.'[76] The transformation of the self, 're-birth', is beyond our power and so cannot be *taken* as an end.

We may, of course, turn away from the religious response in offence: it is, after all, as Kierkegaard frequently remarks, inhuman. And no doubt, in terms of our own preferred resolution, we may consider ourselves all the better off for this. But we cannot claim, as philosophy has tried to do, that such a preferred resolution has any greater justification than other competing ones. Religion can claim this, but only, of course, by abandoning the field of human resolutions and so being unable to provide reasons from within that field for its justification. It can only put to the individual the question of whether he or she will have a meaning for the whole of his or her life or not, and that can only be resolved by the individual for him- or herself.

It may, finally, be asked what happens within Kierkegaard's thought to the historicality of resolutions to the problem of human life. The immanent determinations, in terms of privileging different human capacities or outcomes in the world whose significance depends on certain human desires, characteristic of relative willing, can take many varied forms. Nevertheless, as immanent resolutions, they are according to Kierkegaard incapable of resolving the question of the meaning of human life in its totality, and we have seen that for him this is possible only through a relation to God. In its universal form, the religious understanding, 'Religion A' as it is called in the *Concluding Unscientific Postscript*, leads to a recognition of life's task as one of infinite resignation, the active living of life in terms of the possibilities of one's culture, in so far as these are compatible with God, but only in such a manner that their value is given them through a resignation of humanly determined goods, and so in the resignation of the ultimate significance of results. Where and when this has been an historical actuality as a form of belief, Kierkegaard leaves as a question to be determined by another form of inquiry.[77] His point here is rather that it is a conceptual possibility regardless of historical eventualities, and so could have been present, even if it was not, in antiquity. What we think of as the religions of classical antiquity, Kierkegaard regarded as variants of the aesthetical and not of the religious understanding of existence: 'Paganism is the sensuous, the full development of the sensuous.'[78] That is, the

'God-relationship' here is manifest for the pagan only in what *happens* to him, in the granting of what he *anyway* desires: 'being loved by God is marked by being successful in everything'.[79] Hence God is not the determiner of value, but is rather understood in terms of humanly determined values: 'God is merely the superlative of what it is to be a man.'[80] This is an 'immediate' relation to God, as what grants to humans their desires, whereas only after a break with the human determination of value 'can there be any question of a true God-relationship'.[81] With Christianity, of course, there is a conceptual significance in relation to the historical for Kierkegaard, since Christianity involves faith in the redemption of the self, that the self can and will be totally transformed by God to absolute purity, and this must be announced to man to make faith possible. But the analysis of this distinction of Christian faith from the universally religious, although obviously central for Kierkegaard, is not, I think, of direct relevance here.

In the next chapter I shall consider the thought of Jacques Derrida, not, however, to repeat the Kierkegaardian critique of Heidegger to which it is, I think, still subject, but in order to contrast it with the position of the later Wittgenstein, and so articulate the latter's criticisms of the *philosophical* idea of a 'universal problematic'.

# Chapter 5

# Derrida, Wittgenstein and the question of grounds

In 'The Ends of Man' Derrida quotes Heidegger's statement from 'The Letter on Humanism':

> The devastation of language which is spreading everywhere rapidly . . . is caused by man's essence being put in danger . . . It is only in this way, on the basis of Being, that the absence of native land, in which not only men but the existence of man are lost, begins to be surmounted[1]

and comments:

> The thought of the truth of Being, in whose name Heidegger de-limits humanism and metaphysics nevertheless remains a thought *of* man. In Heidegger's eyes, what is threatened in the extension of metaphysics and technique . . . is the essence of man which should be considered before and beyond its metaphysical determination.[2]

As a thought *of* man, that is, a thought which determines the essence of man, Heidegger's thought remains metaphysical. 'Man', says Derrida, is 'the name of that being who, throughout the history of metaphysics or of onto-theology – in other words, throughout his entire history – has dreamed of full presence, the reassuring foundation, the origin and end of play.'[3] Heidegger too seeks a 'reassuring foundation' within which man can inhabit his 'native land', even if this land is that of Being, rather than of the Being of beings, where man as mortal is thrown into the unhomely. Metaphysics is that mode of thought which determines a *ground* for our ways of thinking and relating to what is, including ourselves. Something can only function as such a ground if it lies, in a certain way, *beyond* those forms of thought and relation which it is to ground, and so, since it is to provide *the* ground for *all* we can relate to, it must lie beyond language. The ground is something already given by relation to which our language is enabled to speak truly: the intellectual structure of the Kosmos which our language can reflect, the thoughts of God we can believe in by faith, or man's given nature as the being who projects the forms of experience, and so forth. The ground for our forms of thought is sought by appeal to something beyond language which can determine those forms of thought as being the right ones, the ones which reveal things, and ourselves, as they and we really are, to the degree possible for us. Such a ground Derrida calls a 'transcendental signified', and Heidegger's appeal to Being is to such a signified, which can return man to his 'essence', his 'proper form' of historical existing. Metaphysics has the character of a *centred* structure:

> The concept of centered structure is in fact the concept of a play based on a fundamental ground, a play constituted on the basis of a fundamental immobility and a reassuring certitude which is itself beyond the realm of play.[4]

That is, within metaphysics, what things and man really are is provided by a determination of their essences, of what distinguishes them one from another. We provide an essence when we determine what the distinguishing character of something is, and so set it off from everything else: we determine it in its essence by differentiating it, by establishing its *difference* from all else. But this particular process of differentiating is, at the same time, a matter of determining *essence*: that is, what things *really* are, so that these differences are not merely differences but the *true* ones, grounded in reality. In order that this should be so, the process of differentiation must proceed from a *ground*, something taken as itself beyond the determination of essence by difference and which can dictate the *way* differences are truly determined. Where that ground, for example, is the self-giving intellectual structure of the Kosmos, differences are to be determined through reflection on the way the realm of becoming intimates that of Being, of what cannot be otherwise; where it becomes man as subject, they are to be determined through the ways in which things can be subsumed under the idea of law, so that man becomes distinguished as the potential master of the world. The determination of essence is first a matter of establishing a *way* of arriving at the differences which will *count* as essence, and that is done by appeal to the ground, which, as source of such differences, and so of the structure, is itself in a way 'beyond essence': 'The center, which is by definition unique, constituted that very thing within a structure which while governing the structure, escapes structurality.'[5] But this makes the position of the 'transcendental signified' contra-dictory, both without and within the structure. As ground, it must lie outside, as determining a particular way of arriving at differences as *the* truth. But it can only function as a ground for our determination of differences if it can be appealed to, and so addressed *in* language. And it can only be spoken of if it can be distinguished from what it is not, and so subject to a process of differentiation. It must, that is, have an 'essence', a difference, which it cannot, however, justify *as* essence. If, for example, we arrive at the essences of things by referring to the way they can be brought under the idea of law, we determine a certain way of arriving at differences as the way of determining what things really are. We do so by referring to the 'essence' of essence. But what justifies counting this *as* the essence of essence? Since all questions of the justification for taking differences as essences are referred to the ground, there is no possible way within the structure of answering this. And since this question can always be raised of any purported ground, it undermines the very possibility of grounding. Furthermore, through this under-mining, it removes the appearance of 'essence' from the system of differences. If there is no ground for the determination of a system of differences as constituting *the* system, there are no essences. But if there are no essences, then there is no longer a justification for speaking of 'man', 'reality', 'truth', and so on. It is not merely that we have no way of justifying counting the idea of law as 'essence', but we have no justification for speaking of there being such essence at all. Since the notions of 'reality', 'truth' and 'man' equally depend upon that of 'essence', the same has to be said of them too. The 'ground' is simply part of the structure, of the system of differences, and cannot play the role of determining a system as *the* system.

The thought of this becomes possible 'in the absence of a center or origin' so that previous forms of thought can be revealed as 'a series of substitutions of center for center'.[6]

Because we today have no such ground, we can see the ground-less character of the centred structures of metaphysical thought. Nevertheless, the ways of thinking and relating to ourselves and all else which we have inherited are metaphysical; that is, they consist of structures of differences organized in terms of a 'ground'. But we are in this language in such a way that the 'ground' can no longer be regarded as such. It now appears as *part* of the structure of differences, incapable of justifying it, and so as an, in a sense, arbitrary determination of that structure as 'correct'. Our contemporary situation for Derrida is one of both belonging and not belonging to such a structure. 'Deconstruction' is a response to this situation, one which intervenes in the structure in order to dislodge the appearance of there being a ground, so as to liberate the play of differences. We have no other forms of thought than those we have inherited in terms of ground. We cannot, as it were, immediately proceed to think in a radically different, ungrounded way. Rather, we must exploit the possibilities which that grounded way of thinking contains but which are hidden from it.

Determinate meanings, as differences, depend upon contrast, upon determining what something is over against what other things are. But if this process has no ground, no ultimate source, then there are no privileged differences. The hierarchy which results from a grounded structure is the product of arresting the possibilities of developing differences in a certain way, of seeing things from a particular vantage point whose privilege is not a matter of justification but of imposition. Differance, which Derrida calls 'the possibility of conceptuality',[7] is the process whereby meaning is produced, and it has a paradoxical structure. 'Differance produces what it forbids, makes possible the very thing it makes impossible.'[8] Meaning is only produced in differences, but in so far as there is no ground for this, no meaning is what it appears to be, namely determinate. It is only present to us in its difference from other meanings, which themselves are only in relation to other differences, and so on *ad infinitum*.

If totalization no longer has any meaning, it is not because the infiniteness of a field cannot be covered by a finite glance or a finite discourse, but because the nature of the field – that of language and a finite language – excludes totalization . . .

> because instead of being an inexhaustible field . . . there is something missing from it: a center which arrests and grounds the play of substitutions . . . The movement of signification adds something . . . but this addition . . . comes . . . to supplement a lack on the part of the signified.[9]

Meaning is only produced through the production of differences: but this process has no given end, no organizing centre. 'But to the extent that meaning presents itself, gathers itself together, says itself and is able to stand there, it erases difference and casts it aside.'[10] It forgets that any difference is only possible through the process of differing which has itself no given termination. But it is the very lack of a ground which provokes the production of differences and so of meaning: that is, they are produced in order that there should be determinate meaning.

> The desire for the intact kernel is desire itself, which is to say that it is irreducible . . . despite the fact that there is *no* intact kernel . . . without this desire . . . no desire would be set moving, likewise without necessity and without what comes along to interrupt and thwart that desire, desire itself would not unfold.[11]

Without the desire for meaning as intact, meanings as differences would not be generated; but without the absence of such meaning, they could not unfold *as* differences. Any particular meaning, a particular difference, is only possible because meaning is produced by a process of differing. But as there is no ground to determine a given structure of differences as *the* truth, any particular meaning is only possible because the sign concerned *can* always be incorporated in another nexus of differences, and so come to mean differently, in a way which cannot, in principle, be limited. Every mark, spoken or written, Derrida says, is constituted as such only by its 'possibility of functioning', its being cut off, at a certain point, from its 'original' context of meaning and so from a saturable and constraining context.[12]

'What is unnameable is the play that brings about the nominal effects, the relatively unitary or atomic structures we call names . . . we must *affirm* it . . . with a certain laughter and with a certain dance.'[13] Man has existed in terms of a centred structure, of a structure of differences that is grounded in some way. To realize the impossibility of ground is to open up that structure of differences to an 'active interpretation', to an exploitation of difference as the production of differences without end: the affirmation of a world of signs without fault, 'without truth, and without origin . . . [which] determines the non-center otherwise than as loss of center', without nostalgia.[14] Such an active interpretation can only operate on the language we have, one formed in terms of a dream 'of deciphering a truth or an origin which escapes play and the order of the sign and which lives the necessity of interpretation as an exile'.[15] It requires, that is, a relation to our language which derives from the recognition of our paradoxical situation: without the desire for the 'intact kernel', for truth and ground, no differences would be produced, and differences are essential to meaning; but given that meaning is always a matter of differences, there can be no ground, no truth. The desire for meaning is *itself paradoxical,* and yet something which, as desire, has to be lived. It is not a paradox which may be removed by thought, by the continued search for meaning, for *meaning itself does not make sense.* Metaphysical thought, as proclamation of ground, 'wants to forget . . . that there has never been an intact kernel'.[16] Derrida's deconstructive readings of philosophical texts intend to reveal them as the products of a paradoxical desire, as determining a truth, a meaning, *only* in such a way that *at the same time* they show its impossibility. What we can do now is remember what the metaphysical tradition tried to forget, and so engage in the deconstruction of our inherited modes of thought, liberating the differences from their 'center' in the prospect of a mode of existence in which we can engage explicitly in the production of meaning though the generation of differences which are always themselves only to provide the source for further differentiation.

Such 'transcendental signifieds' as the *logos,* the self-giving intellectual structure of the Kosmos, the creator God, or the essence of man, served within metaphysics to justify certain ways of thinking about the human and non-human as *correct,* in accordance with the way things really are. The absence of the 'transcendental signified' for Derrida is the lack of anything beyond language which could serve to ground the ways of thinking contained within it. Derrida's 'differance' is the play of difference, which has always constituted, and now can re-place, thought arrested in terms of a 'transcendental signified', which is itself, in fact, 'also in the position of a signifier'.[17] The thought of

> a concept *signified in and of itself,* a concept simply present for thought, independent of a relation to language, that is of a relation to a system of signifiers . . . a 'transcendental signi-fied' which in and of itself, in its essence, would refer to no signifier[18]

is an 'illusion',[19] albeit one which has had powerful historical effects. These have been no less than the entirety of 'Western science and Western philosophy', 'the Western methods of analysis, explication, reading or interpretation'[20] which have been formed in accordance with the conception of thought as a centred structure, and whose history has consisted in a series of 'substitutions of center for center'. 'The history of metaphysics, like the history of the West, is the history [of these sub-stitutions].'[21] The ways of thinking we have inherited have, then, been grounded in such signifieds. Hence, our recognition of the differential nature of meaning can only result for us *now* in revealing the illusion of the 'transcendental signified', in deconstructive operations on our ways of thinking, preparatory for a form of existence which would be lived in terms of the play of difference itself, 'the as yet unnameable which is proclaiming itself and which can do so . . . only under the species of the nonspecies, in the formless, mute, infant and terrifying form of monstrosity'.[22] The very conception of what thinking is under-goes a profound mutation into the constant play of differences, which requires a radical change in the very form of Western existence.

We can recognize, as with the later Heidegger, the char-acteristically Nietzschean structure of this. What is in prospect is existence which has no need to appeal to a ground but would be the joyful affirmation of the absence of 'truth'. Nevertheless, this must be revealed *as* the prospect, that is, as having a *claim* on us and so as 'the truth'. Our perception of the prospect and its claim on us proceed from a position outside it, from *within* the pursuit of truth but at the point where that pursuit under-mines itself through revealing the truth of meaning as its paradoxicality. If metaphysics justifies a given set of differences by appealing to a ground, the nature of essence, Derrida appeals to the paradoxicality of meaning, the impossibility of essence, in order to justify the deconstruction of our structures of meaning and to proclaim the prospect of play as having its *claim* on us. Such a play can be seen by *us* to be in accordance with the 'truth' of meaning, and yet in terms of play there can be no truth since there can be no reflection as to the 'nature' of meaning. Such reflection has undermined itself and in doing so holds before us a prospect which nevertheless we cannot, in admitting its claim, its *truth*, share. In terms of 'truth' of meaning, what is left to us is the liberation of our forms of thought from the hold of the 'transcendental signified' and so the preparation of the way for an existence which would not need it. In this way, Derrida reveals 'what the age demands', and I shall not repeat here Kierkegaard's strictures on this. Rather, through a contrast with the thought of the later Wittgenstein, I would like to suggest certain general problems with the project of 'the universal problematic' of which Derrida's work is, as he himself recognizes, a mutation.

Such a contrast might seem invited by the presence in Wittgenstein's later writings of a line of thought which may appear structurally similar to that of Derrida's, and which has indeed provoked attempts at bringing their thought into close proximity.

> Both aim to dissipate the charm of the picture of meaning as representation, here and now before the private eye or ear of the mind or deposited in a public archive, so potent that every permissible employment of an expression with that meaning is preordained, already signed, sealed and delivered.[23]

For, doesn't Wittgenstein's thought, like Derrida's, attempt to get us to see the illusion of a 'transcendental signified', something beyond language which could justify our use of language?

## II

Wittgenstein remarks in *The Blue Book*:

> It seems to us that there are certain definite mental processes bound up with the workings of language, understanding and

meaning. The signs of our language seem dead without these mental processes. And it seems these can bring about effects no material mechanism could, for example, a thought can agree or disagree with reality, I can think of someone who isn't present, I can imagine him, mean him in a remark which I make about him if he's thousands of miles away or dead.[24]

The meaning of our signs is what enables them to 'anticipate reality', and yet those signs as written or verbal marks appear in themselves to be dead, capable of any interpretation or none, but quite incapable of imposing their own meaning. So we are inclined to think meaning lies in the accompaniment of the use of the sign, in some 'definite mental process' of meaning, which nevertheless has properties which no other 'process' possesses:

> your idea was that that act of meaning the order had in its own way already traversed all those steps: that when you meant it your mind as it were flew ahead and took all the steps before you physically arrived at this or that one . . . it seemed as if they were in some *unique* way predetermined, anticipated – as only the act of meaning can anticipate reality.[25]

Yet this idea is an illusion. When we try to think what such an accompaniment, such a process, might consist in, having a mental image or a picture before the mind's eye, or such a picture together with a method of projection,[26] we see that, however we conceive it, it is still subject to the same problem as apparently accrued to the mere physical sign, and so cannot solve the problem. Anything given behind the sign could itself be variously interpreted and cannot, as it were, determine its own meaning: 'in the course of our argument we give one interpretation after another, as if each one contented us at least for a moment, until we thought of yet another standing behind it'.[27] Any purported 'signified', Derrida would say, has only the status of a 'signifier'.

It is this which precipitates the Derridean response. What this shows is that no 'unitary' meaning 'attaches' to the sign, but its meaning lies in the, in principle, indeterminable sequence of differences in which it may be placed. Meaning is given only in differences, and that these cannot be brought to a termination is what leads us to a new understanding which would dispense with the idea of *the* meaning, seeing it only as an effect of a terminated play of differences in terms of some centre, whose meaning itself is given by the interminable play of differences. Wittgenstein, however, draws a different conclusion: 'What this shows is that there is a way of grasping a rule which is *not* an *interpretation*, but which is exhibited in what we call "obeying the rule" and "going against it" in actual cases.'[28] This is not, as Llewellyn believes, an appeal to 'the immaculate granny of all discourse' who can tender 'recompense and solace' to those 'who feel nervous without' the idea of a transcendental signified, by producing practice as 'home base',[29] as though this were now to be simply substituted for the missing signified. Wittgenstein draws this conclusion because we cannot *understand* the notion of a 'sign', rule, a difference, independently of that of *application*, and application is not an act of interpretation, of the substitution of one set of signs for another. 'The *truth* of my statements is the test of my *understanding* of these statements. That is to say: if I make certain false statements, it becomes uncertain whether I understand them.'[30] If the meaning of an expression is what I can be said to understand, then that 'meaning' is not independent of the *truth* of certain statements that use the expression: if someone appeared to make certain false statements this would be used as *evidence* that he didn't understand the constituent expressions. As Baker and Hacker remark:

> we *define* the series '+2', for example, in terms of the sequence '. . . 998, 1000, 1002, 1004'. Getting this result is a *criterion* for applying the operation '+2'. The rule and its application are internally related, for we define the concept 'following this rule' by reference to *this* result.[31]

Hence, '"obeying a rule" is a practice'.[32] The reference to a practice, to agreement in *action*, in the *application* of expressions, is not a substitute for a 'transcendental signified' since it does not serve to justify certain concepts as the *correct* ones. It is rather a part of saying what it is for there to be what Derrida calls 'signs', and so differences, at all. Wittgenstein does not proclaim 'practice' as 'home base' but as *constitutive* of what we understand as a 'rule', 'definition', and so as a 'difference'. It is not that in order to apply an expression we have to understand it, but that understanding it involves being able to apply it, and that means being able to judge correctly in a certain range of cases.

> If language is to be a means of communication there must be agreement not only in definitions but also . . . in judgements. It is one thing to describe methods of measurement, and another to obtain and state results of measurement. But what we call 'measuring' is partly determined by a certain consistency in results of measurement.[33]

What we call 'measuring' involves a shared, or sharable, way of taking certain expressions, which *consists* partly in agreeing as to the *truth* of a certain range of judgements. The justification for following a rule as I do reaches an end, but not by appealing to something which shows that this is the right interpretation of it. 'If I have exhausted the justifications I have reached bedrock and my spade is turned. Then I am inclined to say "This is simply what I do"'.[34] Here, saying 'this is what I do' is not a justification but an *explanation* of what the rule *is*: what rule we are dealing with is partly determined by the *results*, by acting in this way. Justification comes to an end, 'but the end is not certain propositions striking us immediately as true; that is, it is not a kind of *seeing* on our part; it is our *acting* which lies at the bottom of the language-game'.[35] For, that acting, applying expressions in a certain way, shows what those expressions are.

Wittgenstein's intention in his later thought was 'to bring words back from their metaphysical to their everyday use'. This metaphysical use embodies 'a preconceived idea to which reality *must* correspond', a conception of the 'essence' of 'reality', and so of 'knowledge', 'truth', and related notions. In terms of the determination of these essences, the inadequacies of the ways in which we usually think about ourselves and the world are revealed. But such ideals, Wittgenstein suggests, cannot be justified in their critical role. The reason for this is simply that this critical role is already occupied by the use of these terms in the language-games of which they are a part. That this should be so is a consequence of the internal relation between the meaning of our 'signs' and their application, that understanding that meaning is not independent of the capacity to recognize the *truth* of certain kinds of statement that use the expressions concerned.

Practice can have this internal relation to a rule only if there is a 'matter of course' way in which we take its expression, and it is this which underlies our philosophical inclination to construe meaning as 'anticipating reality': 'The rule can only seem to me to produce all its consequences in advance if I draw them as a matter of course.'[36] Such 'production' is what we indicate when we use the 'logical must': 'If you really follow the rule in multiplying, it *must* come out the same.'[37] The justification for this cannot lie in appeal to the rule, but rather to the resulting value as being produced 'in the same way' as other values which you recognize as *defining* what the rule is. But seeing that it is 'the same' depends on taking those other values in a common way, as does seeing them as 'in accordance with a rule' at all. 'And the "like this" [in "go on like this"] is signified by a number, a value. For at *this* level, the expression of the rule is explained by the value, not the value by the rule.'[38] What the logical 'must' appeals to is a shared application of expressions which we find a 'matter of course' and which we must participate in for us to be said to *understand* the relevant expressions.

But further, Wittgenstein suggests, we could find such application 'matter of course' only if the introduction of such expressions could connect up with ways in which we *already* act as 'a matter of course': 'We react to the cause. We instinctively get rid of the cause if we don't want the effect. We instinctively look for what has been hit to what has hit it. (I am assuming that we do this.)'[39] That is, it is not that we react in these ways to what we *judge* to be the cause, but we react instinctively in this way and this makes it possible for us to form a concept of 'cause' at all. Wittgenstein refers to such reactions as 'the prototype of a way of thinking and not the result of thought.'[40] 'Our language is merely an auxiliary to, and further extension of, this relation. Our language-game is an extension of primitive behaviour (for our language-game in behaviour).'[41] It is 'behaviour', for it is practice, the *application* of expressions, which, one might say, constitutes those expressions as the expressions they are. 'It is what human beings say that is true and false, and they agree in the language they use. This is not agreement in opinions but in form of life.'[42] Agreement in form of life is the sharing of reactions which are the prototypes of our forms of language and of the reactions which constitute the ways of taking expressions, of applying them, which we would produce as their explanation. Such reactions are, of course, *facts* of human nature, just as it is a general fact of nature that lumps of cheese on a balance do not 'suddenly grow or shrink for no obvious reason',[43] and both are required for us to have, for example, a language of measuring weights of cheese. But these 'facts of human nature' do not play a justificatory role here, as if Wittgenstein were appealing to a given human nature in order to establish that certain ways of thinking are 'correct', as being in accordance with that nature. For what these facts are appears only *in* the use of language.

> The consensus of reactions is in this sense prior to language, but the reactions themselves are not language, nor are they languages. Neither does the agreement in reactions come first or anticipate language. It appears as the language does, it is a common way of taking the expressions of the language.[44]

Such shared reactions, to each other, to our environment, and in the application of linguistic expressions which extend these primitive relations, constitute the forms of certainty which characterize our language-games. 'The kind of certainty is the kind of language-game.'[45] This 'certainty' is not a matter of belief, but is rather *definitive* of the kind of language at issue, since it shows us what the expressions concerned are.

> But how *can* previous experience be a ground for assuming that such-and-such will occur later on? The answer is: What general concept have we of grounds for this kind of assumption? This sort of statement about the past is simply what we call a ground for assuming that this will happen in the future – and if you are surprised at our playing such a game I refer you to the *effect* of a past experience (to the fact that a burnt child fears the fire).[46]

Our language of prediction of the future on the basis of the past is a refinement and extension of a reaction: 'The belief that fire will burn me is of the same kind as the fear that it will burn me.'[47] But that fear, that form of certainty, is neither reasonable nor unreasonable:

> I would like to regard this certainty, not as something akin to hastiness or superficiality, but as a form of life. But that means I want to conceive it as something that lies beyond being justified or unjustified, as it were, as something animal.[48]

We can only give reasons in so far as something *counts* as a reason, and that something does, a reference to the past, say, in speaking about the future, does not itself have a reason.

> Isn't it experience that teaches us to judge like *this*, that is, that it is correct to judge like this? But how does experience *teach* us, then? We may derive it from experience, but experience does not direct us to derive anything from experience. If it is the *ground* of our judging like this, and not just the cause, still we do not have a ground for *seeing this in turn as a ground*.[49]

That we have such a language-game depends upon our already behaving in certain ways, as when a child, before it has learnt to talk, looks for the toy it has previously put down. Such behaviour is neither reasonable nor unreasonable, but, as it were, 'something animal'. Language extends these modes of behaviour, and it is this which makes possible our finding certain applications of that language 'natural', 'matter of course': as when the child is enabled to tell us what he is looking for, where he left it, and so on. These 'matters of course' applications of the language are not interpretations of it, since it is by appealing to them that we explain the expressions involved, say *what* expressions they are. Without shared judgements there would be no 'signs', and so no differences, in the Derridean sense.

There is an end to justification, but it does not lie in appealing to a ground which would show that certain specified differences were 'essences', revealed things as they really are. Such a conception presupposes the possibility of differences, as does, in another way, Derrida's own 'differance', the differentiating play which produces them. What Wittgenstein tries to get us to recognize is that without shared judgements, and so forms of action which apply expressions without reason, there would be no possibility of speaking of rules, definitions, differences, and so forth, at all. Such ungrounded ways of acting do not lack a ground, since they make possible anything counting as a reason. Neither, therefore, are they formed through a desire for meaning which looks for a ground and so could be transformed into play by the revelation of the absence of ground. They are not formed at all. The language-game 'is not based on grounds. It is there – like our life.'[50] For such a practice is indeed a part of our life, and so of what must be accepted *as* given.

## III

Derrida speaks of deconstruction as an attempt to give expression to a deep 'mutation in our search for meaning'.[51] That search has in the past been for the essences of ourselves and all else and which has, therefore, understood meaning in terms of a system of differences generated from a centre, a ground which determines differences *as* essences. This search for meaning had the character of a need, to relate to ourselves and what is other than ourselves in terms of truth, through an understanding of what these *really* are. The metaphysical project has the character of an interpretation of ourselves and other beings which is guided by a notion of Being which involves that of truth. The mutation this has now undergone lies in the realization of the interpretive nature of the project itself, so that interpretation can, as it were, now constitute the essential way in which we exist. In this way, Derrida draws out the consequences of Heidegger's thought by undermining the finality involved in the idea of Being, in the very idea of relating to things in terms of what they 'really' are.

Early in his career, Heidegger had formulated this basic assumption thus: 'Something like Being reveals itself to us in the understanding of Being, an understanding that lies at the root of all our comportment towards beings.'[52] When we relate to ourselves or to anything else, we always do so in terms of our understanding of the Being of what we relate to, an understanding which itself involves an understanding of Being. Pre-reflectively, such an understanding encounters beings in terms of the ready-to-hand, in terms, that is, of those purposes we pursue through which we understand our own Being. We are what we do, and other things are encountered within the context of such purposive relations, as being beneficial or detrimental, or as found already there to be used or coped with, and so forth. Only from this basis can beings be revealed in other ways, as when we suspend all purposive relations in order to reveal beings 'worldlessly' in the comportment of theoretical viewing. Metaphysics, for the early Heidegger, has forgotten world, the unobtrusive purposive context within which things are first manifest in their taken-for-grantedness. In doing so, it interprets Being in terms of theoretical comportment, and organizes its general understanding of man and other beings accordingly, thereby leading man to understand himself in an essentially alien manner and not as the being who has constantly to reveal beings in their Being. The revelation of world makes possible a transformation in the understanding of Being through which man can understand himself as the constant task of renewing world. Man is in his Being as creative, as taking over his heritage into a future which is essentially open. Only within the context of such a world can beings be revealed and so available for their interpretations in terms of theoretical comportment as well as the everyday mode of unobtrusiveness. That man understands himself and all else in terms of some fundamental apprehension of Being is required for him to have the overall understanding which he always exhibits. Man is always in some determinate way in 'beings as a whole'. How he is depends on the interpretation of Being which he *lives*. In his later work, metaphysics is regarded by Heidegger as a certain fundamental way in which man has existed during the course of Western civilization determined by thinking of Being as the Being of beings, as a given intelligible structure available in principle to man's intellect. The sequence of interpretations of such a Being constitutes the history of metaphysics and of Western man, which, in our age, breaks down where what is no longer manifests itself as having a determinate structure which we may appeal to in order to govern our lives and our comportment towards things, but rather appears to us only as the material for an ever increasing capacity for prediction and calculation. It is this which reveals metaphysics as a tradition, an historical sequence of interpretation, and thereby man as historical. It now becomes possible for us to think this historicality explicitly so that we may come to exist in terms of the understanding of Being, as such.

Derrida, as we have seen, responds to Heidegger's thought, and in particular to the suggestion of finality in his revelation of historicality as man's essence. All such appeal to essence is an attempt to justify certain modes of thinking as being in accordance with the truth, and it is this project which identifies Heidegger's thought as at one with metaphysics. The thought of meaning as the play of differences, interminable in principle, removes the possibility of speaking of truth and Being except as *effects* of the enforced termination of such play. Contemporary humanity is, therefore, faced with the necessity of living, not in terms of an interpretation of Being, and so in terms of truth, even as historical unconcealing, but in terms of differance, engaging in the play of differences as such. I say 'necessity' here, since Derrida presents his thought as having a *claim* on us, as revealing to us 'what the age demands' through identifying our situation as one in which all our ways of thinking have been formed metaphysically, but where the very perception of this means that we are no longer simply *in* metaphysics. The demand to live in terms of differance, the play of differences, ensues from this diagnosis, which itself depends, therefore, on the assumption that we have to live in terms of some overall interpretation, one which has hitherto been based on the conception of Being and truth.

But what is the justification for this assumption? What we may call the 'philosophical' argument for this I have already mentioned in my earlier discussion of Heidegger. Our relation to ourselves and to anything else is mediated through an understanding of their 'nature', their 'Being'. A human being, unlike an animal, encounters, for example, a tree *as* a tree, and so *as* a living thing which is a part of the non-human world: and he can only do this if he has an implicit *understanding* of the sort of thing a tree is, both as a living thing and as an 'external object'. As understanding, this is an implicit form of *thought*, and as such needs to be raised to its appropriate form in thinking the 'natures' we already understand. But such thought has to be guided by what is to be understood as a 'nature', a general, overriding conception of Being in terms of which the Being of particular kinds of beings can be articulated. Such a determination of the governing notion of Being is, in its expressed form, philosophy, which has, therefore, a ruling role over all other forms of human activity. Man himself, his Being or essence, is to be as the understanding of essence, or a relation to Being, or the desire for meaning: in this lies that conception required for the mediation of our relation to ourselves. In its pristine form, this adequate mediation takes place in philosophy, which thus constitutes man's most proper form of activity. The universal problematic thus answers to a *need* present in human experience. Such experience is always *ruled* by an implicit understanding of the nature of what one encounters: it aspires, therefore, to a condition where such rule would be explicit and man would attain the self-consciousness of which he is capable. That self-consciousness is at its clearest where the governing notion of Being finds its articulated form, in philosophy.

It is this kind of argument which Wittgenstein's work undermines, by denying the model of human experience it is founded on, that of *governance* by what aspires to the condition of thought. Our fundamental relation to ourselves and to all else cannot lie in an understanding of their nature which can be brought to conceptual articulation and so be the subject of interpretation, for this understands that relation as *already*, although implicitly, conceptual and linguistic. But only if we already relate in certain ways to each other and to our environment can there be concepts, 'signs', at all. Our primary relation lies in the 'primitive reactions' of which our language-games are extensions, and the shared reactions involved in our common ways of taking the relevant expressions which show which expressions they are: that is, upon reactions involved in *concept-formation*, and thereby prior to and involved in any conceptual articulation. What is meant by such expressions is given by their use, their application, within language-games which we play as 'something animal' and which do not, therefore, rest upon or are governed by what aspires to, and so needs, conceptual articulation. Hence the idea that our ways of thinking rest upon metaphysical presuppositions is an illusion, as is, therefore, the diagnosis of our 'contemporary situation' by Nietzsche and post-Nietzschean thought as being both within and beyond metaphysics.

Nevertheless, the model of self-determination implicit in the appeal to the universal problematic suggests an alternative motivation which may provide a different kind of justification, which we may call 'existential'. We, it may be said, have to determine how to live, and to live in terms of that determination: the nature of human life aspires to the condition of self-governance. If we arrive at this truth of human life, it will then give us the truth concerning all aspects of life, and so all forms of human experience. In this way, it will provide the measure in terms of which the human relations within which all else can be encountered can be shown as they truly are, and this will show what can be meant by our speaking of the 'truth' about what we can encounter. The necessity for a universal problematic derives from our need for a meaning for our lives as a whole, and one through which we can attain to self-governance. It is this understanding of the problem of human existence which, I think, really underlies the production of resolutions to that problematic and which Kierkegaard's work is intended to undermine.

We could apply Wittgenstein's ideas to Kierkegaard by noting that the notion of 'the problem' of the significance of life is part of a 'language-game' which has its centre in the *first-person* position and which has an ineradicable primacy in relation to the *speaker* of a language. Here, the notions of 'problem', 'reflection', 'resolution', and so forth have a different 'grammar' from that they have in intellectual pursuits, and even there no doubt they differ from case to case. *Self*-reflection is a relation to the previous 'how' of one's life, marking a break having the character of some degree of despair, and which thus faces the individual with a decision, whether to continue in a modified form of the previous 'how' or to make a 'leap' into a new 'how' revealed in the process of reflection. I shall consider the structure of this again in the next chapter. 'Resolution' has thus the character of a resolve, and so of a dissolution of despair, rather than of an 'answer' to a question. And one further remark may be made here. Derrida's work initially appears as a response to the problem of interpretation in relation to texts: why is it that a text seems to generate endless interpretive labour, each interpretation claiming for itself a finality, or a closer approximation to it than previous efforts? Derrida finds a quite general answer to this, in the nature of language as a differential play of signs which precludes totalization. Wittgenstein would of course emphasize the great variety of what may be called 'texts', and would locate the differences in what may be said about them to their roles in our various forms of life, some of which may preclude this proliferation of interpretation. But then for at least certain kinds of text, and perhaps some of those we call 'literary' are among these, this generation of interpretation will be part of the language-game in which they are located. It may be that they play a role, as a certain development, in relation to the notions appropriate to the first person and thus *require* a first-person response. Some such texts may, for example, be one of the ways in which, through our responses to them, we gain an insight into *ourselves*, into the 'how' of our own lives, so that they play a role in 'self-reflection'. Kierkegaard's own texts, as a certain sort of fiction, and so engaged in 'indirect communication', have this character, which, lacking any *actual* authority of an existing individual addressing others, provoke a response which can differ depending on the 'how' of our own lives, whilst at the same time making us aware of this self-understanding and so creating a space within which our lives can take on the form of a question. Perhaps other forms of 'literary text' can play an analogous role too, although an examination of this will have to await another occasion.

# Chapter 6

# Philosophy as hubris

## I

Post-metaphysical thought in Nietzsche, Heidegger and Derrida shows certain central characteristics which have their parallels in Kierkegaard: a 'style' of writing at variance with that of the metaphysical tradition which has its rationale in the 'situatedness' of the thought whose intention is, not the representation of 'the truth', but an 'intervention' into that situation. But for Kierkegaard, these characteristics of post-metaphysical thought would only serve to mark its complicity with the metaphysical project which forgets that the thinker is an existing individual whose questioning about life must have the character of a *self-questioning*, one carried out in the *first person*, which precludes the essential philosophical move of an intellectual inquiry into the 'essence' of the human or into the 'historical situation' of the thinker. In order to obtain a more general Kierkegaardian perspective on the philosophical project, let me rehearse these parallels and their fundamental difference.

Nietzsche's use of aphorisms, stories, poems, the fictional character of Zarathustra, Heidegger's 'etymologies' and 'poetic' thinking, Derrida's 'double-reading', are strategies of writing demanded by the essentially 'situated' character of their thought. Nietzsche situates his thinking in relation to a 'nihilism' which he diagnoses as implicit in contemporary European culture, the immediate manifestation of which is the unbelievability of the Christian God; Heidegger finds himself in the context of the 'age of technology' in which Being has become a mere word and our existence is challenged to the ordering and calculating of beings; whilst Derrida locates his thought in the moment when the question of language enters 'the universal problematic' in the absence of a ground for thinking. These 'situations' locate the thinker in relation to metaphysical thought, revealing it as a *tradition* and so as *history*. Metaphysical thought is thus revealed as a form of *human* existing rather than the revelation of 'The truth'. For Nietzsche, metaphysics reveals itself as the justificatory discourse of life characterized by the will to truth which *needs* justification, for Heidegger, that 'essence is no longer idea' reveals metaphysics as a tradition blind to its own traditionality, whilst for Derrida his thought is a response to the 'historical sedimentation' of thought, the production of the forms of thought we possess through a changing history of the substitution of centre for centre.

But this situation has been *produced* by the internal dynamic of Western culture itself. For Nietzsche, nihilism is 'the necessary consequence of our valuations so far', the secularization of our science, ethics and politics being part of the manifestation of this implicit nihilism and so part of the process by which the supreme value of truth undermines itself. For Heidegger, that beings now address us in a claim to be planned and ordered is a challenge to man, an address of Being, which, although the 'supreme danger' where Being is hidden in an oblivion where philosophy turns into the empirical sciences of man, at the same time opens up the possibility of a 'saving' by revealing metaphysics as tradition and so enabling us to hear Being address us in a different way. For Derrida, the situation is created by the loss of ground, the absence of a 'centre or origin' revealing metaphysics and the 'history of the West' as a series of substitutions of such centres and which can thus provoke thought to address the condition of this internal necessity.

The internal dynamic of Western culture which finds its justificatory discourse in metaphysics *undermines* this discourse itself. Metaphysics begins as the search for an ultimate ground, a point which would bring reflective discourse to a stop, so that an ultimate 'centre' could be appealed to in order to justify our non-philosophical discourses. The pursuit is thus for 'the Truth of truth', which could guarantee our ability to speak truly about the human and the non-human: metaphysics at various times finds this point in the Platonic Good, in Aristotle's God, in the creator God of philosophical Christianity, in the transcendental subject, in Spirit, and so on. As the ultimate ground of truth, this is changeless and so beyond time (or incorporates time within itself in the case of Spirit): hence the historical position from which it is apprehended is either irrelevant, a contingency, or the point of its completion in its own self-consciousness. But the constant necessity within the pursuit of the truth for questioning ultimately turns upon this very pursuit itself through questioning the possibility of *access* to what metaphysics claims to know. As Nietzsche says, 'the value of life cannot be estimated' by a living man, 'because he is party to the dispute, indeed its object, and not the judge of it'. Metaphysics presupposes access to a transcendental position beyond life in order that the truth of life be apprehended. The situatedness of these forms of thought is thus a recognition of 'finitude', the essential lack of access to such a transcendent position, or to its idea as a possibility, which recognition is made possible by this very pursuit of the truth *itself*. Hence, the recognition of this finitude or historicality or history as a series of substitutions of centre for centre, occurs necessarily at a point of hiatus. The situation can only be identified in its *relation* to the pursuit of truth from a position where we are both *within* and *without* metaphysics and the structures of discourse it forms, our inherited forms of thought, formed in terms of the will to truth, of essence as idea, or of a centre, which we still occupy but which can no longer be *believed* in the way they require.

Hence, the diagnosis of the situation *at the same time* reveals the *task* of current thinking: not a continuation of the metaphysical project directed towards the truth, but rather an *intervention* into our inherited forms of thought in order to dislodge them from their metaphysical underpinnings and so make possible a new way for the human to exist. Nietzsche's philosophizing with a hammer, Heidegger's 'destruction' of ontology, the divesting of man and Being of 'those qualities with which metaphysics has endowed them', and Derrida's deconstructive practices, are such forms of interventionary thinking. Hence the issue of 'style': it is required by the new role which thinking must play, that of such intervention rather than the systematic reflective argument to a ground.

We can formulate a parallel structure for Kierkegaard. His use of pseudonyms, and so fictional form, and within this, especially with Climacus' discussions of philosophy, the extensive use of irony and comedy, are at variance with what we expect from philosophy. But this too finds its rationale in his emphasis on the *situatedness* of all thought about existence. Kierkegaard too criticizes the metaphysical orientation towards system, the truth, available at least in ideality, to the human being: 'if an existing individual were really able to transcend himself, the truth would be for him something final and complete; but where is the point at which he is outside himself?' But this is not said to recall the human to its finitude and so to provoke a thinking of historicality through which the task for the present would become manifest. Rather, it is said to *prevent* any such recuperation of the philosophical project by reminding the philosopher that she or he is an *existing* individual whose thought about life must have the character of thought about *her or his own*. Philosophy has forgotten what it means to be a human being, but not 'what it means to be a human being in general . . . but what it means that you and I and he are human beings, each one for himself'. Kierkegaard wishes to remind us that philosophy is written by individual human beings who are *involved* in existence so that their questioning about life can only be a questioning about *their own* life and must therefore have the character of such a questioning in the *first person*. The questioning undertaken by metaphysics and its successors is intended to be *fundamental*, and so to put all concrete ways of living by individuals in question, including, therefore, that of the individual who speaks. But such a radical questioning by the individual of *her own* life must have the character of a radical *despair* which not only must be expressed in the form of her utterance, but would encompass the totality of the individual's life, including her intellectual activities. The philosopher sees the question of the significance of the individual as subsumed under the general question of the significance of human life, whether this is to be understood in terms of 'essence' or as to be determined through the diagnosis of the 'historical situation', and must so regard his own life. But this self-mediation through the general is impossible, since the radicality of the questioning would put *any* activity of the philosopher himself in question.

Philosophy 'has begun by tricking the individuals into becoming objective'.[1] The philosopher forgets that his own thinking is part of his own life, so that there is no way an I can be in a position to engage in an intellectual inquiry which would resolve the question of the significance of his life which he claims to have by virtue of the generality of his questioning. The ethical 'opposes every confusing attempt, like that of proposing ethically to *contemplate* humanity and the world'. Such ethical contemplation is impossible, 'since there is only one kind of ethical contemplation, namely self-contemplation'.[2] The philosophical project, whether understood metaphysically or post-metaphysically, is thus an evasion of the problem the philosopher claims to have, embodying a 'sheer distraction of mind'.[3] Rather, that project itself is a manifestation of the existential condition of the thinker himself, of the implied relation he has to his own life. In embarking on his intellectual inquiry, he subordinates his life, at least in appearance, to the exercise of his intellect, and so exemplifies an adhesion to a capacity he *finds* himself with, a developed reflective intelligence, and so manifests a form of *aesthetic* existence. The aesthetic is the field of differentiation in capacities between individuals, so that there can be many different forms of aesthetic existence. But where, as in philosophy, such a capacity is not only erected into the centre for an individual's life, but claims a universal validity, as in metaphysics, or a validity within an historical position, this marks rather the self-assertion of the human being, not merely to live in terms of some given capacity, but to claim that this is ultimately *justified* so that the human can live a life justified before *itself*. But this is, for an existing individual, impossible, since the radical question would put his or her own life in its entirety in question. Philosophy is thus an expression of *hubris* which is a result of the individual thinker failing to recognize that the question of life must be that of his own and so must be characterized in the appropriate existential form, as despair, which, in relation to the question he claims to have, must be a despair over his life in its totality.

Any questioning of life must have the character of a self-questioning by an I, and the radical form of the philosophical question, of the significance of life itself, can only existentially be heard as the expression of a total despair, and not as the disinterested raising of an intellectual problem. Similarly, any thought or communication concerning life's significance must be heard as proceeding from the context of such a reflection by an I about his or her own life. It is this exigency which provides the rationale for the *form* of Kierkegaard's writings which address philosophy.

The ethical and the ethico-religious, Kierkegaard claims, can only be communicated 'indirectly'. Now, indirect communication generally is the appropriate medium, he says, for the communication of capability as opposed to that of knowledge.[4] In the communication of knowledge 'it is always "the object" which is reflected upon'. The concern is 'with the WHAT which is to be communicated'[5] in relation to which the communicator and the receiver stand in the same subordinate relation: what judges both is the truth of what is said, and this truth is indifferent to them as individuals. They thus speak disinterestedly, in a way which claims for itself an impersonal validity. In the communication of capability, however, Kierkegaard says, the relation is *personal* and there is no object. If you teach a child to write, your concern is that *she* develop the ability, and there is no ability to write independent of particular individuals who have that ability. I have an ability which I wish to communicate to the other: but what that means is that I wish that they *too* be able to write. What matters is *their* being able to do something. I can only 'communicate' here by getting them to do it, by training, where what I *say* has the imperative form 'Do it like this' which is exemplified in *my own* action. 'The communication of capability is in the medium of actuality':[6] it is carried out by my *doing* it, and the other trying to do it for themselves. To sum up: the communication of such 'aesthetic' capability is 'indirect' in that the ability of the teacher is 'communicated' to the pupil only by her coming to be able herself; this communication involves an essentially *personal* relation, therefore, which has the character of training by example and by the pupil's own performance, and so in 'actuality', and which thus involves an *authority* of the teacher in relation to the pupil which derives from the former's developed ability.

Such aesthetic capability is 'knowing how' and communication here is a matter of one who can showing another and getting her to do likewise. But such exercise and development of capacities takes place within the context of a more fundamental 'how': that of how the individuals concerned are related to these capacities themselves which is an aspect of how they live their lives. Now, this 'how' encompasses what Kierkegaard calls the 'existential dialectic', the 'stages' through which the way an individual lives her life may be characterized, the movement between which being a matter of her *taking on* a new 'how' which would resolve, or dissolve, *despair* over the way they have lived their life previously. In order to see what forms of communication are possible here, let me first outline this 'dialectic', bearing in mind that Kierkegaard might already be objecting to the form of this communication! (I shall return to this possible objection in the final chapter.) Aesthetically, an individual regards the significance of her life as dependent on what happens to her, and so in terms of fortune, misfortune and fate: the exercise of their capacities and relations with others depends for its continuance on results. This aesthetic 'how' has the character, however, of an *implicit* assertion of the I. I find myself already disposed towards certain results suggested by my capacities and exercise them on the condition that these results are forthcoming or can be hoped for. But in order that *I* should act, I have to passively *go along* with this disposition, a passivity which can be broken if the results are not forthcoming or appear unlikely to result. Such a break, having the character of a certain degree of despair, may, of course, simply result in an attachment to some other capacity and so a directing myself elsewhere. But it can also provide the opening for a reflection that the significance of the results, and so of the capacities themselves, depended on my attachment to them, and so on the temporary and conditional identification of myself with these capacities through which I had what *I* wanted. Such reflection makes possible the adoption of a new 'how' of life through which the despair over the immediate aesthetic 'how' itself is dissolved, one in which I try to free the satisfaction of *myself* from dependence on external results by 'having my own way', the 'how' of reflective aestheticism, where my capacities become a field of possibility for an enjoyment which I myself determine. But this 'how' contains its own impossibility, since enjoyment may or may not come whatever I do. The life lived 'for enjoyment' can only be successfully pursued unreflectively. The melancholy which haunts the aesthete may thus become a despair and create the opening for the realization that 'having my own way' had the significance it did for me because I had adopted, *chosen*, this strategy, but not explicitly, so that it appeared my freedom lay in the performance of the project itself rather than in my capacity for choice.

Since the project had the significance it had for me because I had implicitly chosen it, the despair over aesthetic reflection may be dissolved through 'choosing choice itself', as Judge William tells A. Here the significance of my life seems to lie in imposing choice upon my capacities regardless of result or enjoyment, by the undertaking of *commitment*. Yet this project cannot be carried out in such a way as to encompass my life in its totality. The issue of which commitments have priority introduces an element of the arbitrary, which is only increased when I realize that such commitments have a general character which cannot encompass the particularities of life. This arbitrariness can only be resolved by an appeal *outside* commitment and so to *myself* as that on which *I* impose commitment. This is, of course, a result of the nature of the project, to impose commitment on myself, which cannot resolve the issue of the significance of my life as such. Ethical despair is thus over the very possibility of myself as the source of the significance of my life, which for its dissolution requires the resignation of such a pretension, a resignation which cannot therefore itself confer significance either. It thus requires a negative movement against my proclivity to regard myself as the source of the significance of my life, that proclivity which has progressively become explicit through the dialectic. Were I to live no longer in such a negative movement, but absolutely without reference, positive or negative, to myself as the source, this could occur only as a 'gift', by 'grace', of a pure selflessness.

In this dialectic, a stage as a determinate 'how' lived in actuality is not contained implicitly in the previous one, since embarking on it requires a 'leap', a determination to live in a way for which *no reason* is provided by the stage one occupies and yet despairs over. Yet *what* is to be taken over in the leap is indeed determined by the nature of that despair itself *if* the individual is to remove it. Despair is the condition of an individual who is both *within* a particular 'how' of life, and so within the reasons it provides, and yet sees its *impossibility* of providing reasons for *her*. Such perception occurs through realizing that the reasons provided by that 'how' have been such for her only because of an implicit understanding of the source of the value of herself which is not recognized by that 'how' itself. Thus the despair marks the realization that one has been living an 'illusion' which requires an explicit and active taking on of that new self-understanding itself. This active move into a new sense of 'reason' thus takes place through a decision which marks an increasing *seriousness* with which one takes the issue of the significance of one's life, of one self. Despair is the moment when the incompatibility between the project, the 'how', and the issue of the significance of my life in its totality, of myself, is experienced, and the progress through the forms of despair is thus the way in which an I can come into an ever increasing recognition of what that issue must mean in terms of self-understanding. The dialectic moves from an implicit recognition of *my* satisfaction as the source of my life's significance in the aesthetic, to an explicit *attempt* to live in terms of this satisfaction secured against contingency (aesthetic reflection) which thus implicitly recognizes my *choice* as source, to an explicit imposition of choice itself as commitment in the ethical. The foundering of the latter reveals the *impossibility* of the general project of taking myself as the source of significance itself, which thus requires living in terms of an explicit recognition of a significance which, impossible of my attainment, would be as the gift of selflessness.

What, then, of the possibilities of communication within this dialectic, leaving for a moment the problem of communication *about* it? (I shall comment on this latter issue in the final chapter.) Communication of aesthetic capability is indirect since the teacher is concerned that the pupil should come to be able to do something themselves. She will communicate by example and an imperative form of speech, 'Do it like this', which marks the position of authority she possesses in virtue of her developed ability in relation to what the pupil is to be brought to be able to do. This relation of authority means that the pupil has reason to do what the teacher says in terms of his own lack of development of the ability concerned. Although indirect in this sense, however, such communication is 'direct' in that the teacher can demonstrate what the pupil is to do *without reference* to either of their *relations* to the ability concerned:[7] whether the pupil simply enjoys it, is doing it out of obedience to his parent's desires, out of fear of the consequences of not doing it, and so on, is irrelevant to what communicated and learnt, as is the teacher's own relation to the ability concerned. Hence the communication, the transmission of ability, can take place through compulsion, through the imposition of an alternative even less desired, however undesirable on other grounds this may be.

But the relation of an I to an I in terms of the 'how' of life itself differs in at least three fundamental ways from this model. First, a 'how' of life, since it encompasses the very relations of the individual to her own capacities, cannot be undertaken by compulsion. Rather, since this 'how' is the way the individual understands her own significance, its acquisition constitutes part of the process of her own self-understanding. It is taken on only in the context of the opening created by a despair over a previous 'how' of life by a decision which at the same time is a coming to a new form of self-understanding. Following from this, and second, this decision cannot have its reasons in her previous state, as her lack of development of an aesthetic capacity can give her reasons to do what the teacher prescribes. An ethical individual like Judge William may provide an example to A and may formulate an existential communication as an imperative 'Choose choice itself'. But A, as an individual living the how of aesthetic reflection, cannot be reasoned into obeying this, since to adopt it renders what he has previously seen as reason, in terms of 'having his own way', unreasonable. A 'leap' is necessary, which can only be taken by the individual herself as a determination in actuality about their life which will alter their very notion of what a reason is through the alteration in their self-understanding. These two features indicate that any communication from another in this context can only be such as to *create* or *provide* a *situation* in which this process of self-examination can occur. And this, third, raises the question of the authority with which one individual may relate to another here. Since the communication concerns the how of life itself, it must proceed from the speaker's relation to their *own* life. The 'existential dialectic' is, we might say, essentially in the *first* person, so that communication is not merely personal, as is that of an ability from one to another, but is from an I in terms of *his or her* existential position to another who can receive it in terms of *his or her* own. When Judge William utters an imperative to his friend he assumes an authority in relation to him, one which he thinks he has in speaking for 'the universally human'. But if one conceives one's life in terms of the developed dialectic, and thus from the position from which one's life is at least questioned by the religious, such authority is necessarily lacking, since there one becomes aware of one's absolute inadequacy in relation to life's significance. The assumption of authority can only proceed from the assumption of a *human* source of significance which one then shares with the other. Where the religious is at least seen in its claim on oneself, then any communication which assumes such an authority, even if what it says is in a certain sense in conformity with the dialectic, denies in *saying* it what it says. The communication must be 'doubly reflected': its mode of saying in relation to another must be in conformity with what is said, which makes it impossible for an I to say to another what she may say to herself.[8] Thus Kierkegaard notes in the *Journals*:

> The communication always dares influence only indirectly 1) because he must always express that he himself is not a master teacher; 2) because he must express that the receiver knows it; 3) because ethically the task is precisely this – that every man comes to stand alone in the God-relationship.[9]

It is because of these exigencies that Kierkegaard developed his pseudonymous method. The pseudonymous writings avoid even an indirect relation in *actuality* of an I to an I since the one who addresses the reader is not an actual individual but a *fiction*, and so the author himself is in the same position as any other reader, left alone entirely in what he does or does not do with what is said: 'The fact that there is a pseudonym is the qualitative expression that it is . . . not I who speak but another, that it is addressed to me just as much as to others'.[10]

## II

Within the various forms of the transmutation of the 'universal problematic', philosophy plays a deciding role in relation to the question of human existence, either constituting its resolution or determining our task in the present historical juncture. Under the latter diagnosis, a different possibility is variously glimpsed of an existence which does not give the priority to truth which characterizes metaphysics. What, then, gives its role to philosophy in relation to the question of human existence is the way the latter has been, and in a transmuted way still is, bound up with the issue of truth. Man can resolve the question only by determining his own truth, but the drive towards this reveals his essential difference as the capacity to know truth itself and which finds fulfilment in knowledge of reality as a whole, in philosophy. Thus, man's self-knowledge is at the same time knowledge of the nature of reality. Post-metaphysical thought puts metaphysics, and so its primary concepts of reality, truth and knowledge, in question through understanding it as the product of a particular form of human existence. Metaphysics articulates the fundamental structures of the interpretation of the human and the non-human of a humanity oriented towards familiarization, being at home in the world, and so of a flight from the threatening, or the openness of the future, or the endless possibility of the generation of differences. These latter notions enable us to conceive of the possibility of a non-metaphysical form of life, one which embraces what metaphysics unknowingly flies before. Such a non-metaphysical form of life would then not need to justify itself in terms of truth, and so would cease to give philosophy its privileged place. Yet this possibility and its claim on us now derive from the continuance of that fundamental questioning which has manifested itself as metaphysics and which is now turned against metaphysics itself. Philosophy thus in its transmuted forms retains its privilege in the current historical juncture, revealing to us both the non-metaphysical possibility in outline and the present task of undermining the metaphysical presuppositions of our thought. Philosophy thus looks forward to its own self-overcoming, but in doing so stresses the centrality for us now, as in the past, of fundamental philosophical questioning in determining the meaning of human existence.

The significance of Wittgenstein's work in this context lies in its dissolving the appearance that the question of the nature of reality, or, therefore, of the nature of the life which gives primacy to this question, arises through a reflection, and so recollection, of what is implied by our non-philosophical ways of thinking and acting. Metaphysical conceptions of the 'nature of reality' are answers to the question of the harmony between thought and reality. What must reality be if there is to be the possibility of true thought about it? It must, it appears, be thought-like, formed in accordance with the ideas, or a series of moments in the coming to self-knowledge of Spirit, and so on. For the later Wittgenstein, such answers are only such to an *apparent* question: 'It is in language that an expectation and its fulfillment make contact'; '"An order orders its own execution." . . . that was a grammatical proposition and it means: If an order runs "Do such-an-such" then executing the order is called "doing such-and-such."'[11] The relation between an expectation and its fulfilment is not a mysterious relation between two entitities, a thought, say, and a situation, but is grammatical, one *within* language itself, not one between language and something external to it. It lies merely in that if you, say, expect 'he will come', then if you do not see *this* as 'fulfilling' that expectation then you have either made a mistake or you are talking of something else. Seeing that situation as fulfilling the expectation is determinative of the signs you have used being *those* signs, that you expected 'he will come'. There is no mysterious relation between two entities, since the 'sign' is not that sign without its having that application, just as there is no mysterious relation between the thoughts of adding two and getting 1002, 1004 and so forth. Rather, that 'add two' is a sign is shown by its having an application, a use, and what sign it is shown by its application. Our getting 1002, 1004, and so on is *definitive* of our using the sign 'add two'. If we don't get that result, we have made a mistake or we are speaking of something else, using a private code, or whatever. The question of the 'harmony between thought and reality' is no real question since we cannot *identify* the relevant terms independently of one another: thoughts are only such in having an application, and what thoughts they are is shown by that application itself. Since there is no real question, not only can there be no genuine metaphysical answers to it, but equally there can be no 'metaphysical presuppositions' involved in the forms of our language. We do not have to, through a redefinition of fundamental questioning, envisage a form of non-metaphysical existence, since that is what we always have had already.

Yet if the problem of the harmony between thought and reality is illusory, can we nevertheless understand how it arises? As the earlier Wittgenstein remarked, it is the problem of the nature of 'all being', and so requires the latter conception. The later Wittgenstein saw this as a result of being misled by the superficial grammatical similarity which makes it appear 'that

language always functions in one way . . . to convey thoughts –
which may be about houses, pains, good and evil, or anything
else you please'.[12] The apparent similarity between, say, 'He
has a house', 'He has a headache' and 'He has a conscience',
and so forth, leads to the assumption that these are particular
cases of a general form, that of the 'proposition'. Since we
speak of 'truth' and 'falsity' in all such cases, and since we can
add to what we say in these ways, 'This is how things are', we
think truth and falsity lie in a relation between the 'proposition' and the situation which would make it true. This then
appears to raise a quite general question about the relation
between our thought and what it is about, which requires us to
give an account of 'all being', the nature of reality, which would
show how truth was possible. Yet even if we accept Wittgenstein's diagnosis of the latter problem as illusory, and the
correctness of his account of how it is initially posed, might we
not still wonder at its motivation? That is, might we not suspect
that the notion of 'all being' is not simply the result of being
misled by superficial grammatical similarities, but rather that
one seizes upon the latter because of a particular construction
one is placing on the notion of 'all being' whose motivation
is itself non-philosophical? Such a suggestion would require
that we bring this notion of 'all being' back from its 'metaphysical' to its 'everyday' use. It may, that is, indeed be a
conception needed to formulate a question which we can non-
philosophically ask, so that the metaphysical construction of it
would proceed from a particular understanding of that question. This is, I think, Kierkegaard's position in calling philosophy 'the human standpoint'. The question at issue for him is
that of *the* meaning of life, which is possible for us to raise as
mortal and so be able to think of our lives as a whole. If we ask
this question, we are asking about the significance of anything
whatever we may relate to, and so to all possible 'being'. But
here what defines the latter is not a purported general form of
language or thought, as the correlate of the general proposi-
tional form, but the general form of the content of our lives,
*whatever* that may be. Here to think about 'all being' is to think
about this content in its absolute generality, and so is to think
about our lives in their totality. But such a question can only
confront us, as existing individuals, as an existential question,
about the value of *our own* lives, about what can give them

significance in their totality. Metaphysics, however, understands the question formulated in terms of 'all being' as intellectual, in order to resolve the question of the meaning of life in terms of its answer, and so subordinates the latter question to the former. This does not, therefore, represent for Kierkegaard a merely intellectual mistake, a misunderstanding of the notion of 'all being', but rather that this misapprehension is a result of a fundamental *existential* error.

The philosophical move first, as we have seen, fails to address the *nature* of the problem of 'the meaning of life', that it is 'existential', one which the individual faces in relation to their *own* life, which rules out the *philosophical* ambition of achieving a result through intellectual reflection in terms of which life may then be lived. Self-reflection, rather, can only make clear to the intellect its inadequacy. But the philosophical resolution does not, however, only misapprehend the nature of the problem. Philosophy tries to determine an answer to the question of life as what would fulfil man's 'Being' or would be appropriate to the historical situation and so appears as a manifestation of 'relative willing', that relation to our lives which judges its meaning in terms of some immanent human capacity or disposition, here that of philosophical reflection. But it represents not merely one further immanent possibility, such as are represented by the aesthetical and ethical resolutions, but one which claims, by its nature, universal validity. In this way, it is a manifestation of the desire that man should be able to *justify* his life in terms of himself. The general character of existential error for Kierkegaard is *pride*, since all relative determinations judge life in terms of some aspect of life which thus asserts its own value as unquestionable. In philosophy, however, this takes the form not of unquestioning assertion but of a claim to *ultimate justification*. It is, then, for Kierkegaard, the *hubris* of the human, in which man does not just, out of pride, determine the meaning of his life, but claims a right to do so. And this is revealed in the conception of the resolution within metaphysics of the problem of human existence as *autonomy*.

Seen in this way, Plato's thought, for example, would *proceed* from the desire to determine the meaning of human life in terms that would render it autonomous, whilst the *appearance* of that thought is to justify such an understanding. Let us briefly review the Platonic project in this light.

'Our inquiry' says Plato in the *Republic* 'concerns the greatest of all things, the good life and the bad life.'[13] A man who lived the good life would be *eudaimon*, and *eudaimonia* constitutes the end for our lives: 'We don't need to ask for what end one wishes eudaimonia, when one does, for that answer seems final [*telos*].'[14] Man is a being who desires *an* end for his life as a whole. If an animal can be said to pursue an end in its life, then this is something we impute to it, but, as Aristotle said, 'Man alone possesses speech and speech is designed to indicate the advantageous, the harmful, the right and the wrong. Man alone has perception of good and bad and right and wrong and the other character qualities.'[15] Man is aware, in a way animals cannot be, of having a life and so of being faced by the task of giving it a unity, so that it will be *his* rather than a sequence of events which he merely experiences. Man's task, Socrates remarks, is to attain 'self-mastery and beautiful order' and to make 'of himself a unity, one man instead of many'.[16] He has the problem of ruling his life, rather than spontaneously moving towards his end, as one may suppose of animals, and so Aristotle remarked, 'a man is or is chiefly the part of himself having authority, and a good man values this part of himself most'.[17] That 'part' is man's capacity to formulate the conception of an end for one's life as a whole and which underlies the possibility of the inquiry Plato is engaged upon: 'It belongs to the rational part to rule, being wise and exercising forethought on behalf of the entire soul.'[18] Such an end is 'that which every soul pursues and for its sake does all that it does', since each individual desires to live his life as his own. Because this is 'the greatest of all things', 'when it comes to the good nobody is content with the possession of the appearance but all men seek the reality and the semblance no one holds in esteem'.[19] Yet men are 'baffled and unable to apprehend its nature adequately' having 'only an intuition [*apomanteuomenos*, announced by a prophet] of it'.[20] This intuition follows from the capacity men have for forming the conception of an end for their lives as a whole: what they are baffled by is what that conception really involves and so what form of life is adequate to it. Since the task, however, is to *make* of himself 'one man instead of many', this question is directed towards a life which would *rule itself*.

Men do not just react to their environment on the promptings of their instinctive desires, but act in the light thrown by a consciousness of their ends. This capacity means that they do not merely live, but have a conception of their lives, and so of a unity through which their lives would express the unity of the I, of the soul. It is the *ergon*, the function, of the soul to manage, rule and deliberate,[21] and it can fulfil this function only if it makes of its given nature a unity, becoming 'one man instead of many'. The problem is to identify which of one's capacities is to be given priority so that one's nature as a whole achieves unity: and that requires a capacity which is directed towards a *true* end, one which is unchanging, always the same. Plato identifies the stages through which the soul comes to apprehend the nature of this end in the *Symposium*.[22] The end proposed by our individual given desires, pleasure, is no one thing but changes as one desire overcomes another, whilst that proposed by our common bodily nature, physical well-being, is apprehended by the body merely sensuously, both changing with our disposition and lacking any conception of its end in terms of which we could unify ourselves. That suggested by our socialized character, social excellence, *arete*, changes as the conventions and traditions of our *polis* or land do, whilst the unchanging truth of mathematics, although indeed providing an unchanging end, is not pursued knowingly, in the self-conscious knowledge of the nature of such truth and its fulfilment of our capacity to live in terms of our conception of *an end* as such. 'Those who are uneducated and inexperienced in truth do not have a single aim and purpose in life by which all their actions, public and private, must be directed.'[23] It is because of this that the capacity for rule which constitutes the soul is identical with that of learning and knowledge:[24] it fulfils itself in the self-knowledge which is philosophy. The philosopher is, as the consummation of the nature of the human being, *kalos kagathos* ('noble/fine and good', the term aristocrats used to refer to themselves!).[25] Socrates is a man who desires to know whether 'I am a monster more complicated and more furious than Typhon or a gentler and simpler nature to whom a divine and quiet lot is given by nature [*physis*].'[26] Such knowledge is achieved by knowing the nature of *the problem of human existence* and what can resolve it. That problem is one of self-rule, of making oneself a unity, which can be achieved through giving priority to that capacity whose end is knowledge of the nature of truth itself. Only a life organized in this way is formed knowingly directed towards an unchanging end, and so can achieve self-conscious unity: only such a life is truly self-ruling.

If man is to be autonomous, to rule himself, he must know the truth of human life and why it is the truth, and govern his life accordingly. But only the philosopher has, or aspires to, this self-conscious clarity, since his task is precisely to understand the truth of truth itself. Only this activity can constitute the self-conscious ruling of oneself in terms of truth. The notion of the *eidos* itself derives from this, since this is what we can intellectually apprehend in order to rule the world intellectually, to know it in so far as it can be known, and to rule ourselves individually and socially. As what can be intellectually apprehended, it apportions the world and man to the reach of man's capacities. The appearance within Plato's thought of the justification of man's end as contemplation of truth is just that, since its fundamental notions of truth and the idea and its procedure of recollection, are determined by the desire for autonomy itself. And in this sense, the accounts of metaphysics in Nietzsche and Heidegger have their validity, since these emphasize that metaphysics results from a particular understanding of human life and so cannot justify it.

Yet the post-metaphysical forms of thought, although revealing autonomy and its associated ideas as the result of a particular human project, are themselves a continuation of the 'universal problematic'. They emerge through a questioning of metaphysics itself, but one which repeats the structure of *philosophical* reflection. They wish to show that if reason is true to itself, it must put itself in question, in a move which reveals the dependency of its rational structures, which are articulated and grounded in metaphysics, upon a more fundamental reference. Such 'dependency', of course, is not on a ground for truth, but rather indicates that metaphysics is a *limited manifestation* of what cannot be thought metaphysically and which thus cannot recognize its limits and so itself. It is a form of Will, or historicality, or language, which is precluded by that very form from recognizing itself. Whereas the desire for autonomy culminates in the subordination of the human to a rational structure apprehensible by the human intellect thus making 'self-rule' possible, the *situating* of autonomy locates the human in relation to what encompasses reason. This revelation opens up the possibility of a non-metaphysical form of existence in its *claim* on us, and determines the present task of undermining the hold of metaphysical conceptions in terms of which life has been lived. This dual revelation is the result of reflective thought, but at the moment when the notion of autonomy itself is undermined. What is in prospect is not autonomy but the absorption of the human into the very forces which made possible the limited apprehension of the human at all, into the will of life itself, the hold of Being, or the differential structure of language itself. The structure of such thought thus on the one hand maintains the adequacy of reflective thought to determine our 'present' position and so the task binding on us now, whilst looking towards a loss of the 'human' in the impersonal. It would thus for Kierkegaard still embody the intellectual pretensions of metaphysics in relation to the question of human existence, whilst revealing in its most naked form what the desire for autonomy disguised, the impetus towards the subordination of the individual, who alone can ask the question of life or indeed any question at all, to the impersonal and general. That question, for Kierkegaard, asked by the individual and so about *her own life* in its totality, precludes giving a priority to *any* human capacity, so that the most which reflective thought can accomplish is the realization of its own inadequacy. This inadequacy *reveals* itself, but is not recognized, in the very trajectory of all such thinking towards the *subordination* of the individual to the impersonal whether in the form of the structure of the *logos*, of will, Being or language. What such thought reveals is the distraction of the individual from her/himself, from the very existence of the I who alone can pose the question of life or engage in the questioning that is philosophy. The philosopher forgets himself in order to bow down before the idols projected by his own intellect. What is evinced here, in philosophy as 'the human standpoint', is the paradoxical movement of the self-assertion of the human which can only take place as a *giving* of itself, and so subordinates itself to a phantasm of its own making. This necessity of giving marks the unthought *existentiality* of the individual who must carry out this thinking and which reveals the inadequacy of any human capacity to provide the object to which life in its totality could be given, an inadequacy which can only be recognized by giving up the desire for such an object at all. Such resignation is thus not the descent into a 'loss of meaning', a 'nihilism', which is only possible as a defeat of the desire for humanly determined significance which must therefore still be present, but a significance which life can take on as the surrendering of such desire itself.

# Chapter 7

# Philosophy always comes too late
## Levinas and Kierkegaard

Of all modern European thinkers, Levinas perhaps is closest to Kierkegaard. They share a critique of philosophy which argues that the latter, in the name of autonomy, subordinates the individual to the impersonal. In this way, philosophy forgets the first-person position from which the philosopher her/himself speaks. This position can only be understood in *ethical* terms, so that ethics refuses the imperialism of philosophy. But the rejection of the impersonal, the general, leads to the centrality for reflection upon the first-person position of what can only appear as paradox. Such paradox appears at the moment when, for the I to be as I, a transcendence of conceptuality is necessary which thus cannot be described in terms acceptable to the logic of concepts. Do such fundamental similarities then hold out the prospect of a rapprochement between Kierkegaard and contemporary Continental thought?

## I

Levinas' critique of the philosophical tradition finds its first extended development in *Totality and Infinity*. In that work, Levinas argues that Western philosophy is dominated by the concept of totality. It purports to give us knowledge of the nature of reality and thus of the ultimate measure for all that is. As such, it has been an ontology, an account of the nature of being, and thus a knowledge. Since it addresses the nature of Being itself, it cannot draw its resources from anything which is, cannot make any fundamental reference to existing beings, and thus asserts the primacy of Being over beings. As such, it is essentially a reflection on the a priori, what is prior to any encounter with beings. This reflection thus has the form of a discovery within the thinker of the resources for the resolution of the question of Being, so that I as thinker receive nothing but what was in me. In this way, 'the ideal of autonomy guides philosophy':[1] the nature of reality is discovered as the appropriate object of my powers, and so the 'I think' comes down to 'I can'.[2] Encounter with what is is mediated through a conception of its Being, and so ultimately through a conception of Being itself, notions implicit in non-reflective experience and which are to be brought to explicitness in philosophy. (This structure is not fundamentally altered where, as in Heidegger, a reflection is further undertaken into the conditions for the metaphysical determination of Being in terms of timelessness.) Such a structure implies that philosophy is an 'egology', so that reality is ultimately referred to the capacities of the I which does the reflective thinking. But since all encounter with existents on the part of such an I, including oneself as the particular individual one is, must be mediated through a conception of their being, and so of the Being of beings in general (or of Being itself, of the differential structure of language, etc.), 'the individual abdicates into the general that is thought, or Being as light in which existents become intelligible'.[3] Both I myself and the other person become subordinated to a general conception, of the psyche, soul, subject, particular Dasein, and so forth. The 'autonomy' aimed at by philosophy becomes the subordination of the thinker and the other to an *impersonal* rational structure, or, in Heidegger's case, to the priority of impersonal Being, which nevertheless is available to the grasp of human thought (or which summons it). Philosophy as ontology is thus a philosophy of power, 'an appropriation of what is, an exploitation of reality'.[4]

What this structure forgets, however, is the first-person position from which the thinker always speaks, the thinker as, Kierkegaard would say, an 'existing individual'. This is not addressed by the reference to 'finitude' in post-metaphysical thought, where the historical situatedness of all thought is articulated which precludes the absolute knowing of the totality sought by traditional philosophy. The conception of the human as Dasein, as always 'thrown' into an historical 'there' within which it must *be* as long as it lives, remains a *conception* through which the thinker mediates his own existence and that of others. Ontology, fundamental or otherwise, however, is only produced as a response to a question. But a question which *I* ask is asked of *another*, who must, therefore, have already *addressed* me prior to any determinate question. Such an address, being prior to any question which could result in the formulation of a response in terms of conceptuality, must come from a position *beyond* conceptuality; and as an address to me, it can only come from another person. Further, as an address to me which is prior to conceptuality, the I which is addressed must too be beyond and behind conceptuality. There is a prior structure of the relation of the I to the human Other which denies mediation through concepts and in which the I is addressed by the Other, *summoned* to respond, and so subordinated to the Other's call. Thus, the 'alterity of the Other . . . is prior to all imperialism of the Same', that imperialism reflected in the philosophical ideal of autonomy, and the 'I, who have no concept in common with the Other, am like him without genus'.[5] Such a relation cannot, therefore, be 'totalized': the I and the Other can neither be subsumed under a concept, nor defined in opposition to each other in terms of some more encompassing structure which would presuppose their conceptualization. The Other is not other in relation to some already determined conditions of identity of the I, nor is the I to be determined in terms of such conceptual conditions itself. Rather, to be Other is the very *content* of the Other, whilst 'to be I is to have Identity as one's content'.[6] The Other is other *absolutely*, and not relative to some other term, just as the I is the Same absolutely and not only in relation to something else. To have identity as one's content means to *exist* in the form of 'identifying oneself', in being the 'primal work of identification',[7] to exist as the work of 'separation'.

The first-person position is not a self-relation mediated by a representation, a concept of the I, but is, one might say, always already underway in a spontaneity, or as Kierkegaard would say, in passion. Such a movement, life, must always be going out, and thus have a relation to what is other, whilst, proceeding as identification, 'in recovering its identity throughout all that happens to it',[8] it suspends 'the very alterity of what is at first other and other relative to me'.[9] This passionate relation to what is other is thus 'accomplished as enjoyment or happiness',[10] an essentially *personal* relation which does not look outside itself for its significance but is as love of life itself, as self-sufficiency. This relation to what is other Levinas calls 'living from', a relation in which need, and so dependence on what is other, is at the same time the source of happiness and enjoyment, of the exercise of my powers upon the other within which its otherness is transmuted into the field for my enjoyment. But within this relation alterity nevertheless constantly makes itself felt through insecurity, happiness and enjoyment occurring as a 'happy chance'[11] always likely to be withdrawn. To *remain* as the Same, to exist as the process of identification, is to appropriate this revelation of alterity itself through labour and possession, in which the I comes to dwell in a realm of familiarity.[12] The other becomes domesticated through becoming a realm of stable things fixed by words. This familiarity thus involves the emergence of language, of discourse and so of a relation to the human Other. The familiarity 'that spreads over the face of things', an intimacy, a being at home in the world, is a being at home *with someone.* The recollection of myself, the self-consciousness involved in *remaining* the Same in a familiar world, from within my life as living from, as enjoyment and happiness, the spontaneity of life, involves a relation with what I do *not* live from, the relation with the human Other with whom I share a familiar world. This first revelation of the Other as the Other with whom I share a Home is called by Levinas the 'feminine Other'. The formation of the familiar world, as a response to the insecurity of 'living from' as enjoyment, means that the form this world takes is as a creation of security, so that the Other whose relation to the I is necessary for such a stable environment is characterized by *frailty.* It is the 'thou' of familiarity and the insecurity of need.

The I which has no essential content but is as the process of identification, of the rendering of the other into the Same, now *lives from* the representations that are provided through the relation to the familiar Other in the home. The common possession of the contents of the home thus *possesses* the I and precipitates a move to refuse possession and so establish the I in its separation, in its radical uniqueness beyond conceptuality. But such a movement, which is an act of separation, of the assertion of the I, can only take place as a *giving* of what I possess: 'only thus could I situate myself absolutely above my engagement in the non-I'.[13] But for this I must be called into question by the Other who lacks any commonality with myself, to whom I could give the world I possess. Not part of my world, and yet summoning me to offer what I possess, and thus questioning the possession, the Other speaks from a height.[14]

The I accomplishes its radical separation, an existing which refuses a concept, a genus, and is not for itself one of a kind, only in separating itself from its world. But for this it must be addressed from a position of height which calls for the gift of its world: it must be addressed by the absolutely Other, beyond its world and conceptuality in general, who puts that world and the I in question, but who, since I am *addressed*, is the *human* Other. The I can only be as radically separate, as an unsurpassable individuality, in a relation which, paradoxically, requires the very giving up of egoism, which is the transformation of alterity into the Same. 'The I which arises in enjoyment as a separated being having apart in itself the centre around which its existence gravitates, is confirmed in its singularity by purging itself of this gravitation, purges itself interminably.'[15] The I is thus confirmed in its singularity in infinite responsibility for the Other in which this responsibility is irreducibly *mine*, 'for which no one can replace me and from which no one can release me . . . by this election the I is accomplished *qua* I'.[16] The I becomes I, the irreducible singularity, only as infinite and irreplaceable responsibility, as the never-ending giving of what I possess, the *content* I have acquired, to the Other. The I accomplishes its singularity in giving its content: but it can only do this if it is put in question by another for whom it is never-endingly, infinitely, responsible. The I becomes I through the sacrifice of egoism.

The I and the Other exist in a sense beyond and prior to conceptuality, the one as the very upsurge of the love of life which is irreducibly personal, the Other as the putting of the I in question, a summons to responsibility, to giving without return. Such a relation is 'primordially enacted as conversation',[17] a conversation which has already taken place prior to any actual discourse. Such a giving of the world possessed initiates a *common* world, one offered for all. To see 'things in themselves' rather than in their relation to my possession, is to submit them to the viewpoint of the Other, to open them to questioning. 'Universalization is the offering of the world to the Other',[18] through which concepts emerge. Concepts are a response to the question of 'What it is'. This question is put to someone, and this in response to a summons addressed to the I by the Other, 'He to whom the question is put has already presented himself without being a content – as a face.'[19] The face is the address of the Other, beyond conceptuality, without genus, which puts the I in question and so lies behind any response in terms of justification. The answer in terms of 'quiddities', concepts, always refers to a system or structure of concepts, the impersonal structures of reason that emerge in a discourse between I and the Other, within which the things the I lives from are placed in the perspective of the Other, thematized, and so subject to questioning.[20] But the emergence of such structures presupposes what lies beyond any such structure, the relation of the I with the Other. 'Objectivity is posited in a discourse, conversation, which proposes the world – this proposition is held between two points which do not constitute a system, a totality. To have a meaning [here] is to teach or be taught.'[21] 'Pre-existing the disclosure of being in general taken as basis of knowledge and as meaning of being is the relation with the existent that expresses himself', that is, who is in the form of a summons to responsibility and so justification.[22] Thus, 'pre-existing the plane of ontology is the ethical plane'.[23] Ethics, as the relation of infinite responsibility of the I for the Other, is prior to ontology, the reflection upon impersonal rational structures. It is thus first philosophy. And in it the priority of the relation between existents, the I and the Other, over Being is asserted.

And this, of course, applies equally to the above account. Reflection can become aware of the relation between I and the Other, but it does so as a response to the questioning, the summoning to responsibility and apologia of the I by the Other which has already taken place.[24] In this way, the *thematization* of the I and the Other in their relation must always miss its mark: it must always be undone, unsaid, for any such thematization must always miss what lies behind thematization itself. What such thematizing discourse does is to return us to our *living* responsibility for the Other, within which alone the I and the Other stand in their appropriate ethical relation of infinite responsibility of the I for the Other. For discourse is most often not one in which the interlocutor is related to *as* the Other, and so as addressing me from a height from which I can be summoned to endless responsibility, but rather is approached in terms of a *category*, thus denying his presence to us prior to all conceptuality, in the nakedness, destitution of the face. Such discourse Levinas calls 'rhetoric', and his own thought thus is meant to serve to recall us to our responsibility and so away from all rhetorical relations, including, of course, those of philosophy which address the Other only in terms of an ontological category.

## II

The difficulties of speaking or writing about this 'primal relation' become central in Levinas' later work *Otherwise than Being or Beyond Essence*. What can be spoken or written about is what can be made *present* to the hearer or reader. And it is essential to what can be said to be that it can enter in this way into the said: 'entities *are*, and their manifestation in the said is their true essence . . . To enter into being and truth is to enter into the said; being is inseparable from its meaning! It is spoken.'[25] Being in this way is what can be thematized, enter as the object of discourse and be spoken about. But, Levinas says, 'there is question of the said and being only because saying or responsibility requires justice'.[26] Even at this quite formal level, it is clear that saying, responsibility and justice, whatever their sense, can only be thematized themselves by a certain 'abuse' of language, for they indicate 'conditions' for the very possibility of thematization itself.

Whatever can be said to be, being, manifests itself in something said. But such manifestation takes place only in the context of a question, and this itself in a dialogue, the exchange of questions and answers.[27] Being is thus disclosed within *lived* experience.[28] As such, questions are posed by me, by the I, of someone. But in order for such a question to be posed, I must already, in a sense, have been addressed by the Other, summoned to speak. Thus, the I has 'to do with the Other *before* the other appears in any way to a consciousness'.[29] It has an 'allegiance' to the Other, as a summons to respond. This relation, that of the Same to the Other, has already always taken place prior to any relating of me to another, any concrete relations or actual thematization of anything, and thus prior to any consciousness of the Other. As such, it has 'taken place' in a time *other* than 'clock time', the time within which beings can manifest themselves and actual encounters between me and others can take place, a 'diachronic temporality, outside, beyond or above, the time recuperable by reminiscence, in which consciousness abides and converses, and in which being and entities show themselves in experience'.[30] The address has always already taken place in a 'past' which was never present: 'A past more ancient than any present, a past which was never present'.[31]

The I is thus affected by the Other, as a response to the Other's summons, before any question.[32] Subjectivity has a structure in which the I has an allegiance to the Other prior to any consciousness of the Other or self-consciousness. I am always already responsible to the Other, always already summoned to respond to speak. It is this always prior relation that is 'saying', and the said always occurs within it. This summons, as always having taken place no matter what actual response I make, is without limit, infinite, and so summons me to infinite responsibility for the Other. Such a summons can only come from 'an absolutely heteronomous call',[33] one which *commands* me, and so comes from a *height*, and before which I am *absolutely* responsible, unable to be replaced by anyone else. Here the I is divested of all conceptuality, 'of all that can be common to me and another man, who would thus be capable of replacing me. I am then called upon in my uniqueness as someone for whom no one else can substitute himself.'[34] The I in its absolute singularity is as infinite responsibility for the Other. And the Other in his absolute singularity, having no concept in common with me, is as the summons to this responsibility. The uniqueness of the I does not lie in any quality the I could have, and which I could then share with others, but in 'the unexceptionable requisition of responsibility',[35] that the summons is addressed to *me* and can only be answered by *me*, that I am 'called upon in my uniqueness as someone for whom no one else can substitute himself'.[36] The I is *first* for the Other, as an *ethical* relation.

But as such the I is summoned to *give* infinitely. Thus the summons commands *egoism*. To give one must have a self to give, to be able to give oneself in what one gives the Other. And for this one must have become a concrete ego: 'enjoyment is the singularization of an ego . . . it is the very work of egoism'.[37] This love of life through which I become an individual, the process of identification which is 'more identical than any identification of a term in the said',[38] is necessary for the giving to which the relation with the Other summons me: 'giving has meaning only as a tearing from oneself despite oneself . . . Only a subject that eats can be for-the-Other.'[39]

But this summons to respond at the same time involves 'the third party', the other who is also a neighbour, one who addresses me, and who is a neighbour of the Other.[40] Just as the relation with the Other requires egoism, so that it may be deposed,[41] so too it requires justice, that is, the formation of concepts through which you and I and the others can be subsumed under a common term through which comparison, co-existence and order can be established. Through the 'comparison of the incomparable', the concept of the subject for whom there can be an object and so a theme can emerge, and thereby a concern for truth. Thus, being, what is, which is essentially disclosed in the said, is revealed as 'a function of justice'.[42] What is, being, is disclosed in dialogue between an I and the Other, an unequal relation in which what I possess is put in question. But what emerges in the dialogue, as the said, claims universal validity, and so a bindingness on *all*, who are thus subsumed under a common term, as subjects in relation to the object which is the theme. The impersonal structures of reason are thus demanded, but by a prior structure which serves to prevent their ossification and tyranny. The notions through which that prior structure have been articulated become through the command to justice the more familiar concepts of the structure of rationality: the infinite responsibility of the I for the Other becomes co-existence concretized as responsibilities in an historical world which can be formulated. The 'diachronic time', the always already past which cannot become and has never been present within which the Same-Other relation occurs, becomes the continuous, indefinite time of history, which can be remembered and so made present in a theme. The Same, the I of the primal relation with the Other, becomes the ego capable of discourse directed to a theme with others, related to an object, and who is capable of reflection back to a principle.[43] But although this structure of the *logos* is essential, it is so as demanded by the Same-Other relation which 'happens' in that other time. There the demand of the Other to the I is infinite and thus without possibility of finality, of satisfaction. It is this which destabilizes both all structures of knowledge, as the impetus to constant movement beyond the present, and all structures of social justice, in the criticism of any *de facto* situation. The hidden relation provides the basis for a never-ending critique of any actuality in the relations between human beings, or between them and their world, and motivates the cry of injustice which is always possible where the particularities of the individual case are mechanically subsumed under universal laws. Discretion and mercy are demanded equally with the universal structures of justice, as is the constant movement towards self-critique.

Yet that primal relation can be spoken of, as here, only by an abuse of language.[44] For in being spoken of, the attempt is made to make it present, to disclose the matter in what is said. But the primal relation is what lies beyond and behind *all* thematization in a time which is other than the time within which what lies in the future can appear in the present and be recollected as having been in the past: it is as always having occurred in a 'past more ancient than any present, a past which was never present'.[45] The relation defies thematization, and yet at the same time demands it: 'it must let itself be seen, undergo the ascendancy of being. Ethics itself, in its saying which is a responsibility, requires this hold'.[46] The responsibility to the Other requires the giving of the world of the I, and so the activity of reflection upon the grounds of that world, and so beyond ground to the condition for all thematization in the primal relation. But this thematization, the formulation of the saying in the said, here fails irredeemably: 'the one-for-the-Other . . . indeed shows itself in the said, but does so only . . . betrayed, foreign to the said of being; it shows itself in it as a contradiction'.[47] The thematization takes place only in terms which, as far as the logic of the realm of the said is concerned, are contradictory, undermine the possibility of a unitary sense. 'A past which was never present' utilizes the concepts of 'clock time' but in a way which defies their logic: we cannot *conceive* a past which was not a past present. Subjectivity which 'is struc-tured as the Other in the Same' utilizes the concepts of relation and of the terms between which the relation exists, which thus have an identity prior to the relation. But the Same and the Other of the primal relation are not identities, and so there is nothing for there to be a relation between. And so forth.

Whenever the attempt is made to bring the saying into the said, the result is a said which involves contradiction, thus disturbing the logic of the said itself. In this way the saying appears in the only way it can, as the *disturbance* of this logic, and thus as the source of the movements, towards ever greater justice, towards mercy and discretion, towards greater knowledge, which at the concrete level disturb and upset the achievement of the said at any time. We are compelled by reflection to recognize the necessity for both the logic of the said *and* its disturbance, and thus to attempt to bring to language the source of this necessity, an attempt which in its perpetual failure keeps us alive to the relation to the Other which is infinite responsibility. We must incessantly unsay the said to which the saying is reduced, and we do so by returning from the book within which it is written to the living nature of our responsibility for the Other (which may, of course, result in, among other things, another book).[48]

## III

Both Kierkegaard's and Levinas' critiques of philosophy focus on the latter's treatment of the individual human being who must always speak in the *first person*. For philosophy, the I becomes the individual interpreted as a particular case of a generality. Philosophy thinks the particular only in terms of Being, so that one's relation to any individual, including oneself, is always mediated through a knowledge, albeit implicit, of that kind of being, and so through an understanding of Being in general. (This structure is not really altered where the metaphysical orientation towards the Being of beings is itself interrogated in terms of Being as the temporal horizon upon which anything that can be said to be can appear, or where language becomes the field of differential play which allows as an 'effect' the encounter with what is.) Since what is can only appear through such mediation, philosophy as knowledge of Being, or as the bringing to language of the question of Being, or as an apprehension of language as differential play, provides what is necessary to raise our relation to what is to self-consciousness or to situate us in terms of our 'historical' situation. Such knowledge or self-situation provides the *critical* position from which we can see things 'as they are' (even if this is as an effect of differential play) and so sit in judgement on non-philosophical forms of thought or engage in an historically conscious situating of such forms of thought in the prospect of a non-metaphysical form of life. Philosophy thus privileges knowledge and itself as the access to the fundamental critique of all other forms of thought. In doing so, it provides us with the appropriate conception of the human, through which we can relate to *ourselves* and either provide a foundation for ethics or a critique of ethics which opens up the prospect of another form of human life. Philosophy only *returns* to the I *as* psyche, soul, subject, Dasein, or moment of arrested difference in the play of language, and so through a detour through Being, however understood.

But the very structure of this thought for both Kierkegaard and Levinas ignores the first-person position from which the philosopher must himself speak. The essential character of this 'position' is that I am not for myself a particular case of a generality: and it is this which requires for both thinkers a reference to a 'transcendence' which itself precludes conceptuality and which therefore involves us in a paradoxicality when we try to speak about it. For both Kierkegaard and Levinas, I resist subsumption under a generality, a feature which can initially be seen in the fact that I should have to *relate myself* to any purported generality, a relating which could not, therefore, be absorbed *within* it. For Kierkegaard, I am the one who acts, decides, commits myself, am, therefore, *passionately* involved. I must first engage with activities or relations with others or with objects in passion for there to be any question of decisions, actions or beliefs for which one could have reason within them. Such engagement manifests itself, for the most part, in the way in which I *give* myself to such activities and relations, an engagement which thus admits of *degree*, from the aesthetic return to self, to the commitment of self in the ethical, to the resignation of the self in the religious. It is in terms of such engagement that the notion of 'significance' in relation to life seen in terms of the first-person position is to be understood, and with that the associated notions of 'problems' and their 'resolution'. The latter themselves thus admit of degree. To despair of a particular aesthetic return to self, to have such a 'problem' with one's relation to some activity or relationship, and turn to another, is not itself to despair of the aesthetic return itself. That more radical form of despair, and so of a more radical problem with the significance of one's life, is precipitated in recognizing the distinction between myself and the concrete forms of life which I have spontaneously taken on, and can only be 'resolved' through relinquishing such return in the undertaking of ethical self-commitment. But this can itself be the source of *radical* despair, over the significance of my life in its *totality*, for self-commitment sees such significance as still flowing from the exercise of my capacities and thus does not encompass my life as a whole. In such exercise, I as the imposer of commitment am separated from myself as the field of such imposition. Such a self-reflexive relation does not, therefore, constitute the form through which my life could be meaningful as a whole, beyond the dialectic of *any return* to self. The problem of *the* significance of one's life has the character, that is, of an all encompassing despair. The source of this despair, as all encompassing, derives therefore from an attachment to the very exercise of one's capacities, which thus points towards the 'resolution' of the problem as lying in absolute detachment, but one which I am not *capable*, in terms of my capacities, of achieving, and which I can only *recognize* in the practice of what Kierkegaard calls infinite resignation. The dialectic of despair is the result of the *resistance* of the I to generality, the impossibility of my identifying myself either as the concrete form of my life in the aesthetic or as the I who imposes the form of the I on myself in the ethical. This resistance, however, leads to the absolute despair in which the exercise of my capacities *tout court* is seen to be inadequate in relation to the problem of the significance of my life, since any such exercise would itself involve a split within myself. The 'resolution' of such despair would thus involve a life without objective, for *nothing*, since any such objective would have an essential reference to my own powers. Yet the absence of objectivity would be the absence *too* of the I as the source of significance, and so would involve the loss of the self in terms of which *I* can despair of the significance of my life. Such a life could then only be *given*. The resistance of the I to generality must itself be given up in the recognition of absolute inadequacy, nothingness, in the face of the question which my life is, in the infinite resignation of humanly deter-mined significance, which thus implies that significance in its most extreme form would lie in the very loss of the self who despairs and who can take on 'infinite resignation'. But this is

*unthinkable*, for the I who despairs and takes on infinite resignation thereby recognizes the *absolute inadequacy* of their powers
in relation to the significance of their life. To attempt to think
it would itself *contradict* that very recognition itself. To think
one understands this is, Kierkegaard says, to show one doesn't:
it would itself mark a lack of infinite resignation. Such thinking
attempts to go beyond the most that is possible for the intellect,
to recognize the inadequacy of the I to achieve a *fully* meaningful existence of itself. The recognition of this inadequacy, and
the infinite resignation which embodies it, is the only relation
we can have to an *unthinkable* transcendence of the I. The
relation to transcendence has for us only the *negative* movement, in action and in thought, of recognizing human nothingness in its regard.

To see one's life in terms of infinite resignation is to see it as
'created', as beyond a humanly determined significance. The
world appears as creation only through this radical rejection of
humanly imposed significance. This is therefore not to see it as
'meaningless' which is the way it appears in a despair over a
human valuing to which one is still attached, but as essentially
beyond all human projection of significance. This 'beyond' in
relation to *my* life and the world can only appear as a negation,
to be *lived* in resignation of humanly determined values and so
beyond my thinking which is always an aspect of my life itself.
'God' does not therefore indicate an object of thought, but
rather marks the recognition of myself and the world as
'created'. 'God is the God of the living', says Kierkegaard,[49] that
is, of the 'I'. 'Immanently (in the imaginative medium of
abstraction) God does not exist or is not present [*er ikke til*]; he
is [*er*] – only for the existing individual [*existerende*] is God
present.'[50] This doesn't mean that 'God' is a 'subjective' notion,
a Humean colouring cast by our feelings over an indifferent
world, since the word 'God' is only uttered meaningfully where
the I recognizes the *inadequacy* of the subjective and the
objective in relation to the problem which their life is. A
'relation to God' can only be *lived*, in expressing this inadequacy
in one's own life. To 'think about God' is to think about one's
life in terms of this inadequacy, to think of it as 'created', not to
address a 'theme', an object appropriate to the capacities of
one's thinking.

'Human reason has boundaries; that is where the negative

concepts are found.'[51] The religious concepts are found at the boundaries of human reasoning about the significance of life, which is always a reasoning about *one's own* life: at the point where the inadequacy of the human, of oneself, of the 'I', to the question of one's life is revealed.

> But people have a . . . conceited notion about human reason, especially in our age, where one never thinks of a thinker, a reasonable man, but thinks of pure reason and the like, which simply does not exist, since no one, be he professor or what he will, is pure reason. Pure reason is something fantastical.'[52]

The flight to 'pure reason' or its contemporary mutations is a flight from the 'I': 'let us then ask . . . "Who is to write . . . such a system?" "Surely a human being . . . an existing individual".[53] For the existing individual, for the 'I', to ask the question which is to be resolved through reason, thinking, deconstruction, or whatever, is necessarily to put her own life in its totality in question: how could this be addressed by her own thought? The 'maximum is, reasons can be given for the impossibility of giving reasons',[54] and so the necessity which then appears of *living* this inadequacy or of asserting oneself in the clear-sighted apprehension of what one is doing and so not claiming it as 'the truth' or what our 'historical situation' demands, chimeras of the intellect.

For Levinas too the resistance of the I to conceptuality first manifests itself as love of life, as passionate involvement, as the passionate upsurge of the I beyond and prior to conceptuality, in the work of individuation, which is as the very resistance to thematization and so the generality of the concept. The I who questions in philosophy therefore cannot be absorbed into the concepts that activity may produce. Rather, philosophy as the thematizing of Being, already takes place in relation to the summons directed to the I by the Other, between poles which cannot themselves be thematized. The ethical relation of the Same–Other, of the address by the Other to the I which summons the I to infinite responsibility, to non-ending, unsatisfiable, response, is prior to any thematization or any concrete relation. The ethical relation is thus prior to ontology as a reflection upon the structures of rationality, structures which we produce through the summons to justice by the Other of the I. For both Kierkegaard and Levinas, philosophy comes too late. What is primary is, for Kierkegaard the passionate involvement of the I which is therefore the subject of ethical critique, of the degree of passion with which life is lived, or for Levinas, the ethical relation of the I and the Other. Ethics thus resists philosophical imperialism, the claim to take ethics under its own jurisdiction: philosophy, rather, is subject to *ethical* criticism.

There is a parallel too in Levinas to the essential para-doxicality in which the resistance to conceptuality of the I results, although with a crucial difference. For Kierkegaard, the paradoxicality involved in an attempt to think tran-scendence is a result of the inappropriateness of a cognitive relation to transcendence: the negative relation can only be lived and does not require a conception of transcendence but of the inadequacy of human life to resolve its own question. For Levinas, however, there is a necessity to think transcendence, even though this thought must always miss its mark. This necessity derives from the nature of the transcending itself, that it is a going of the I towards the *human* Other in infinite responsibility. When the I reflects, for Levinas, this is a response to a summons to justification and so ultimately to philosophical reflection and the reflection which goes behind philosophy to the recognition that I can never be justified before the Other, that the I is addressed prior to its being an I, to its becoming a concrete self. This reflection can only be carried out in an 'abuse' of language, so that bringing the ethical relation into the said is itself required by the relation, by the summons of the Other. The form of Levinas' discourse thus follows that of philosophical reflection, which is itself a response to the summons to justification, to apologia, which comes from the Other, but without philosophy being aware of it. Levinas thus goes beyond or behind philosophy in the attempt to bring the ethical relation of saying into the said through a paradoxical use of language, thus showing this relation as the *condition* for all other relations, and so of thematization in general. This regression upon conditions is what makes Levinas' discourse, as he himself insists, *philo-sophical*, albeit in a new, and more fundamental, form.

The form of Kierkegaard's writings is, however, quite differ-ent. They are characterized, as we have seen, by 'indirect communication', for they attempt to create a situation within which the reader is faced by a question, that of the significance of *their own* lives, to which only they can respond. What the communication shows is the variety of forms the relation of the I to the content of life can take in increasing degrees of intensity, and which thus faces the reader, as another I, with the question of the relation he or she has with his or her own life. In this way, it is shown what would be involved for one's life to have meaning in its totality, whilst recognizing that to see this and yet to decline to have anything to do with it is not to be involved in an *intellectual* error. For Levinas, however, the ethical relation is one which one discovers one is *committed to already* by the discourse through which one lives one's life. There is here a process of recollection, and thus a revelation of the logical, or rather pre-logical, commitments of one's position to which, as living through discourse, there is no alternative. Hence, Levinas presents this as *binding* on all who speak, whether they realize it or not: the ethical relation has a 'force' that convinces even 'the people who do not wish to listen'.[55] In this sense, one can be argued into one's responsibilities, since they ultimately derive from the ethical relation of the Same–Other, and it is here, in showing this point of ultimate justification, that the importance of Levinas' work lies. The philosophical pedigree of this structure of thought is clear enough. But if this is so, then responsibilities *require* such derivation, such 'grounding' in what underlies any ground. And in that case, they require an intellectual inquiry in order to determine their bindingness on *me*: it is crucial, as Levinas says, to establish 'whether we are duped by morality'.[56] The problem with this for Kierkegaard is not merely that if this schema, which is fundamentally shared with philosophy, is accepted, then the intellectual individual able to follow the argument appears in a superior position *ethically* to those who are not, which would suggest that the position privileges the intellect and so cannot encompass a relation to life in its *totality*, but also rather that this would *preclude there being any responsibilities at all.* For, one's adherence to the proposed responsibilities would depend on the appropriate intellectual underpinning, but this must always be a matter of argument whose results could only be held *hypothetically*, able to be overturned by future discussion. But then the responsibilities themselves could only be held in the same way, *conditionally*, and so not as *commitments* of *myself* and so *not as responsibilities*. For Kierkegaard responsibilities cannot rest on a ground, even of the Levinasian kind: they *are* only *as* commitments, either in the ethical sense of self-imposition or as ensuing from the commitment of myself to an unthinkable transcendence which requires of me infinite resignation. Hence the indirect form of Kierkegaard's writings: they do not attempt to argue one into a position but merely to make clear what is involved in a *rejection* of a return to self, of an immanent determination of the significance of one's life, one form of which is *precisely the desire for an intellectual ground.* To attempt to argue the reader into such a position would prevent the possibility of the individual engaging in such a rejection of immanence, since it would appeal to the verdict of the intellect. Levinas, Kierkegaard might argue, attempts to demonstrate that the life of giving without return is one to which, unwittingly, one is already committed in reason, or rather through what reason itself presupposes: but to argue this is precisely to prevent one undertaking, or 'imitating', since for Kierkegaard it is beyond human powers, such a life, for there would always be the reservation that the intellectual 'ground' may be found wanting. Life as infinite giving *cannot be justified*, but can only be desired through a giving up of *all* desire for justification. It then appears as something which must be *given*, as beyond human powers, and so in a relation to what is *absolutely* other to the human, to a transcendence which cannot be thought, even in an abuse of language, but only *worshipped*, that relation to one's life which *enacts* the impossibility for the human of living for nothing. The recognition of this does not require intellectual activity, although that may be involved in order to remove the barriers presented to its recognition erected by the pretensions of the intellect itself. What it requires, rather, is humility, the recognition of one's nothingness before the question which one's life is, and which is not an indifference or a despair which would embody a judgement in terms of human valuations.

The I is 'beyond conceptuality' in that the way one's life can be given significance in its totality is one *beyond* justification. The dialectic from the aesthetic, to the ethical to the religious is one, not of seeking ever more transparent justification, but the progressive *giving up* of the demand of the I for justification, and so of any sense of a return to self. The sense which justification, and so any sense of responsibility, can then have derives from the extent to which I involve myself in this progressive sacrifice of self-assertion. There can be no *reason* for this sacrifice: its progression has the character of an increasing *love*, whose ultimate 'for nothing' is revealed as beyond my powers and thus requiring a transformation *into* love, into a living for nothing, beyond justification and reason. But at any point in this progression, the responsibilities or justification I can recognize ultimately appeal *beyond* justification, to the *giving* of the I which lacks justification if is to be such giving at all.

# Chapter 8

# A concluding revocation

In the *Journals* we find a remark which is enough to make any writer on Kierkegaard uneasy about their own work:

> 'The fact of the matter is that there ought not to be teaching; what I have to say may not be taught; by being taught it turns into something entirely different . . . the assistant professors want to swallow an existential thinker in order to obtain blood and life-warmth in paragraphs for a while.[1]

Does the present work fall foul of this condemnation?

We have seen that Kierkegaard claims that all ethical and ethico-religious communication can only be indirect. It would be convenient for me to say that I have not been concerned with speaking from *within* the existential dialectic but only *about* it, in marking the difference between the way philosophy, on the one hand, and Kierkegaard, on the other, treat the issue of the significance of human life. But this would, I think, be seen by Kierkegaard as an evasion. The pseudonym Johannes Climacus not only points to the 'contradiction' involved in directly asserting that the 'Truth is inwardness' and so forth, which said by an individual who at least recognizes the religious would contradict his lack of authority, but also that 'It would again be a contradiction to assert' that 'it is a fraud which brings him into contradiction with his entire thought . . . because in spite of the double reflection in the content the form would be direct'.[2] Now it is tempting here to say that Climacus himself says just this and a great deal more which I have, of course, used in my own presentation. His own justification for doing this appears initially to be that he is only 'an outsider' in relation to the religious and to Christianity in particular, so that he is engaged in understanding the nature of Christianity as an existential communication.[3] It might, therefore, seem possible for me to claim an appropriate distance from which the existential dialectic and its philosophical opponents could be expounded. But the distance Climacus claims is *personal*: 'the whole work has to do with me myself, solely and simply with me'.[4] And indeed, so that 'no one . . . takes the pains to appeal to it as an authority', he appends 'a piece of information to the effect that everything is so to be understood that it is understood to be revoked', so that 'the book has not only a conclusion but a Revocation'.[5] The work is, one might say, Climacus thinking about his own life in relation to the addresses made to him by philosophy on the one hand and Christianity on the other. It thus takes place in relation to 'an imagined reader', the other we speak with in our soliloquies who 'understands one at once and line by line' and to whom 'one can talk . . . in perfect confidence'.[6] It is the soliloquy of a fictional I occupying a particular existential position, that of the *humorist*[7] on the threshold of the religious, 'the boundary that separates the ethical from the religious'[8] from which the comedy of human pretension to their own significance can be seen whilst the seriousness of undertaking living this insignificance is not embarked on but presents itself for decision. In reading the book, we thus occupy the position of this imagined reader in relation to the 'I', and so *rehearse*, since this is fiction, how life, not as an object but as lived, appears from this position, which as existential requires decision. By entering the soliloquy, we ourselves are thus *questioned*, but by *ourselves*, since the work is not the reflection of an actual I, and so not by an external authority. For a period, the actual 'how' of our own existence is broken, not by despair, an engagement with the existential dialectic in actuality, but by becoming in imagination the other partner in a soliloquy where decision is called for and so becoming questioned in the 'how' of our own lives.

Kierkegaard would, I think, object to the sort of 'distance' which appears required by the form of discourse I have used. That discourse has, in attempting an 'exposition' of the existential dialectic and so a direct communication, presupposed a position *outside* it in 'disinterest'. But such a position is subject to ethical criticism itself: it is inappropriate for an existing individual, and so inappropriate *tout court*. The only appro-

priate mode, which recognizes that all reflection upon existence is by an existing individual and so concerns *them*, and thus
must take place within the existential dialectic itself where no
individual can assume a position of authority if the claim of the
religious is recognized, is *fictional*. 'If existence is the essential
and truth is inwardness . . . it is also good that it be said in the
right way. But this right way is precisely the art that makes being
such an author very difficult'.[9] Kierkegaard would have thought
that I have not fully appreciated that difficulty, and therefore
the extent of the influence of philosophy, which extends beyond
its projects and can still mark the very form of one's writing. Yet
to be brought to despair over oneself as an author about these
concerns, one has to pass through a certain 'how', and so
through a certain temptation to write in a particular way. The
book has, at least, a personal justification, if ultimately for
Kierkegaard it must be found wanting.

# Notes

ABBREVIATIONS

| | |
|------|------|
| *AC* | Nietzsche, *The Anti-Christ* |
| *BGE* | Nietzsche, *Beyond Good and Evil* |
| *BP* | Heidegger, *The Basic Problems of Phenomenology* |
| *BT* | Heidegger, *Being and Time* |
| *BW* | Heidegger, *Basic Writings* |
| *CA* | Kierkegaard *The Concept of Anxiety* |
| CE | Wittgenstein, 'Cause and Effect' |
| *CUP* | Kierkegaard, *Concluding Unscientific Postscript* |
| D | Derrida, 'Differance' in *Speech and Phenomena* |
| *E* | Derrida, *The Ear of the Other* |
| *EH* | Nietzsche, *Ecce Homo* |
| EM | Derrida, 'The Ends of Man' |
| *E/O* | Kierkegaard, *Either/Or* |
| *FLN* | Weil, *First and Last Notebooks* |
| *FT* | Kierkegaard, *Fear and Trembling* |
| *GG* | Weil, *Gravity and Grace* |
| *GM* | Nietzsche, *The Genealogy of Morals* |
| *GS* | Nietzsche, *The Gay Science* |
| *HCT* | Heidegger, *The History of the Concept of Time* |
| *ID* | Heidegger, *Identity and Difference* |
| *IM* | Heidegger, *An Introduction to Metaphysics* |
| *J* | Kierkegaard, *Journals and Papers* |
| *MFL* | Heidegger, *The Metaphysical Foundations of Logic* |
| *NB* | Weil, *Notebooks* |
| *NR* | Weil, *The Need for Roots* |
| *OC* | Wittgenstein, *On Certainty* |
| *OG* | Derrida, *Of Grammatology* |

| | |
|---|---|
| *OL* | Weil, *Oppression and Liberty* |
| *OTB* | Levinas, *Otherwise Than Being or Beyond Essence* |
| *P* | Derrida, *Positions* |
| *PF* | Kierkegaard, *Philosophical Fragments* |
| *PI* | Wittgenstein, *Philosophical Investigations* |
| *PR* | Hegel, *Lectures on the Philosophy of Religion* |
| *PT* | Heidegger, *The Piety of Thinking* |
| *QT* | Heidegger, *The Question of Technology* |
| *R* | Plato, *The Republic* |
| *S* | Plato, *Symposium* |
| *SD* | Kierkegaard, *The Sickness unto Death* |
| SEC | Derrida, 'Signature Event Context' |
| SSP | Derrida, 'Structure, Sign and Play' |
| *T* | Plato, *Timaeus* |
| *TAI* | Levinas, *Totality and Infinity* |
| *TC* | Kierkegaard, *Training in Christianity* |
| *TI* | Nietzsche, *The Twilight of the Idols* |
| *TSZ* | Nietzsche, *Thus Spake Zarathustra* |
| *WG* | Weil, *Waiting on God* |
| *WL* | Kierkegaard, *Works of Love* |
| *WP* | Nietzsche, *The Will to Power* |
| *Z* | Wittgenstein, *Zettel* |

## INTRODUCTION

1 Plato, *The Republic* trans. P. Shorey, London: Heinemann, 1978, 473D. (Hereafter *R.*)

2 G.W.F. Hegel, *Lectures on the Philosophy of Religion*, 3 vols, ed. P. Hodgson, Berkeley: University of California Press, 1984 pp. 84, 88, 89. (Hereafter *PR.*)

3 F. Nietzsche, *Ecce Homo*, trans. R.J. Hollingdale, Harmondsworth: Penguin, 1979, p. 117.

4 M. Heidegger, 'Letter on Humanism' in *Basic Writings*, ed. D. Krell, London: Routledge & Kegan Paul, 1978, pp. 203, 193. (Hereafter *BW.*)

5 M. Heidegger, *Early Greek Thinking*, trans. D. Krell and F. Capuzzi, London: Harper and Row, 1975, p. 58,

6 J. Derrida, *Of Grammatology*, trans. G. Spivak, Baltimore: Johns Hopkins University Press, 1978, pp. 46, 50.

7 J. Derrida, *Positions*, trans. A. Bass, London: Athlone Press, 1987, p. 19.

8 R. Kearney, 'Dialogue with Jacques Derrida' in *Dialogues with Contemporary Continental Thinkers*, Manchester: Manchester University Press, 1984, p. 118.

9 *R* 514a and following.
10 J. Derrida, 'Structure, Sign and Play' in R. Macksey and E. Donato (eds), *The Structuralist Controversy*, London: Johns Hopkins University Press, 1972. (Hereafter *SSP.*)
11 That this is a recurrent theme in Wittgenstein's work has been well brought out in the writings of Frank Cioffi. See, for example, 'When do Empirical Methods bypass "The Problems Which Trouble Us"?' in A. Phillips Griffiths (ed.), *Philosophy and Literature* Cambridge: Cambridge University Press 1983; 'Information, Contemplation and Social Life' in G. Vesey (ed.) *The Proper Study*, Macmillan, 1970.
12 S. Kierkegaard, *Concluding Unscientific Postscript*, trans. D. Swenson and W. Lowrie, Princeton: Princeton University Press, 1968, p. 275. (Hereafter *CUP.*)

## 1 KIERKEGAARD AND THE METAPHYSICAL PROJECT

1 S. Kierkegaard, *Concluding Unscientific Postcript*, trans, D, Swenson and W. Lowrie, Princeton: Princeton University Press, 1968, p. 184, fn.
2 Aristotle, *Rhetoric*, Trans. J. Freese, London: Heinemann, 1975, 1.1371.a21
3 Plato, *Phaedo*, trans. H. Fowler, London: Heinemann, 1977, 96b.
4 Ibid., 97c.
5 Ibid., 98c.
6 Ibid., 99c.
7 Ibid., 99e.
8 Ibid., 100c.
9 Ibid., 103e.
10 Ibid., 102b.
11 Ibid., 102d.
12 L. Wittgenstein, *Philosophical Investigations* trans. G. E. M. Anscombe, Oxford: Blackwell, 1968, I.429. (Hereafter *PI.*)
13 Ibid., I.437.
14 L. Wittgenstein, *Notebooks 1914–1916*, ed. G. H. von Wright and G. E. M. Anscombe, with an English translation by G. E. M. Anscombe, Oxford: Blackwell, 1961, entry 22.1.15, p. 74.
15 Plato, *The Republic* trans. P. Shorey, London: Heinemann, 1978, 576a.
16 Compare Aristotle's remarks in the *Poetics*: 'not only philosophers, but all men, enjoy getting to understand something . . . therefore they like to see these pictures, because in looking at them they come to understand something and can infer what each thing is, can say, for instance, "This man in the picture is so-and-so"' (1448b; trans. in D.A. Russell and M. Winterbottom, *Ancient Literary Criticism*, Oxford: Oxford University Press, 1983, p. 94).
17 *R* 507c.
18 Plato, *Timaeus*, trans. R. Bury, London: Heinemann, 1975, 51a. (Hereafter *T.*)

19  *T* 50d–e.
20  *T.* 51b.
21  Plato, *Philebus*, trans. W. Lamb, London: Heinemann, 1975, 54c.
22  *R* 519c.
23  *R* 508e.
24  *R* 532b.
25  Plato, *Gorgias*, trans. W. Lamb, London: Heinemann, 1975, 508a.
26  *R* 537c.
27  *R* 537b.
28  Plato, *Sophist*, trans. H. Fowler, London: Heinemann, 1977, 254.
29  *R* 475e.
30  *T* 28a.
31  *T* 77b.
32  Plato, *Phaedrus*, trans. H. Fowler, London: Heinemann, 1977, 249b–c.
33  *T* 90d.
34  *R* 505a.
35  *R* 519c.
36  Plato, *Phaedo*, 79a.
37  *Phaedo* 67c.
38  *R* 443d.
39  *R* 441e.
40  *R* 581b–c.
41  *R* 506a. This may also be read as referring to the Good as what makes possible all knowledge and so is itself beyond knowing.
42  G. W. F. Hegel, *Lectures on the Philosophy of Religion*, vol. 1, P. Hodgson, Berkeley: University of California Press, 1984, p. 280.
43  *PR* 3, p. 283.
44  *PR* 3, p. 304.
45  *PR* 1, p. 84.
46  *PR* 1, p. 139.
47  *PR* 1, p. 302.
48  *PR* 1, p. 243.
49  *PR* 1, p. 250.
50  *PR* 3, p. 280.
51  *PR* 3, p. 312.
52  *PR* 1, p. 88.
53  *PR* 1, p. 84.
54  *PR* 1, p. 379.
55  *PR* 1, p. 143.
56  S. Kierkegaard *Journals and Papers*, ed. and trans. H. and E. Hong, Bloomington: Indiana University Press, 1970, 3253. (Hereafter *J*.)
57  *J* 3276.
58  *PR* 1, p. 101.
59  *PR* 3, p. 284.
60  *J* 653.
61  *CUP*, p. 24.
62  *CUP*, p. 23.
63  *CUP*, p. 86.

64  *CUP*, p. 147.
65  *CUP*, p. 68.
66  *CUP*, p. 272, fn.
67  *CUP*, p. 108.
68  *CUP*, p. 109.
69  *CUP*, p. 280.
70  *CUP*, p. 79.
71  *CUP*, p. 115.
72  *CUP*, p. 79.
73  *CUP*, p. 284.
74  *CUP*, p. 79.
75  *CUP*, p. 84.
76  *CUP*, p. 177.
77  *J* 1050.
78  *CUP*, p. 80.
79  *CUP*, p. 107.

## 2 KIERKEGAARD, HEIDEGGER AND THE PROBLEM OF EXISTENCE

1  M. Heidegger, *Being and Time*, trans. J. MacQuarrie, Oxford: Blackwell, 1967, p. 67. (Hereafter *BT*.)
2  S. Kierkegaard, *The Sickness unto Death* (hereafter *SD*), passage translated in S. Kierkegaard, *Works of Love*, trans. H. and E. Hong, London: Harper, 1962, p. 370. (Hereafter *WL*.)
3  M. Heidegger, *Basic Writings*, ed. D.F. Krell, London: Routledge, 1978, p. 53. (Hereafter *BW*.)
4  S. Kierkegaard, *Concluding Unscientific Postscript*, trans. D. Swenson and W. Lowrie, Princeton: Princeton University Press, 1968, p. 79.
5  *BT*, pp. 387–8.
6  S. Kierkegaard, *The Sickness unto Death*, in *Fear and Trembling* and *The Sickness unto Death* trans. W. Lowrie, Princeton: Princeton University Press, 1974, p. 184.
7  *SD*, p.186.
8  *BT*, p. 232.
9  S. Kierkegaard, *The Concept of Anxiety*, trans. R. Thomte, Princeton: Princeton University Press, 1980, p. 74. (Hereafter *CA*.)
10  Draft for *CA*, *CA*, p. 200.
11  *BT*, p. 333.
12  *BT*, p. 343.
13  *CUP*, p. 217.
14  *BT*, p. 494.
15  M. Heidegger, *The Piety of Thinking*, trans. J.G. Hart and J.C. Maraldo, Bloomington: Indiana University Press, 1976, p. 10. (Hereafter *PT*.)
16  *PT*, p. 21.
17  *PT*, p. 20.
18  *PT*, p. 9.

19  *PT*, p. 21.
20  *BW*, p. 41.
21  *BW*, p. 46.
22  M. Heidegger, *The Basic Problems of Phenomenology*, trans. A. Hofstadter, Bloomington: Indiana University Press, 1982, p. 10. (Hereafter *BP.*)
23  *BP*, p. 16.
24  *BW*, p. 54.
25  M. Heidegger, *The Metaphysical Foundations of Logic*, trans. M. Heim, Bloomington: Indiana University Press, 1984, p. 16. (Hereafter *MFL.*)
26  S. Kierkegaard, *Philosophical Fragments*, trans. D. Swenson, Princeton: Princeton University Press, 1974, p. 9. (Hereafter *PF.*)
27  M. Heidegger, *The History of the Concept of Time*, trans. T. Kiesel, Bloomington: Indiana University Press, 1985, p. 279. (Hereafter *HCT.*)
28  *CUP*, p. 107.
29  *CUP*, p. 79.
30  *CUP*, p. 78.
31  *CUP*, p. 217.
32  *CUP*, p. 176.
33  *CUP*, p. 109.
34  *CUP*, p. 136.
35  *CUP*, p. 135.
36  Ibid.
37  *CUP*, p. 279.
38  *CUP*, p. 280.
39  *CUP*, p. 134.
40  Ibid.
41  *CUP*, p. 280.
42  *CUP*, p. 109.
43  *CUP*, p. 86.
44  *CUP*, p. 276.
45  *CUP*, p. 147.
46  *CUP*, p. 256.
47  *CUP*, p. 388.
48  S. Kierkegaard, *Either/Or*, vol 2, trans. W. Lowrie, New York: Anchor, 1959, p. 255. (Hereafter *E/O.*)
49  *CUP*, p. 507.
50  *CUP*, p. 115.
51  *CUP*, p. 115.
52  *CUP*, p. 177.
53  *J* 3081.
54  *PF*, p. 52.
55  *J* 106.
56  *J* 1405.
57  *CUP*, p. 78.
58  S. Weil, *Notebooks*, vol. 1, trans. A. Wills, London: Routledge & Kegan Paul, 1976, p. 545. (Hereafter *NB.*)

59  S. Weil, *Gravity and Grace*, trans. E. Cranford, London: Routledge & Kegan Paul, 1963 p. 3. (Hereafter *GG*.)
60  *NB*, p. 237.
61  *GG*, p. 13.
62  Ibid.
63  *PF*, p. 55
64  *WL*, p.355.
65  *CUP*, p. 382
66  *CUP*, p. 353.
67  *CUP*, p. 197.
68  *CUP*, p. 412.
69  *PF*, p. 55.
70  *CUP*, p. 412.
71  S. Kierkegaard, *Training in Christianity*, trans. W. Lowrie, Princeton: Princeton University Press, 1972, p. 121. (Hereafter *TC*.)
72  *J* 1608.
73  *J* 1449.
74  *CUP*, p. 367.
75  S. Kierkegaard, *Fear and Trembling* in *Fear and Trembling* and *The Sickness into Death*; trans. W. Lowrie, Princeton: Princeton University Press, 1974, p. 48. (Hereafter *FT*.)
76  *J* 46.
77  *CUP*, p. 459.
78  *CUP*, p. 551.
79  *CUP*, p. 223.
80  *CUP*, p. 226.
81  *CUP*, pp. 216–17.
82  *CUP*, p. 346.
83  *CUP*, p. 247.
84  *CUP*, p. 226.
85  *CUP*, p. 551.
86  *CUP*, p. 31.
87  *J* 656.
88  *J* 653.
89  *CUP*, p. 280.
90  *CUP*, p. 151.
91  *CUP*, p. 280.
92  *PT*, p. 21.

## 3 HAPPINESS, SELF-AFFIRMATION AND GOD: NIETZSCHE AND KIERKEGAARD

1  R.M. Hare, *Freedom and Reason*, Oxford: Oxford University Press, 1963, p. 157.
2  J. Mackie, *Ethics*, Harmondsworth: Penguin, 1977, p. 170
3  F. Nietzsche, *The Twilight of the Idols*, trans. R. J. Hollingdale, Harmondsworth: Penguin, 1978, p. 45. (Hereafter *TI*).
4  F. Nietzsche, *The Will to Power*, trans. W. Kaufmann and R. J.

Hollingdale, New York: Random House, 1968, pp. 7, 9. (Hereafter *WP.*)

5  F. Nietzsche, *The Gay Science*, trans. W. Kaufmann, New York: Vintage Books, 1974, p. 279. (Hereafter *GS.*)

6  *WP*, p. 44.

7  *WP*, p. 45.

8  Ibid.

9  Ibid.

10  *WP*, p. 156.

11  *WP*, p. 45.

12  *WP*, p. 9.

13  *WP*, p. 10.

14  *WP*, p. 12.

15  *TI*, pp. 40–1.

16  *WP*, p. 13.

17  *TI*, p. 30.

18  *TI*, p. 45.

19  *WP*, p. 18.

20  *TI*, pp. 45–6.

21  *WP*, p. 318.

22  *GS*, p. 328.

23  *WP*, p. 196.

24  *WP*, p. 157.

25  F. Nietzsche, *The Genealogy of Morals*, trans. F. Golffing, New York: Anchor, 1956, p. 179. (Hereafter called *GM.*)

26  *WP*, p. 235.

27  *WP*, p. 235.

28  *WP*, p. 235.

29  *WP*, p. 279.

30  Ibid.

31  Ibid.

32  *WP*, p. 276.

33  Ibid.

34  *GM*, p. 297.

35  F. Nietzsche, *Beyond Good and Evil*, trans. R. Hollingdale, Harmondsworth: Penguin, 1979, p.15. (Hereafter *BGE.*)

36  Ibid.

37  *BGE*, p. 90.

38  *BGE*, p. 123.

39  *BGE*, p. 64.

40  *WP*, p. 196

41  F. Nietzsche, *Thus Spoke Zarathustra*, trans. R.J. Hollingdale, Harmondsworth: Penguin, 1978, p. 100. (Hereafter *TSZ.*)

42  *WP*, p. 279.

43  *WP*, p. 129.

44  F. Nietzsche, *The Anti-Christ*, trans. R.J. Hollingdale, Harmondsworth: Penguin, 1978, p.179. (Hereafter *AC.*)

45  TI, p. 108.

46  *GM*, p. 191.

47 *WP*, p. 154.
48 *WP*, p. 162.
49 *TSZ*, p. 100.
50 *GS*, p. 255.
51 TI, p. 93.
52 *GS*, p. 266.
53 *WP*, p. 252.
54 *WP*, p. 500.
55 *WP*, p. 453.
56 *WP*, pp. 318–19.
57 TI, p. 91.
58 *AC*, p. 173.
59 Ibid.
60 TI, p. 54.
61 *WP*, p. 378.
62 *GM*, p. 255.
63 *WP*, p. 288.
64 F. Nietzsche, *Ecce Homo*, trans. R.J. Hollingdale, Harmondsworth: Penguin, 1979 p. 128. (Hereafter *EH*.)
65 *AC*, p. 150.
66 *EH*, p. 82.
67 *TSZ*, pp. 54–5
68 Ibid.
69 *GS*, p. 242.
70 *GS*, p. 192, and see also *AC* p. 126.
71 *GS*, p. 290.
72 *TSZ*, p. 100.
73 *AC*, p. 141.
74 S. Kierkegaard, *Either/Or*, 2 vols, vol. 1, trans W. Lowrie, Anchor, 1959, p. 37. (Hereafter *E/O*.)
75 *E/O*, vol. 1, p. 295.
76 *E/O* vol. 1, p. 30.
77 *E/O* vol. 1, p. 300.
78 *E/O* vol. 1, p. 26.
79 *E/O* vol. 2, p. 15.
80 *E/O* vol. 1, pp. 24–5.
81 *E/O* vol.1, p. 285.
82 *E/O* vol. 2, p. 92.
83 *E/O* vol. 1, p. 290.
84 *E/O* vol. 2, p. 163.
85 S. Kierkegaard, *Concluding Unscientific Postscript*, trans. D. Swenson and W. Lowrie, Princeton: Princeton University Press, 1968, p. 85.
86 *CUP*, p. 281.
87 Ibid.
88 *CUP*, p. 285.
89 *CUP*, p. 78.
90 *CUP*, p. 281.
91 *CUP*, p. 313.
92 TI, 40.

93  *CUP,* 176.
94  *CUP,* 109.
95  S. Weil, *Oppression and Liberty,* trans. A. Wills and J. Petrie, Routledge & Kegan Paul, 1972, p. 157. (Hereafter *OL.*)
96  *CUP,* p. 339.
97  *CUP,* p. 19.
98  *CUP,* p. 412.
99  S. Kierkegaard, *Fear and Trembling,* in *Fear and Trembling* and *The Sickness Unto Death,* trans. W. Lowrie, Princeton: Princeton University Press, 1974, p. 59.
100  *CUP,* p. 388.
101  *FT,* p. 60.
102  *FT,* p. 61.
103  *CUP,* p. 256.
104  S. Weil, *GG,* p. 3.
105  S. Weil, *First and Last Notebooks,* trans. R. Rees, Oxford: Oxford University Press, 1970, p. 288. (Hereafter *FLN.*)
106  *J* 3081.
107  *CUP,* p. 514.
108  *CUP,* p. 517.
109  *FT,* p. 57.
110  *J* 2333.
111  *FT,* p. 61.
112  S. Kierkegaard, *Philosophical Fragments,* trans. D. Swenson, Princeton: Princeton University Press, 1974, p. 79.
113  *FT,* p. 48.
114  *FLN,* p. 316.
115  *TC,* p. 121.
116  *J* 4901.
117  *CUP,* p. 412.
118  *CUP,* p. 231.
119  *OL,* p. 157.
120  S. Weil, *The Need for Roots,* trans. A. F. Wills, London: Routledge & Kegan Paul, 1978. p. 6. (Hereafter *NR.*)
121  Simone Weil gives a sketch of these needs seen in relation to man's eternal destiny in *The Need for Roots.*
122  S. Weil, *Notebooks,* vol. 1, trans. A. Wills, London: Routledge & Kegan Paul, 1976, p. 282.
123  NB, p. 365.
124  Ibid.
125  S. Weil, *Waiting on God,* trans. E. Crauford, Glasgow: Fontana, 1977, p. 115. (Hereafter *WG.*)

## 4 GOD AND HEIDEGGER'S LATER THOUGHT

1  M. Heidegger, 'The Age of the World Picture' in *The Question Concerning Technology,* trans. W. Lovitt, London: Harper and Row, 1977, p. 116. (Hereafter *QT.*)

2   M. Heidegger,'The Onto-theo-logical Constitution of Metaphysics' in *Identity and Difference*, (hereafter *ID*), trans., J. Stambaugh, London: Harper and Row, 1974, p. 51.

3   M. Heidegger,'What are Poets For?' in *Poetry, Language, Thought*, trans. A. Hofstadter, London: Harper and Row, 1975, p. 91.

4   Ibid, p. 92.

5   M. Heidegger, 'The End of Philosophy and the Task of Thinking' in *Basic Writings*, ed. D. Krell, Routledge & Kegan Paul, 1978, p. 376.

6   M. Heidegger, *An Introduction to Metaphysics*, London: Yale University Press, 1975, p. 45. (Hereafter *IM*.)

7   *BW*, p. 377.

8   *IM*, p. 50.

9   Heidegger, 'The Age of the World Picture', p. 117.

10  M Heidegger, 'Letter on Humanism' in *BW*, p. 230.

11  Heidegger, 'The Onto-theo-logical Constitution of Metaphysics', p. 72.

12  Quoted in B. Welte, 'God in Heidegger's Thought, *Philosophy Today*, 26, 1982, p. 98.

13  M. Heidegger, 'Only a God can Save Us' in T. Sheehan (ed.), *Heidegger: The Man and the Thinker*, Chicago: Precedent Press, 1981, pp. 45–70.

14  M. Heidegger, 'Poetically Man Dwells' in *Poetry Language Thought*, p. 225.

15  J. Derrida, 'The Ends of Man', *Philosophical and Phenomenological Research*, 30, p. 53.

16  M. Heidegger, *Nietzsche*, vol. 2, trans. D. Krell, San Francisco: Harper and Row, 1984, p. 192.

17  M. Heidegger, *Nietzsche*, vol. 4, trans. F. Capuzzi, San Francisco: Harper and Row, 1982, p. 97.

18  M Heidegger, 'Metaphysics as History of Being' in *The End of Philosophy*, trans. J. Stambaugh, New York: Souvenir Press, 1975, p. 23.

19  Ibid., p. 23.

20  Heidegger 'The Onto-theo-logical Constitution of Metaphysics' in *ID*, p. 72.

21  St. T. Aquinas, *Commentary on Four Books of Sentences*, Prologue q. 1, a. 1, c; quoted in M. T. Clark (ed.) *An Aquinas Reader*, London: Hodder and Stoughton, 1974, p. 411.

22  Heidegger *Nietzsche*, vol.4, p. 89.

23  Ibid. pp. 89, 90.

24  Ibid. p. 28.

25  Ibid. p. 99.

26  Ibid. p. 98.

27  Ibid. p. 99.

28  Ibid. p. 99.

29  *ID*, pp. 34–5.

30  *QT*, p. 17.

31  *QT*, p. 27.

32  Ibid.

33  *QT*, p. 30.
34  M Heidegger 'Metaphysics as History of Being' *The End of Philosophy*, p. 4.
35  *IM*, p. 107.
36  Ibid., p. 164.
37  Ibid., p. 44.
38  Ibid., p. 41.
39  Ibid., p. 167.
40  Ibid., p. 63.
41  M Heidegger 'A Dialogue on Language', in *On the Way to Language*, trans. P.D. Hertz, London: Harper and Row, 1982, p. 38.
42  *BW*, p. 387.
43  *BW*, p. 390.
44  *BW*, pp. 349–50.
45  M. Heidegger, 'Poetically Man Dwells' in *Poetry Language Thought*, p. 222.
46  Ibid.
47  *BW*, p. 325.
48  M. Heidegger, *The Piety of Thinking*, trans. J.G. Hart and J.C. Maraldo, Bloomington: Indiana University Press, 1976, p. 48.
49  S. Kierkegaard, *CUP*, trans. D. Swenson and W. Lowrie, Princeton: Princeton University Press, 1968, p. 275.
50  *CUP*, p. 280.
51  *CUP*, p. 145.
52  *CUP*, p. 181.
53  S. Kierkegaard, *Journals and Papers*, trans. H. and E. Hong, Bloomington: Indiana University Press, 1975, 1405.
54  *BW*, p. 53.
55  M. Heidegger, *BT*, trans. J. MacQuarrie, Oxford: Blackwell, 1967, note 6 to div. 2, Sect. 45, p. 494.
56  *ID*, p. 37.
57  M. Heidegger, 'Letter on Humanism' in *BW*, p. 203.
58  Heidegger, 'Letter on Humanism' in *BW*, p. 239.
59  M. Heidegger, 'The Turning' in *QT*, p. 47.
60  Heidegger, 'Letter on Humanism' in *BW*, p. 240.
61  *CUP*, p. 129.
62  *CUP*, p. 135.
63  *J* 649.
64  *CUP*, p. 33.
65  S. Kierkegaard, *FT* and *The Sickness unto Death*, trans. W. Lowrie, Princeton: Princeton University Press, 1974, p. 130.
66  *CUP*, p. 147.
67  *CUP*, p. 452.
68  S. Kierkegaard, *Philosophical Fragments*, trans. D. Swenson, Princeton, 1974, p. 55.
69  *CUP*, p. 353.
70  *CUP*, p. 382.
71  *CUP*, p. 412.
72  *CUP*, p. 280.

73 *J*1611.
74 S. Weil, *NB*, trans. A. Willis, London: Routledge & Kegan Paul, 1976, p. 146.
75 *J*14.
76 *NB*, p. 110.
77 *CUP*, p. 474.
78 *J*3059.
79 *J*1433.
80 *J*3062.
81 *CUP*, p. 218.

## 5 DERRIDA, WITTGENSTEIN AND THE QUESTION OF GROUNDS

1 J. Derrida 'The Ends of Man' in *Philosophical and Phenomenological Research*, 30, 1969, p. 50. (Hereafter EM.)
2 Ibid.
3 J. Derrida 'Structure, Sign and Play' in R. Macksey and E. Donato (eds), *The Structuralist Controversy*, London: Johns Hopkins University Press, 1972, p. 292. (Hereafter *SSP*.)
4 SSP, p. 279.
5 Ibid.
6 Ibid.
7 J. Derrida, 'Differance' in *Speech and Phenomena* trans. D. Allison, Evanston, Illinois: North Western University Press, 1973, p. 138. (Hereafter D.)
8 J. Derrida *Of Grammatology* Baltimore: Johns Hopkins University Press, 1976, p. 143. (Hereafter *OG*.)
9 SSP, p. 289.
10 J. Derrida *Dissemination*, trans. B. Johnson, Chicago: University of Chicago Press, 1981, p. 351.
11 J. Derrida *The Ear of the Other*, ed. C. McDonald, New York: Schocken, 1985, pp. 115–16. (Hereafter *E*.)
12 J. Derrida 'Signature Event Context' in *Margins of Philosophy*, trans. A. Bass, Brighton: Harvester, 1986, p. 320. (Hereafter SEC.)
13 D, p. 159.
14 SSP, p. 264.
15 SSP, p. 292.
16 *E*, p. 115.
17 OG, p. 20.
18 J. Derrida, *Positions*, trans. A. Bass, London: Athlone Press, 1987, p. 19. (Hereafter *P*.)
19 OG, p. 20.
20 SSP, p. 278.
21 Ibid., pp. 279–80.
22 J. Derrida, *Writing and Difference*, trans. A. Bass, RKP, 1978, p. 293.
23 J. Llewellyn, *Derrida on the Threshold of Sense*, London: Macmillan, 1986, p. 107.

24 L. Wittgenstein, *The Blue and Brown Books*, Oxford: Blackwell, 1958, p. 4.
25 L. Wittgenstein, *Philosophical Investigations*, trans. G.E.M. Anscombe, Oxford: Blackwell, 1968, I88. (Hereafter *PI*.)
26 *PI*, I 139, 141.
27 *PI*, I 201.
28 Ibid.
29 Llewellyn, *Derrida on the Threshold of Sense*, pp. 111–12.
30 L. Wittgenstein *On Certainty* trans. D. Paul and G.E.M. Anscombe Oxford: Blackwell, 1969, sect. 80. (Hereafter *OC*.)
31 G.P. Baker and P.M.S. Hacker *Wittgenstein: Rules, Grammar and Necessity*, Oxford: Blackwell, 1985, p. 149.
32 *PI*. I 202.
33 *PI*. I 242.
34 *PI*. I 217.
35 *OC*, sect. 204.
36 *PI*. I 238.
37 L. Wittgenstein *Zettel*, trans. G.E.M. Anscombe, Oxford: Blackwell, 1967, sect. 299. (Hereafter *Z*.)
38 *Z*, sect. 301
39 L. Wittgenstein 'Cause and Effect', *Philosophia*, 6, pp. 409–45. (Hereafter CE.)
40 *Z*. sect. 541.
41 *Z*. sect. 545.
42 *PI*, I 241.
43 *PI*, I 142.
44 Rush Rees, *Discussions of Wittgenstein*, RKP 1970, pp. 56–7.
45 *PI*, II, xi, p. 224.
46 *PI*, I 480.
47 *PI*, I 473.
48 OC sects 358–9.
49 OC sect. 130.
50 OC sect. 559.
51 R. Kearney, *Dialogues with Contemporary Continental Thinkers*, Manchester: Manchester University Press, 1984, p. 121.
52 M. Heidegger, *BP*, trans. A. Hofstadter, Bloomington: Indiana University Press, 1982, p. 16.

# 6 PHILOSOPHY AS HUBRIS

1 S. Kierkegaard, *CUP*, trans. D. Swenson and W. Lowrie, Princeton: Princeton University Press, 1968, p. 34.
2 *CUP*, p. 284.
3 *CUP*, p. 110.
4 S. Kierkegaard, *J*, H. and E. Hong, Bloomington: Indiana University Press, 1970, 651.
5 *J* 657.
6 *J* 651.

7  *J* 651.
8  *CUP*, p. 69.
9  *J* 649.19.
10  *J* 6528.
11  L. Wittgenstein, *PI*, trans. G.E.M. Anscombe, Oxford: Blackwell, 1968, I 445, 458.
12  *PI* I. 304.
13  Plato, *R*, trans. P. Shorey, London: Heinemann, 1978, 578c.
14  S205a.
15  Aristotle, *The Politics*, trans. T.A. Sinclair, Harmondsworth: Penguin, 1967, 1.1.10.
16  *R* 443d.
17  Aristotle, *Nicomachean Ethics*, trans. H. Rackham, London: Heinemann, 1975, 9.8.6.
18  *R* 441e.
19  *R* 505d–e.
20  Ibid.
21  *R* 353d.
22  Plato, *Symposium*, trans. W. Lamb, London: Heinemann, 1975, 210d.
23  *R* 519c.
24  *R* 581b–c.
25  *R* 490a.
26  Plato, *Phaedrus*, trans. H. Fowler, London: Heinemann, 1977, 230a

## 7  PHILOSOPHY ALWAYS COMES TOO LATE: LEVINAS AND KIERKEGAARD

1  E. Levinas, *Totality and Infinity*, trans. A. Lingis, The Hague: Martinus Nijhoff, 1979, p.24. (Hereafter *TAI*.)
2  *TAI*, p. 46.
3  *TAI*, p. 42.
4  *TAI*, p. 46.
5  *TAI*, p. 39.
6  *TAI*, p. 36.
7  *TAI*, p. 36.
8  *TAI*, p. 36.
9  *TAI*, p. 38.
10  *TAI*, p. 299.
11  *TAI* p. 141.
12  *TAI* p. 128.
13  *TAI*, p. 171.
14  *TAI*, p. 75.
15  *TAI* p. 244.
16  *TAI*, p. 245.
17  *TAI*, p. 42.
18  *TAI*, p. 174.
19  *TAI*, p. 177.
20  *TAI*, p. 210.

21  *TAI*, p. 97.
22  *TAI*, p. 208.
23  *TAI* p. 201.
24  *TAI* p. 81.
25  E. Levinas, *Otherwise than Being or Beyond Essence*, trans. A. Lingis, The Hague: Martinus Nijhoff, 1981. (Hereafter *OTB*.)
26  *OTB*, p. 45.
27  *OTB*, p. 111.
28  *OTB*, p. 31.
29  *OTB*, p. 25.
30  *OTB*, p. 85.
31  *OTB*, p. 25.
32  *OTB*, p. 25.
33  *OTB*, p. 53.
34  *OTB*, p. 59.
35  *OTB*, p. 53.
36  *OTB*, p. 59.
37  *OTB*, p. 73.
38  *OTB*, p. 74.
39  *OTB*, p. 74.
40  *OTB*, p. 157.
41  *OTB*, p. 51.
42  *OTB*, p. 162.
43  *OTB*, p. 162.
44  *OTB*, p. 194, fn.
45  *OTB*, p. 25.
46  *OTB*, p. 44.
47  *OTB*, p. 135.
48  *OTB*, p. 181.
49  S. Kierkegaard, *CUP*, trans. D. Swenson and W. Lowrie, Princeton: Princeton University Press, p. 140.
50  S. Kierkegaard, *J*, ed. and trans. and E. Hong, Bloomington: Indiana University Press, p. 1347.
51  *J* 7.
52  *J* 7.
53  *CUP*, p. 109.
54  *J* 4897.
55  *TAI*, p. 201.
56  *TAI*, p. 21.

## 8  A CONCLUDING REVOCATION

1  S. Kierkegaard, *J*, ed. and trans. H. E. Hong, Bloomington: Indiana University Press, p. 646.
2  S. Kierkegaard, *CUP*, trans. D. Swenson and W. Lowrie, Princeton: Princeton University Press, 1968, p. 69.
3  *CUP*, p. 19.
4  *CUP*, p. 545.

5 *CUP*, p. 547.
6 *CUP*, p. 548.
7 *CUP*, p. 404.
8 *CUP*, p. 498.
9 *J* 633.

# References

Aristotle: *The Politics*, trans. T. A. Sinclair, Harmondsworth: Penguin, 1967.

Aristotle: *Nicomachean Ethics*, trans. H. Rackham, Heinemann, 1975.

Aristotle: *Rhetoric*, trans. J. Freese, Heinemann, 1975.

Baker, G.P. and Hacker, P.M.S.: *Wittgenstein: Rules, Grammar and Necessity*, Blackwell, 1985.

Cioffi, F.: 'Information, Contemplation and Social Life' in G. Vesey (ed.), *The Proper Study*, London: Macmillan, 1970

Cioffi, F.: 'When do Empirical Methods Bypass "The Problems Which Trouble Us"?' in A. Phillips Griffiths (ed.), *Philosophy and Literature*, Cambridge: Cambridge University Press, 1983.

Clark, M.T.: *An Aquinas Reader*, London: Hodder and Stoughton, 1974.

Derrida, J.: 'The Ends of Man' in *Philosophical and Phenomenological Research*, 30, 1969, pp. 31–57.

Derrida, J. 'Structure, Sign and Play' in R. Macksey and E. Donato (eds), *The Structuralist Controversy*, London: Johns Hopkins University Press, 1972, pp. 247–72.

Derrida, J.: 'Differance' in *Speech and Phenomena*, trans. D. Allison, Evanston, Illinois: Northwestern University Press, 1973.

Derrida, J.: *Speech and Phenomena*, trans. D. Allison, Evanston, Illinois: North Western University Press, 1973.

Derrida, J.: *Of Grammatology*, trans. G. Spivak, Baltimore: Johns Hopkins University Press, 1978.

Derrida, J.: *Writing and Difference*, trans. A. Bass, Routledge & Kegan Paul, 1978.

Derrida, J.: *Dissemination*, trans. B. Johnson, Chicago: University of Chicago Press, 1981.

Derrida, J.: *The Ear of the Other*, ed. C. McDonald, New York: Schocken, 1985.

Derrida, J.: *Margins of Philosophy*, trans. A. Bass, Brighton: Harvester, 1986.

Derrida, J.: 'Signature Event Context' *Margins of Philosophy*, trans. A. Bass, Brighton, Harvester, 1986.

Derrida, J.: *Positions*, trans. A. Bass, London: Athlone Press, 1987.

Hare, R.M.: *Freedom and Reason*, Oxford: Oxford University Press, 1963.

Hegel, G.W.F.: *Lectures on the Philosophy of Religion*, 3 vols, ed. P. Hodgson, Berkeley: University of California Press, 1984.

Heidegger, M.: *Early Greek Thinking*, trans. D. Krell and F. Capuzzi, London: Harper and Row, 1975.

Heidegger, M.: *Being and Time*, trans. J. Macquarrie, Blackwell, 1967.

Heidegger, M.: *Identity and Difference*, trans. J. Stambaugh, London: Harper, 1974.

Heidegger, M.: *An Introduction to Metaphysics*, London: Yale University Press, 1975.

Heidegger, M.: *Poetry, Language, Thought*, trans. A. Hofstadter, London: Harper, 1975.

Heidegger, M.: *The End of Philosophy*, trans. J. Stambaugh, New York: Souvenir Press, 1975.

Heidegger, M.: *The Piety of Thinking*, trans. J.G. Hart and J.C. Maraldo, Indiana 1976.

Heidegger, M.: *The Question Concerning Technology*, trans. W. Lovitt, London: Harper and Row, 1977.

Heidegger, M.: *Basic Writings*, ed. D. Krell, London: Routledge & Kegan Paul, 1978.

Heidegger, M.: 'Only a God can Save Us', in T. Sheehan (ed.) *Heidegger: The Man and the Thinker*, Chicago: Precedent Press, 1981, pp. 45–70.

Heidegger, M.: *Nietzsche*, vol. 4, trans. F. Capuzzi, San Francisco: Harper, 1982.

Heidegger, M.: *On the Way to Language*, trans. P.D. Hertz, London: Harper, 1982.

Heidegger, M.: *The Basic Problems of Phenomenology*, trans. A. Hofstadter, Indiana, 1982.

Heidegger, M.: *Nietzsche*, vol. 2, trans. D. Krell, San Francisco: Harper, 1984.

Heidegger, M.: *The Metaphysical Foundations of Logic*, trans. M. Heim, Indiana, 1984.

Heidegger, M.: *The History of the Concept of Time*, trans. T. Kiesel, Indiana, 1985.

Kearney, R.: *Dialogues with Contemporary Continental Thinkers*, Manchester: University Press, Manchester 1984.

Kierkegaard, S.: *Either/Or*, 2 vols, trans. W. Lowrie, New York: Anchor, 1959.

Kierkegaard, S.: *Works of Love*, trans. H. and E. Hong, London: Harper, 1962.

Kierkegaard, S.: *Concluding Unscientific Postscript*, trans. D. Swenson and W. Lawrie, Princeton: Princeton University Press, 1968.

Kierkegaard, S.: *Journals and Papers*, ed. and trans. H. and E. Hong, Bloomington: Indiana University Press, 1970.

Kierkegaard, S.: *Training in Christianity*, trans. W. Lowrie, Princeton: Princeton University Press, 1972.

Kierkegaard, S.: *Fear and Trembling* and *The Sickness unto Death*, trans. W. Lowrie, Princeton: Princeton University Press, 1974.

Kierkegaard, S.: *Philosophical Fragments*, trans. D. Swenson, Princeton: Princeton University Press, 1974.

Kierkegaard, S.: *The Concept of Anxiety*, trans. R. Thomte, Princeton: Princeton University Press, 1980.

Levinas, E.: *Totality and Infinity*, trans. A. Lingis, the Hague: Martinus Nijhoff, 1979.

Levinas, E.: *Otherwise than Being or Beyond Essence*, trans. A. Lingis, The Hague: Martinus Nijhoff, 1981.

Llewellyn, J.: *Derrida on the Threshold of Sense*, London: Macmillan, 1986.

Mackie, J.: *Ethics*, Penguin, 1977.

Macksey, R. and Donato, E.: *The Structuralist Controversy*, London: Johns Hopkins University Press, 1972.

Nietzsche, F.: *The Genealogy of Morals*, trans. F. Goffling, New York: Anchor, 1956.

Nietzsche, F.: *The Will to Power*, trans. W. Kaufmann and R.J. Hollingdale, New York: Random House, 1968.

Nietzsche, F.: *The Gay Science*, trans. W. Kaufmann, New York: Vintage Books, 1974.

Nietzsche, F.: *The Anti-Christ*, trans. R.J. Hollingdale, Harmondsworth: Penguin, 1978.

Nietzsche, F.: *The Twilight of the Idols*, trans. R.J. Hollingdale, Harmondsworth: Penguin, 1978.

Nietzsche, F.: *Thus Spake Zarathustra*, trans. R.J.Hollingdale, Harmondsworth: Penguin, 1978.

Nietzsche, F.: *Beyond Good and Evil*, trans. R.J. Hollingdale, Harmondsworth: Penguin, 1979.

Nietzsche, F.: *Ecce Homo*, trans. R.J. Hollingdale, Penguin, 1979.

Plato: *Gorgias*, trans. W. Lamb, Heinemann, 1975.

Plato: *Symposium*, trans. W. Lamb, London: Heinemann, 1975

Plato: *Philebus*, trans. W. Lamb, Heinemann, 1975.

Plato: *Timaeus*, trans. R. Bury, Heinemann, 1975.

Plato: *Phaedo*, trans. H. Fowler, Heinemann, 1977.

Plato: *Phaedrus*, trans. H. Fowler, Heinemann, 1977.

Plato: *Sophist*, trans. H. Fowler, Heinemann, 1977.

Plato: *The Republic*, trans. P. Shorey, Heinemann, 1978.

Rees, R.: *Discussions of Wittgenstein*, 1970.

Russell, D.A. and Winterbottom, M.: *Ancient Literary Criticism*, Oxford: Oxford University Press, 1983.

Sheehan, T. (ed.): *Heidegger: The Man and the Thinker*, Chicago: Precedent Press, 1981.

Weil, S.: *Gravity and Grace*, trans. E. Crauford, 1963.

Weil, S.: *First and Last Notebooks*, trans. R. Rees, Oxford: Oxford University Press, 1970.

Weil, S.: *Oppression and Liberty*, trans. A. Wills and J. Petrie, 1972.

Weil, S.: *Notebooks*, vol. 1, trans. A. Wills, Routledge & Kegan Paul, 1976.

Weil, S.: *Waiting on God*, trans. E. Crauford, Glasgow: Fontana, 1977.

Weil, S.: *Gateway to God*, ed. D. Raper, London: Fontana, 1978.

Weil, S.: *The Need for Roots*, trans. A.F. Wills, London: Routledge & Kegan Paul, 1978.

Welte, B.: 'God in Heidegger's Thought', in *Philosophy Today*, 26, 1982, pp. 85–100.

Wittgenstein, L.: *The Blue and Brown Boods*, Oxford: Blackwell, 1958.

Wittgenstein, L.: *Notebooks 1914–16*, ed. G.H. von Wright and G.E.M. Anscombe, with an English translation by G.E.M. Anscombe, Oxford: Blackwell, 1961.

Wittgenstein, L.: *Zettel*, trans. G.E.M. Anscombe, Oxford: Blackwell, 1967.

Wittgenstein, L.: *Philosophical Investigations*, trans. G.E.M. Anscombe, Oxford: Blackwell, 1968.

Wittgenstein, L.: *On Certainty*, trans. D. Paul and G.E.M. Anscombe, Oxford: Blackwell, 1969.

Wittgenstein, L.: 'Cause and Effect' in *Philosophia*, 6, pp. 409–45, 1976.

# Index